PARIS, *PARIS*

JOURNEY INTO THE CITY OF LIGHT

The Places, People
and Phenomena of Paris
in Thirty Essays

DAVID DOWNIE

Foreword by Diane Johnson

Thirty Original Black & White Photographs
by Alison Harris

Like all great cities and yet unlike any other Paris is alive and fluttering, it changes with the light, buffeted by Seine-basin breezes. This place called Paris is at once the imaginary land of literature and film, a distant view through shifting, misty lenses, and a vibrant contemporary city where a kaleidoscope of millions seems bent on the grand conspiracy of enjoying life. ***Paris, Paris: Journey into the City of Light*** paints a portrait in thirty perennial essays of the world's favorite city.

First published in the United States of America in 2005 by
Transatlantic Press
27,800 North Highway One, Fort Bragg, CA 95437 and
58 Boulevard de Ménilmontant 75020 Paris, France

ISBN 0-9769251-0-9

Designed by Barbara Torgoff   email: barbara@torgoff.com
Printed in the United States of America
U.S. sales and distribution: MEP-Distribooks www.distribooks.com

Front cover photo: Portrait of the author at dusk, Louvre Pyramid, 1989
Back cover: Dog at bistro table, 2004. Spine: Eiffel Tower, 1999

Visit our websites: **www.ParisParisTheBook.com**
www.TransatlanticPress.com

PARIS, *PARIS*

Foreword by Diane Johnson
By Way of Introduction

PARIS PLACES

A Day in the Park: The Luxembourg Gardens 3
Island in the Seine: Île-Saint-Louis 11
A Lively City of the Dead: Père-Lachaise 19
François' Follies 27
Buttes-Chaumont and Montsouris: The Art of the Faux 35
Going Underground 43
It's the Water: the Seine 51
The Place des Vosges 59
Belly Ache: Les Halles 67
Go East, Young Frenchman! 75

PARIS PEOPLE

Coco Chanel 87
Les Bouquinistes 95
Midnight, Montmartre and Modigliani 103
The Boat People of the Seine 111
Meeting Moreau 119
The Perils of Pompidou 127
Past Masters: Keepers of the Craft 135
Dear Dead Vincent Van Gogh 145
Beaumarchais' Marais 155
Madame X's Seduction School 163

PARIS PHENOMENA

In the Spring 171
The Janus City or Why the Year 1900 Lives On 177
La Ville Lumière: Paris, City of Light 187
Philosophy au Lait 195
The Michelin Man Cometh: The Star System 201
Sidewalk Sundae: What Makes Paris, Paris 211
Vie de Chien: A Dog's Life 219
Why the Marais Changed its Spots 227
Night Walking 235
Life's a Café 243

Acknowledgements

For his encouragement, enthusiasm and wise counsel, we give special thanks to Steven Barclay. We are also deeply grateful to Edward Behr of The Art of Eating, Barbara Bray, Romana Downie, Mark Eversman of Paris Notes, Don George, Anne Harris, Odile Hellier of The Village Voice, Diane Johnson, David Malone, Alice Martell, Kimmo Pasanen, Elaine and Bill Petrocelli of Book Passage, Polly Platt, Gloria Spivak, Paul Taylor, and Becky and David Tepfer.

David Downie's travel and food features have been published in over fifty leading newspapers and magazines worldwide. His books include: The Irreverent Guide to Amsterdam (Frommer's), Enchanted Liguria: A Celebration of the Culture, Lifestyle and Food of the Italian Riviera (Rizzoli International), La Tour de l'Immonde (Baleine, Paris), Cooking the Roman Way: Authentic Recipes from the Home Cooks and Trattorias of Rome (HarperCollins).

Alison Harris' photography appears in top magazines and books featuring food, travel and portraiture (among them Marcella Hazan's Marcella Cucina, Sophia Loren's Recipes & Memories, and Anne Willan's The Good Cook).

Foreword

Of all the books about Paris published each year, not one that I can remember tells you where to find the famous Art Nouveau public toilets in the place de la Madeleine, let alone telling you what to look for in the cemetery of Père-Lachaise. David Downie has a delightful sensibility and the most delighted eye, the most perseverance, and the perfect French, *bien sûr,* and these allow him to uncover secrets. Uncover them he has, the secrets of this fascinating city, and not the ones you'll read anywhere else. Did you know those ugly brown posts that keep Parisians from parking on the sidewalks are *bittes*, which is slang for what I guess we would call "pricks?" To take this book as a guidebook, walk out with it as he did and follow his path, is to have adventures, and to see a side of Paris anyone could see, but hardly anyone does.

Suppose you aren't in Paris? Or you're in Paris on a rainy day? Just to sit inside and read this book will transport you, for Downie is above all a wonderful, and wonderfully well-read writer. The essays are delightful as essays, but come fine weather I also recommend following his programs to the letter – a day of looking at the Paris of 1900, for instance. It's still here. You'll eat at Julien, have a coffee at Angélina, go to the movies at La Pagode, look at the Palais des Mirages at the Musée Grévin, the wax museum, where he counsels skipping the wax statues to admire this wonder rescued from the 1900 Exposition Universelle.

Or if 1900 is too recent, try the Paris of Beaumarchais, the playwright who invented Figaro, in the days of Louis XV and XVI. Downie tells you how to get into his historic Hôtel Amelot de Bisseuil, little changed since Beaumarchais' day, to get a glimpse of the remarkable sculpture of the courtyard before the concierge throws you out. You'll learn about the topography of the Buttes-Chaumont, the gorgeous park in the 19th arrondissement, far from the tourist track; it has a bridge by Eiffel and cliffs built to emulate the famous cliffs of Étretat.

What of the man who has served up this delicious array of treats? Something of a gourmet, for one thing, and a fabled cook. I was familiar with his cookbook, *Cooking the Roman Way,* but now I see that the same qualities that make someone love cookery make him love the odd bit of information, the smorgasbord of observations, the taste of the something curious in the scenes before him. Beside a scholar and a gifted *flâneur*, you always want a food-lover to be your guide when possible, and Downie is all three.

And the photographs. Paris must be the most photographed place in the world, from Doisneau to Cartier-Bresson. These beautiful studies by Alison Harris extend that literature with a powerful formal talent. Her camera's loving dissection of details that the busy traveler might not notice for himself, makes of this book a splendid object in itself, a sort of bibliophilic gem.

Diane Johnson, Paris

Paris, *Paris*
By Way of Introduction

Paris is the kind of city butterfly catchers have trouble netting, tacking down and studying. Like all great cities and yet unlike any other, Paris is alive and fluttering, it changes with the light, buffeted by Seine-basin breezes. This place called Paris is at once the city of literature and film, an imagined land, a distant view through shifting, misty lenses, the leftover tang of Jean-Paul Sartre's cigarettes clinging to the mirrored walls of a Saint-Germain-des-Prés café, and the city where I and over two million others pay taxes, re-heel shoes, and shop for cabbages or cleaning fluids.

The tourist brochures and winking websites, the breathless conspiracy thrillers, cinematic fables, and confessional chronicles set in Paris, each offer a view of the city's districts that someone will recognize. Nearly all such views neglect the burgeoning, unexpurgated Paris of last century's housing projects built within and beyond the beltway. My office is in the unfashionable 20th arrondissement. Its windows offer a kaleidoscopic vision of that Paris, a city of Asians, Africans and Eastern Europeans. I gaze upon their city, walk through it, work in their midst, but do not know them or it with anything approaching intimacy. The same applies to the gilded 7th arrondissement – a world of old money, old families, old furniture, old objets d'art, and very old, very heavy leather-bound cultural baggage.

The Paris of this book is not a product of the 7th or 20th arrondissement. In its irreverent, erratic way it flutters from one place, person or phenomenon to the next, touching on aspects of history, alighting on the contemporary, choosing flowers both perfumed and evil-smelling.

The book's emphatic title refers to the Paris of the English speaker, and, in italics, the *Paris* of Parisians. They are cities apart. For a Frenchman, "Paris, *Paris*" sets words at play: *paris* is the plural of *pari*, meaning bet, challenge, risk, wager. Elevate the "p" to upper case and you get a city that's a roll of the dice, a life-wager, a challenge as formidable to meet as Manhattan is to a Mongolian or Miamian.

Beyond its linguistic ambiguity the name "Paris" has a peculiar, pleasing resonance. I often hear it in my head even when I don't actually hear it with my ears, for instance when I ride in the Plexiglas nosecone of the Météor high-speed subway, line number fourteen. I enjoy the subway's swooshing headlong rush down dark tunnels, and the verbal massage the PA system provides.

If you take Météor from, say, the Place de la Madeleine to the Gare de Lyon train station, at each stop you'll hear an unmistakable female voice sing out the stops not once, but twice, with a variation in tone and emphasis. "Pyramides," says the voice of Paris, smooth with self-assurance, before the train pulls into the station. *"Pyramides,"* the voice repeats as the doors slide open, impatient now, a disembodied Catherine Deneuve riding crop in hand.

The change is subtle, not so much marking an accent as a shift to those ambiguous italics. Up and down the futuristic subway's line, the names sing out modulated, *slightly* reformulated, and on several other subway lines, too, including the number three, which is what I ride from the Marais apartment where my wife and I live, to my office near Père-Lachaise cemetery. Or is it, *Père-Lachaise*?

For months, perhaps years, this peculiar duotone subway refrain played in my head without me knowing it, an earworm whispering not station stops but the words "Paris, *Paris*" – words that to me came to signify the great wager, the subway stop of my life, where I got off the train I'd been riding aimlessly, and made my stand.

Perhaps because I came to Paris expecting no favors, with few illusions, and a generous dose of curiosity, I have yet to feel the betrayal some visitors and transitory residents distill into vague resentment. Paris has no monopoly on grumpy waiters, horizontal pollution, or enraged drivers, nor, in my experience, do the elusive, mythical Parisians focus their supposed disdain on any one nationality. I've been privileged to hunt for Paris in many places, with many people, including the occasional Parisian, for nearly twenty years, and these essays are part of my catch. My vision of the city still blurs from Paris to *Paris* in my daily pursuit of fluttering wings. Happily, I don't want to pin them down and anyway, Paris always manages to fly away.

PARIS PLACES

Luxembourg Gardens, Shadow of Chairs, 1994

A Day in the Park: The Luxembourg Gardens

"[Y]ou shall meete some walkes & retirements full of Gallants & Ladys, in others melancholy Fryers, in others studious Scholars, in others jolly Citizens; some sitting & lying on the Grasse, others, running, & jumping, some playing at bowles, & ball, others dancing & singing; and all this without the least disturbance..."

John Evelyn's diary, April 1, 1644

"The gardens shall be open from sunrise to sunset all year, but never before 7am." So reads one of the nine articles of the Règlement du Jardin du Luxembourg, that most sublime of Paris parks that greens the Left Bank between the Latin Quarter and Montparnasse. Like countless enthusiasts who've visited the gardens in the last four centuries, I've stood at dawn before the wrought-iron gates waiting for the black-caped *gardiens* to let me in. On warm summer evenings, when the sun and moon meet in the canopy of horse-chestnut trees west of the Palais du Luxembourg, I've hidden in the shadows, savoring the dusky light, until the guards have ushered me out of those tall, uncompromising gates.

You are denied sunrises and sunsets at the Luxembourg (and the pleasures of the night) but little else worth mentioning. In their own way, the gardens are a perfect world: sixty acres of terraced woods and walks, fountains and pools, with sweeping perspectives along alleys of surgically clipped trees. There's an old-fashioned music stand, a quaint café, a restaurant and several snack bars. City and country embrace to seduce you. A day spent loitering here teaches you more about Paris and its inhabitants than many a scholarly tome.

Some Parisians make a science of studying people's behavior in the Luxembourg gardens. Not long ago, a friend of mine boasted that he could tell the time of day by the breathlessness of the before-work joggers, the ruddiness of the lunch-time loafers and the decibel levels of the babies, maids and beaming young mothers out for an afternoon stroll. I challenged his boast but had to admit that, though I'd been to the gardens many times (they're only a half-hour's walk from where I live), I'd never actually spent a day there. And I resolved to do just that.

I arrived at the park from the Place de l'Odéon one morning (not before 7am!) and walked straight to a wooden kiosk near the gate. A handful of these kiosks are scattered around the gardens. At them you find a map and a poster showing the species of tree – elm, sycamore, ginkgo, giant sequoia – that grow here, with names in French and Latin, for the benefit of budding botanists. You also find a brief history, in four languages, of the Luxembourg palace and its grounds.

To save you the time and trouble, I'll summarize that history. Legend has it that the gardens stand over the ancient Roman encampment of Emperor Julian the Apostate (331 to 363 AD). But there's no trace of it. From Julian's day to the 11th century, the area was farmed. The farms are also long gone. In the 1200s, Saint Louis gave part of the neighborhood to the Carthusian monks. Alas, the monastery is gone, too.

As for the flower-spangled, sun-washed gardens we know today, their life began in the early 1600s as a green garland adorning the palace built by architect Salomon de Brosse for Henri IV's widowed queen, Marie de Médicis, née Maria de' Medici, a Florentine. She wanted an Italian-style palazzo to remind her of the Pitti Palace back home. Instead, she wound up with rusticated stonework grafted onto the archetypal Île-de-France château, surrounded by formal French gardens.

Jostled by breathless joggers, I strolled from the wooden kiosk to the Fontaine de Médicis and sat down beside it. This oblong pool is flanked by a rank of ancient sycamores draped with ivy bows, a sort of living garland motif. No matter what the season, it's cool and damp here. The moody setting seems to attract a soulful breed of visitor. On one side of the pool sat a solitary young man pretending to read *Le Monde*. Across from him posed a comely young woman, the real object of his attention. She looked wistfully at the white marble sculptures of Acis and Galatea embracing rapturously in the fountain's grotto. Above them lurks the menacing Polyphemus, a greenish bronze monster twice their size. The young woman's eyes swept over the pool to the ivy garlands, to the half-opened newspaper and finally to the young man's handsome face. Each time her gaze fell upon him, *Le Monde* trembled.

My thoughts returned to the luckless Marie de Médicis, who so loved this fountain. She moved into her palace in 1625 while the plaster was still wet and was expelled from France shortly thereafter by her thankless son Louis XIII. The name of the Duc de Tingry-Luxembourg, the property's former owner, was revived, and Marie de Médicis' forgotten. The palace then passed through the hands of the Duc d'Orléans, the Duchesse de Guise, Louis XIV and several less illustrious heirs. The only notable incidents in the gardens during these centuries seem to have been the visits of Watteau, who painted many a sensual canvas here, and the late-night summertime orgies of the Duchesse de Berry. She had all the gates but one walled up so she could frolic "with the sort of abandon that requires accomplices and not witnesses."

I was just about to leave Marie's fountain when along came a teetering octogenarian, led unsteadily by her young grandson. "Where are the goldfish?" demanded the boy, waving a stick. "They must be at the other end," whispered the woman. And they shuffled along together, stepping around the nervous young woman and attracting the attention of the *Le Monde* reader. He folded his newspaper then edged around the pool. "Aren't you Sylvie?" he asked. She said a friend of hers was named Sylvie. Perhaps they'd met at Sylvie's house? "Yes," replied the eager young man. "That's it... Shall we have a coffee? It's damp by this fountain." And the two walked awkwardly toward the park café in a nearby grove of flowering horse-chestnut trees.

Meanwhile, there were no goldfish to be found at either end of the fountain. The elderly woman and her grandson headed toward the so-called Great Octagonal Pool – the garden's centerpiece – facing the rear of the Palais du Luxembourg. I followed, settling into an old armchair to sniff the sea of flowers and watch the world go by.

It's hard to imagine this place as a prison. Yet during the Revolution, the grounds were sealed and hundreds of royalists and sympathizers interned. Guests included Danton, the painter David, and Tom Paine (who voted against the execution of Louis XVI). Paine spent many a day wandering the gardens' alleys, trying to find a way out, and by luck escaped the guillotine. Few others did.

Revolutionaries also ransacked the palace. A series of monumental paintings by Rubens depicting the life of Marie de Médicis that had hung here for centuries were packed off to the Louvre, where you can see them to this day.

Since then, with brief interruptions, the building has housed the French Senate. The grounds were expanded under Napoléon I, who destroyed the Carthusian monastery, and reduced in the 1860s under Napoléon III, who ordered his infamous prefect, Baron Georges Eugène Haussmann, to rebuild the neighborhood from scratch. Haussmann would have paved the gardens over had not 12,000 angry citizens poured into the streets to stop him. Instead he moved the Fontaine de Médicis to its present location and ran a road or two across the grounds.

But Haussmann and his team did bequeath the park its handsome round music stand, gingerbread café, beekeeper's bungalow and most of the compound's other charming 19th-century elements. My favorites are the pale-green metal garden chairs, about which I've developed a theory. Each kind of chair seems to have its own personality and to attract people of corresponding character. Some are upright and grave, others are slung back at a suggestive angle, still others have generous round seats decorated with delicate pinhole patterns and armrests shaped like arabesques. These I think of as grandmother chairs. They are comforting and weathered. There aren't many left, a dozen perhaps, and only thoughtful, mature strollers with a nostalgic twinkle in their eyes seem to choose them.

On a weekday morning like today, when the gardens aren't too crowded and there are plenty of chairs to go around, you can guess what sort of person will choose what sort of chair, where. Sun gods and goddesses lope down the gravel lanes then drape themselves over the low-slung kind, usually in the vicinity of the Orangerie, a heat sink dotted with orange trees and outsized potted palms. Chess players favor a combination of one upright, armless chair (for their boards) faced by armchairs. They set up in the grove of paulownia trees and play under a rain of mauve blossoms. Amorous couples prefer secluded lanes and lean two armless chairs side by side. The empty chairs, left as arranged by their last occupants, tell of trysts, duels and roundtable talks.

From my comfortable grandmother chair by the octagonal pool, I watched as children played with old-fashioned wooden sailboats, pushing them into the pool with long wooden poles. A sinister-looking man of middle age with a radio-controlled submarine chortled as his sub prowled just below the surface.

The wizened woman who rents the sailboats displays dozens of the battered little craft on the cart she wheels out rain or shine. She is known to be fierce, defending her boats from the abuse of rambunctious children. Every once in a while, a submarine or powerboat rams a sailboat and she flies into a rage.

Children often misuse the poles she supplies and take a poke at the pool's enormous old carp. Witness the fish-hunting grandson I'd seen earlier at the Fontaine de Médicis: the boat woman has summoned a park guard and ordered him to subdue the child and confiscate his stick.

As the grandmother and her chastened grandson slunk off, I remarked to a neighbor in an upright chair that the *gardien* was perhaps too strict.

"Monsieur," my neighbor remonstrated, "the rules must be enforced." A chorus of Gallic voices agreed. "Rules, rules, rules," echoed the stiff chairs.

With that mild reproach coloring my cheeks, I stole away to the park café, installed myself under the leafy horse-chestnut trees at a wobbly metal table, and soothed my pride with a sandwich and a beer. The beer was cool and refreshing, the sandwich tough as rubber and the prices extortionate. Still, a brass band was playing under the music stand's canopy, the sun slanted through the budding grove, and I couldn't help enjoying myself.

I hadn't been there five minutes when a battalion of *gardiens* appeared for their break. Paunchy and of indeterminate age, they ordered rough red wine and soon it was flowing like the Médicis fountain. The *gardiens* wear dark blue uniforms with brass buttons and matching képis. In winter, they wrap themselves in dark blue overcoats or heavy black capes and look like avenging angels. They carry walkie-talkies and whistles and are not shy about using either. Peep-pee-EEP – get off the lawn! Peep-peep-pee-EEP – don't pick the flowers! Put away that camera – no photos allowed with a tripod!

Some afternoons, the birds can't compete with the *gardiens'* shrilling. But now, as they ate and drank and smoked luxuriantly, they seemed entirely human. Every kingdom must have its rules and someone to enforce them.

Later, as I wandered around the romantic English garden west of the main esplanade, I reflected upon this simple fact. Without the *règlement*, would the Luxembourg lose its magic? As it is, no one pilfers the pears grown by botanists on the pocketsize orchard's espaliered trees.

Or throws smoke bombs at the beehives kept by the Société Centrale d'Apiculture, whose courses on beekeeping, devised to bring Parisians into contact with nature, have been a fixture since the 1860s. Were they allowed on the lush yet delicate lawns, would the gleeful thousands of students from the Lycée Montaigne facing the park soon wear the grass thin? One 19th-century chronicler remarked that so many high school and college students have always come here that if there were parrots in the trees they'd speak Latin – though the current language of choice seems to be Franglais, that admix of French and English, spiked nowadays with Arabic.

Not far from a bronze statue of a stag and deer, and the busts of a score of forgotten men, famous in their day, stands a marble sculpture of Watteau posed beside a buxom demi-monde. He seems pleased, at home, as do the drunken Bacchus, falling off his mule, and the ecstatic Pan across the esplanade, whose lithe figure when glimpsed from the palace seems artfully framed by the Panthéon.

I took another turn around the grounds, this time to admire the monuments to Baudelaire, Verlaine, Gérard de Nerval and Delacroix. These weren't military men or industrialists. Demigods, poets and artists, like guardian spirits, have always inhabited this park. At their feet, children spin on an old merry-go-round, or pedal antique tricycles made to look like horses and royal carriages. Ponies troop up and down, followed by zealous road-apple sweepers armed with worn brooms. Businessmen and bus drivers unknot their ties and troubles and play bowls in the shade of spreading trees.

As I drank in this cheerful spectacle, the bells of nearby Saint-Sulpice tolled four o'clock. Soon the gardens were swarming with perambulators, *poussettes, cochecillos de niño, carrozzine* and whatever else the au pairs and young mothers choose to call a baby carriage in the Babel of languages they speak. Could it be the daycare centers had just closed? Soon scores of starched-looking matrons from the luxurious apartments bordering the park were chatting away with immigrant maids and young bourgeois babysitters.

The words of Louis-Sébastien Mercier, written over 200 years ago, sprang to mind: "This peaceful garden is free from the extravagance of the city, and immodest and libertine behavior is never seen nor heard ... the garden is full yet silence reigns." In truth, there is more joyous laughter in the Luxembourg nowadays than reverential silence, and I'll bet there always has been.

Before I knew it, the sun was dipping into the trees and the whistles of the *gardiens* had begun to blow. Children froze in their games. Lovers released their passionate embraces. Chess players stopped their clocks. And slowly, reluctantly, we took our leave as dusk spread above. I watched from outside the gates as gardeners, rarely seen by day, set to work with shovels and rakes, readying the Luxembourg for dawn.

Île-Saint-Louis, 1990

Island in the Seine

"If you walk along the streets of the Île-Saint-Louis, do not ask why you feel gripped by a sort of nervous sadness. For its cause you have only to look at the solitude of the place, at the gloomy aspect of its houses and its large empty mansions..."

Honoré de Balzac

A spectacular stone gangplank leaps across five arches to link Paris' Right Bank with an unsinkable luxury liner midstream in the Seine. The gangplank is the Pont Marie, an early 1600s bridge. The ship is the Île-Saint-Louis, an island measuring less than half a mile from tip to tip but packed with history, mystery and atmosphere. Peopled primarily by rich, retiring islanders its narrow streets are lined by dozens of historic townhouses and ringed at water level by cobbled quays stippled with poplars. The cathedral of Notre-Dame on the noisy Île-de-la-Cité squats within shouting distance, across a wide footbridge that doubles most of the year as a stage for mimes, fire-eaters and a Captain Ahab look-alike squeezing an old accordion. Beyond the Pont Marie spreads the Marais, its fashion boutiques and art galleries fanning eastwards, amid landmark mansions, to the Place des Vosges and Bastille.

At first glance the physical distance isolating the Île-Saint-Louis from mainland Paris may seem negligible, yet the island manages to preserve a peculiar identity, defined more often than not by mixed metaphor. To some it's Mount Olympus, where writers and artists from Voltaire and Restif de la Bretonne to Théophile Gautier, Charles Baudelaire, Camille Claudel, Dos Passos and the inevitable Hemingway have lived, worked and loved. The envious call it a self-contained, self-satisfied biosphere for native bluebloods and transplanted plutocrats. Property values and rents are among the city's highest. Baron Guy and Marie-Hélène de Rothschild – and, until his recent death, their friend, the reclusive tastemaker Alexis von Rosenberg, Baron de Redé – lord over the island's upstream end from the gilded salons of the Hôtel Lambert, built in 1642 by royal architect

Louis Le Vau and, as befits such a manse, surrounded by high walls few mortals ever breach.

To most Parisians, though, the isle has long been perceived as a cruise ship in both shape and spirit, so much so that in 1935 cosmetics queen Helena Rubinstein knocked down a 1640s mansion to build herself a sleekly hideous house with transatlantic-style porthole windows at 24 Quai de Béthune (former French president Georges Pompidou lived there, and his widow still does). Nancy Cunard, of the shipping fortune, occupied number 2 Rue Le Regrattier, and Ford Maddox Ford's *Transatlantic Review* published Pound, Conrad, Cummings, Stein, Joyce and others at 29 Quai d'Anjou.

Rejecting nautical references my wife Alison thinks of the island as an open-air cloister, its sunny side facing south, its northern side lichen-frosted, cool and shady. That makes sense: the isle is quieter and moodier, its quays more secluded, than just about anywhere else in town, the result of the locals' political muscle, which has helped maintain a system of one-way streets and bridges designed to thwart all but the savviest of cabbies.

Habitués saunter over expecting not bustle and must-see monuments but an eddying, slow Seine churned by riverboats and dotted with seagulls, ducks and the occasional lost Canadian goose. There are benches shaded by sycamores and weeping willows, lazy anglers of uneatable bottom fish, sunbathers and moon gazers, picnickers and pairs of lovers tangled atop crumbling parapets. Quiet? Admittedly, the once-dusty Polish library, with Chopin memorabilia, has been given a lick of paint, but its operating hours are relaxed and, frankly, few set foot in it. The church of Saint-Louis-en-l'île used to be remarkable only for its gilt clock, but now has a 3,000-pipe organ specially designed for baroque music. You practically have to beg to get into the Hôtel de Lauzun, a townhouse owned by the city, for a view from on high. Add in a handful of cafés with outdoor terraces facing Notre-Dame, a travel bookshop run by a colorful woman who seems to love to turn away customers, an unusual fishing and fly-tying establishment called La Maison de la Mouche (the fly house), a few cozily pricey hotels and undistinguished restaurants that cater to the compatriots Hemingway disdained, and that's about it.

Oh, three-star chef Antoine Westermann of Strasbourg's Buerehiesel did open a darkly chic restaurant, Mon Vieil Ami, not long ago, but whether it manages to regild the island's culinary reputation is an open question. After all, the famous, some might say notorious, Nôs Ancetres les Gaulois, for decades the archetype of pseudo Gallic kitsch, is practically next door, serving fare where the operative word is "Gaul."

It's precisely the unrushed, backwater-ish quality of the island that's appealing. A stroll around this metaphorical luxury liner's deck is often the twilight highlight of my day, and not simply because I live a few hundred yards east of the Pont Marie and its mainland metro station – no grubby subway has ever sullied the Île-Saint-Louis itself. For one thing this is big-sky country with low buildings, a wide river and unleaded ocean breezes blowing up from Le Havre. The best views in town of Notre-Dame's buttressed back, and the Pantheon's massive dome, are through the leaves of the poplar trees lining the Quai d'Orléans. There are architectural details galore: carved keystones, masks, rusty mooring rings, stone garlands. The turreted, statue-encrusted Hôtel de Ville, alias city hall, seems much more than an 1870s fake when glimpsed at dusk from the island's Quai de Bourbon, named not for sour mash but for the royal dynasty that produced the bigwig pre-Revolutionary series of king Louis, including number XIII (1601 to 1643).

It was this otherwise unremarkable monarch who, in 1614, gave developer Christophe Marie and his partners the go-ahead to build the Pont Marie and transform the island from cow pasture to aristocratic playground. Marie devised the novel grid of streets girded by stone embankments. As I do my daily shuffle around this early masterpiece of real estate speculation, hands clasped behind my back, I spot the same regulars, pedigrees on each end of the leash, circling slowly, lifting their eyes or legs to the mossy old mansions. They weave warily among the hordes of ice cream pilgrims slurping cones on the island's busiest cross streets, the Rue des Deux Iles and Rue Saint-Louis-en-l'île. Much to the chagrin of islanders with genealogical trees as complex as the spreading old sycamores knotted around my favorite spot, the isle's downstream prow, among gastronomes and guidebook authors the Île-Saint-Louis is celebrated today more for its luscious Berthillon *glaces et sorbets* than for its architectural or literary past.

That past is written in stone, made easy to read for non-specialists by plaques mounted on about half the landmark townhouses, nearly all of them designed in the mid 1600s for royal tax collectors and others with a license to steal. The plaques provide names and birth dates, followed by a few pithy words that can lead you a merry romp through the history books. Here's what you find at number 22 Quai de Béthune, facing the Latin Quarter: "Hôtel Lefebvre de la Malmaison, conseiller au Parlement, 1645. Baudelaire y vecut 1842-43." Deciphered, the plaque tells you the mansion's name (Hôtel Lefebvre de la Malmaison), the owner's occupation as councilor at Parliament, the construction date and the fact that poet Charles *Les-Fleurs-du-Mal* Baudelaire lived here in the mid 19th century. The façade doesn't stir the imagination. But you can't help wondering if it was within these walls or at Baudelaire's other island abode, among the hashish-smokers of the Hôtel de Lauzun, that the tormented genius penned the lines *Luxe, calme et volupté* – luxury, peace and sensuous indulgence – so often associated with the paintings of Matisse. Is it a coincidence, you might ask yourself, that while here, or perhaps while remembering his time on the Île-Saint-Louis, Baudelaire wrote of the mythical island Cythère, sad and bleak, an "Eldorado of all the old fools?"

Baudelaire wasn't talking about a Cadillac but rather referring to Voltaire's imaginary golden paradise in *Candide*. It's a two-fold reference: Voltaire also lived on the island, in the 1740s, ensconced with his lady friend the Marquise du Châtelet in the Rothschild's current residence, the Hôtel de Lambert. There's no plaque to this affect chez Rothschild, nor is there anything to indicate that from 1949 until his death in 2005, the once-flamboyant and later reclusive Baron de Redé, lover of the wealthy Arturo Lopez-Willshaw and soul mate of the Baroness Rothschild, lived in the mansion's magnificent second-floor apartment, among precious antiques and artworks. Meanwhile Lopez-Willshaw's wife-of-convenience, Patricia, had, as one reporter put it, "her own romantic distractions." Baudelaire's distractions included installing his mulatto mistress and muse Jeanne Duval, alias the Black Venus, nearby at 6 Rue Le Regrattier. Scratch the surface and seamy stories well up all over the island.

At number 15 Quai de Bourbon, facing the church of Saint Gervais, the painter and poet Emile Bernard (1868-1941) lived and worked. He founded of the Pont-Aven Group of Symbolists. The plaque doesn't tell you that in his studio, under the gilt beams, court painter Philippe de Champaigne labored in the mid-1600s, his official residence two doors upstream at number 11.

Sculptor Camille Claudel, Rodin's protégé and mercurial lover, had a ground-floor studio from 1899 to 1913 at number 19 Quai de Bourbon. Islanders still grimace when recalling that, for several months after the movie *Camille Claudel* came out, the sidewalks were impassable because of the mobs paying homage to the mad artist, who died in an asylum. You can't get into the studio, but you can see one of the sculptures she made here, *Maturity*, an allegory of human mortality, at the Musée d'Orsay.

Another curiosity exhumed from the history books is that the 1659 townhouse capping the Quai de Bourbon goes by the name "House of the Centaur", because of the pair of low-relief sculptures on the façade showing Hercules fighting Nessus, the savage mythical beast, half man, half horse. For years Madame Louise Faure-Favier held her literary salon here, hosting poet Guillaume Apollinaire, painter Marie Laurencin, writer Francis Carco and critic Max Jacob, Picasso's penniless friend. The centaurs overlook a pocketsize park, which is a popular picnic and panoramic spot, and my wife and I come here often for the view. The mansion's current occupants apparently enjoy entertaining. On more than one occasion we have watched as society women in tailleurs and gentlemen in tuxes mingled under a second floor ballroom's painted ceiling.

It was this kind of wordly tableau, possibly in this same building, that inspired 18th-century author Nicolas-Edme Restif de la Bretonne to invent a new literary genre, the nighttime prowl, writing about it from 1786 onwards in *Les Nuits de Paris ou Le Spectateur nocturne,* a rambling account of 1,001 nights on Paris' streets. His ramblings often started from the Île-Saint-Louis where he lived.

Taking nighttime walks around the island, with a magic lantern show of interiors, is my preferred form of voyeurism. Another, equally fun by day or night, is to poke around the shady courtyards of the island's largely impenetrable mansions. Electronic coded locks called *digicodes* keep the rabble out. But I've discovered two methods to subvert them: wait outside and when someone leaves, confidently stride in, or, two, follow local mail carriers (with passkeys) on their rounds, starting about 10am. Stealth and subterfuge transform innocent exploration into an adventure. They once got me into number 15 Quai de Bourbon after years of cat-and-mouse with the concierge. Hidden in the wide cobbled courtyard I discovered a stone staircase with elaborate ironwork railings. On the roof above rises a two-story gable fitted out with a pulley – presumably to hoist furniture or intruders like me.

By systematically testing the island's doors I've found a few that are nearly always open. The best belongs to the Hôtel de Chenizot, at number 51 Rue Saint-Louis-en-l'île. Giant griffins uphold a balcony over the studded door. Step in and at the back of the first crumbling court you see a low-relief Rococo floral burst. Keystones carved with heads peer down at you. The rusticated sections of the mansion date to the 1640s. The taller additions are from 1719, when Jean-François Guyot de Chenizot, a royal tax collector from Rouen, redecorated. The building then spiraled downward, becoming, in succession, a wine warehouse, the residence of Paris' archbishop, a gendarmes' barracks, a warehouse again, and a moldering apartment house. Today the leprous plaster hides the requisite sweeping staircases and a rear court with a weathered sundial – and two art galleries, one of them also a tearoom. Atmosphere oozes from the place like wet mortar between bricks.

There is a third method I have mastered for penetrating the isle's inner sancta: take a guided tour. This can turn mystery into mere history, but it's the only way to get inside the sole townhouse whose interior is accessible to the public, the Hôtel de Lauzun. Here you actually taste a crumb of the upper crust's lifestyle under the Bourbon Louis – numbers XIII to XVI. The building's history is lavished upon you, like it or not, by a loquacious Cicerone. A potted version of it might run as follows. Charles Chamois, a military architect, designed the Hôtel de Lauzun in 1657 for a rather boring cavalry commissioner named Grüyn, whose boar-head coat of arms shows up on fireplaces and wall decorations (apparently Grüyn was not known for horsing around). Much racier a character, the Duc de Lauzun lived here from 1682 to 1684, shacked up with Louis XIV's first cousin, alias La Grande Mademoiselle. That's why the Lauzun name stuck.

Surprisingly the townhouse has survived almost intact, naturally without anything the heirs could un-nail and sell, meaning period furniture and original paintings. However, the venerable Versailles parquet creaks satisfyingly underfoot. Several tons of gold glitter from delicately decorated beams and walls, and when light pours through the many-paned windows the effect is blinding. Baudelaire and Gautier slummed here in the 1840s when the gilding had gone black, no doubt in part because of the hash fumes spewed by adepts of the Club des Hachichins (pronounced Ha-She-Shans). Baudelaire's hashish-induced hallucinatory poetic visions – of nude women and cloudscapes – apparently derive in part from the mansion's Music Room, a salon garlanded with dreamy plasterwork damsels.

Love Conquers Time was the title given to a second-story ceiling decoration but alas, it has succumbed to the centuries. The catalogue of short-lived unions enacted beneath it, and in the island's many other similar townhouses, suggests au contraire that Time Conquers All. That's not a bad motto for the Île-Saint-Louis, though I can think of an even better one, given the isle's ostensibly unchanging qualities – its stony mansions and merry-go-round of wealthy inhabitants. It's a saying coined by French wit Alphonse Karr in 1849: "The more things change, the more they stay the same."

Père-Lachaise, Cupid, 2005

A Lively City of the Dead: Père-Lachaise Cemetery

"I rarely go out, but when I do wander,
I go to cheer myself up in Père-Lachaise."
Honoré de Balzac, 1819

A fascination with death, what the French call *nécrophilie*, takes many forms, one of them so common it afflicts some two million individuals who each year enter the hallowed gates of Père-Lachaise cemetery in Paris' 20th arrondissement. Hilly, wooded, with winding paths knotted around crumbling tombs, this is without doubt the most celebrated monumental city of the dead in Europe. Surprisingly it stands within the limits of the sprawling French capital. It also happens to be about 150 yards as the raven flies from my office, so I've become a regular Père-Lachaise habitué. I love many things about the place: the greenery, the lack of cars, the expansive views from looping gravel lanes and, of course, the sepulchral monuments. Père-Lachaise quietly merges ancient and modern death cults, thereby assuring itself perennial status on the top-ten list of Paris tourist sights. Peak attendance nowadays is on the newly fashionable Halloween, an Anglo-Saxon holiday, and on November 1st and 2nd, the traditional All Saints and All Souls days. But the procession to Père-Lachaise of curious funerary pilgrims knows no season and braves all weather.

Amid the cemetery's hundred lush acres stand faux Egyptian pyramids, mock Greek or Roman temples, and neo-Gothic chapels erected during the heyday of Romanticism nearly 200 years ago, when the cemetery opened for business. These are my favorite monuments, and their setting is wonderfully evocative. Moss-grown, lichen-frosted and shaded by venerable, voracious vegetation, the graveyard's first tombs were made in imitation of the antique, specifically of Rome's tomb-lined Via Appia Antica. They too are now antiques – proof that time can render true what begins as falsehood.

Scattered between these proto-memorials are Second Empire neo-classical piles worthy of Paris' notorious 1853-to-1870 Prefect, Baron Georges-Eugène Haussmann. Fewer in number but more remarkable are the eerily delicate Art Nouveau fantasies from the turn of the 19th century. The modernist Le Corbusier-style slabs salted around are devoid, like that worthy Swiss genius, of any perceptible humor or humanity. Each tomb faithfully mirrors the times in which it was conceived. There are even a handful of postmodern pastiches – a cat's cradle of Plexiglass, steel and stone, for example – expressing the confused brutalism of recent decades.

The cemetery's upper third marches across a plateau crowned, outside the cemetery's walls, by the egregious Place Gambetta. In keeping with the precepts of the 1850s when this section was developed, the layout is a deadening, dull grid. Had it been easy, or even possible, Baron Haussmann's minions would have done in the 1850s to Père-Lachaise what they did to Paris as a whole: tear up the meandering alleys and asymmetrical tombs, replacing them with an efficient checkerboard of plots for the disposal of the dead. But the modernizers failed, much to the relief of nostalgic lovers of Vieux Paris such as Victor Hugo, or Joris Karl Huysmans. In his 1880 *Croquis parisiens*, Huysmans lashed out against the "tediousness" of Haussmann-style symmetry, seeing in the higgledy-piggledy Père-Lachaise and its rural surroundings "a haven longed for by aching souls..."

Ironically, the thousand-plus seditious Communards massacred by Napoléon III's troops amid Père-Lachaise's tombs in 1871 are buried in the cemetery's symmetrical Second Empire section. Haussmann, enemy of Communards and old Paris alike, wound up in Division 4, an older, less symmetrical area. He lies near such utterly un-Haussmannlike free spirits as Rossini and Alfred de Musset. Subversive Colette, lover of women and weaver of intrigue, is practically his neighbor. There is no such thing as justice, poetic or otherwise, in death, the great equalizer.

What has preserved unpredictable Père-Lachaise from the compulsive straighteners such as Haussmann is a legal concept that, like religious faith, defies logic and in so doing attempts to deny the temporal nature of human life and institutions. That concept is the *concession à perpetuité*, literally a concession granted forever by the city of Paris to families who own plots at Père-Lachaise. This was a novelty in the late 1700s, when the plan to create cemeteries outside Paris was hatched. Until then nearly everyone was thrown into common graves: only important churchmen, nobles and the very rich rated individual burials, usually inside a church, under the paving stones.

But new ideas on hygiene arising from the Enlightenment's scientific advances, plus a renewed familiarity with the burial practices of the ancient Romans, led Paris' administrators to ban inner-city cemeteries and under-floor burials in favor of sites beyond the city walls. The immediate stimulus for these reforms, however, came from the collapse of the cemetery of the Innocents (in the square of the same name near today's Les Halles shopping center). When the bones and rotting corpses of millions of Parisians – about 700 years' worth – burst through the graveyard's walls into the surrounding neighborhood, administrators scrambled. They built the catacombs in abandoned quarries. Later, in 1804, they inaugurated the Cimetière de l'Est. "Eastern Cemetery" is the official name of Père-Lachaise to this day.

It may be hard to credit but in 1804 the site stood beyond Paris' walls in rolling countryside. Known by various names, including Mont Louis, the area had been covered since at least the Middle Ages by woods, vineyards, orchards and market gardens. In the mid-1600s Jesuit father François d'Aix de la Chaise, better known as Père Lachaise, became Louis XIV's confessor. An ambitious, worldly fellow, Lachaise eventually prevailed on the monarch to help him buy Mont Louis and turn it into the country resort of Paris' Jesuit brothers. Included in the deal was a nice little chateau for Lachaise's personal use, perched at the hill's highest point. The Jesuits were evicted in the 1760s and Mont Louis passed through the hands of several private owners. Paris' municipal authorities eventually bought it and created a graveyard to serve the city's eastern arrondissements. Later still, the same authorities demolished Père Lachaise's chateau. Since about 1820 a chapel has stood on the site.

What's in a name? François d'Aix de la Chaise isn't buried in the cemetery that bears his name. Apparently, when it first opened, the clinical-sounding *Cimetière de l'Est* didn't seem like the ideal place to bury loved ones. For this reason the site's earliest developers hit upon the scheme of calling it Père-Lachaise, to give it a hallowed if Jesuitical ring. Then as now religiosity was an effective marketing tool. The cemetery was not consecrated ground under the Jesuits and is not consecrated today. By law French municipal graveyards must welcome all sects, creeds and religions, as well as agnostics and atheists.

These same developers used another clever marketing ploy to promote the cemetery. It involved relocating the tombs of a few famous dead, so that potential clients would be able to say, "Well, if Père-Lachaise is good enough for abbots and royalty it's good enough for me." The first celebrity corpses whisked to the cemetery were in fact those of the luckless abbot Abelard and his pupil Héloïse, the 12th-century lovers whose tragic tale of emasculation (his) and enforced separation (mutual) was the rage among early 1800s Romantics. Abelard and Héloïse's towering neo-Gothic tomb, still one of the most spectacular in Père-Lachaise, is the highlight of Division 7, the cemetery's oldest section. For similar promotional reasons, Louise de Lorraine, king Henri III's widow, was shifted to Père-Lachaise from the convent of the Capucines, perhaps in a bid to entice Royalist customers. (Her tomb was later dismantled). To make intellectuals and artists feel welcome, Molière and La Fontaine were disinterred from the Saint Joseph and Innocents cemeteries, respectively, and placed in new tombs in Division 26, high on a hill. Never mind that the bones of both playwright and author had been mixed with those of other skeletons in a common grave; their tombs are in fact cenotaphs, since no one can be sure whose remains they hold.

Soon after these transfers, another celebrated playwright was dug up and moved to Père-Lachaise: Caron de Beaumarchais, author of *Le Mariage de Figaro*. His original grave in the garden of his townhouse on what is now the Boulevard Beaumarchais stood in the way of progress, so the move was both convenient and necessary.

Though business was slow at first the twin ploys of the Jesuit's name and the famous transplanted skeletons eventually worked. By the 1810s Père-Lachaise had become *the* resting place for families of high social standing or aspiration, those, in other words, with the money to buy a perpetual concession and build a monumental tomb. People spoke of the cemetery's most desirable neighborhoods, paralleling them to Paris' *beaux quartiers*. That explains why the roster of 19th- and 20th-century marquee names with a slice of Père-Lachaise is a Who's Who of France.

Among my favorite residents are botanist-agronomist Auguste Parmentier of potato fame (his tomb is surrounded by potato plants), essayist Louis-Sébastien Mercier (author of *Tableau de Paris* and *Le Nouveau Paris*), military heroes Maréchal Ney and Kellermann (both rate a Paris street in their honor), not to mention Chopin, Balzac, David, Gustave Doré, Oscar Wilde, Guillaume Apollinaire, Amedeo Modigliani, Marcel Proust, Edith Piaf, Gertrude Stein and Yves Montand. Just about every distinguished poet, writer, musician, composer, statesman, military hero, doctor, actor, playwright, scientist, blueblood, industrialist and plutocrat of the last 200 years lucky enough to have died in or near Paris is buried here – Montparnasse's celebrated cemetery is nothing in comparison.

But it's not merely the one million illustrious occupants of the 70,000 tombs strewn picturesquely along ten miles of paths veining the cemetery's panoramic parklands that draw visitors to this preternaturally Parisian necropolis. There is an additional, intangible attraction I notice each time I wander here: the cult of the dead, the fascination, sometimes morbid, that the living feel toward the related phenomena of death, time passing, and collective memory. This fascination takes many forms, and Père-Lachaise accommodates them all, embracing the rites of conventional Catholics, Jews and Moslems, Buddhists, Zoroastrians and adepts of black magic. Even believers in the transmigration of the soul are well served. For the delectation of Spiritists there is the flower-strewn sepulchral monument, perpetually besieged, dedicated to Allan Kardek, father of this curious creed. His tomb is in Division 44 near the crematorium and every time I pass it, Kardek's followers are there by the dozen. They lay hands on the tomb and, they claim, communicate with their master.

Nature and the elements play a big part in the Romantic spell Père-Lachaise casts on visitors. Magnificent trees sprout from graves, consuming them one particle at a time. Ravenous roots and trunks bear up bits of stone, iron or bone. The most astonishing sepulcher-devouring tree I know is an arm span-wide purple beech on the Chemin du Dragon (in Division 27). Its gray, elephantine roots have been delving for decades into the Duhoulley family plot. They have obliterated at least one other tomb and are inching towards its neighbors.

If you are looking for an X Files-style frisson, I suggest you take a look at the imposing sepulcher in Division 8 of Etienne Gaspard Robertson (1763-1837), a magician. Winged skulls, like demonic cherubs, perch at each corner of the massive tomb. Adepts of black masses swear the skulls swirl into the air with Robertson on moonless nights. In keeping with the symbolism of superstition, there are real, live feral cats and owls in many a ruined family chapel. Some nest in the bows of ancient horse chestnut trees. They scurry and flap in the twilight as they feed off the countless rodents that day-trippers seldom see. I have had the honor of seeing the rats and cats, owls and bats, having, on several occasions, been among the last visitors escorted out at nightfall.

Friends who know I've had an office near Père-Lachaise since the early 1990s often ask me what it's like to live or work in the cemetery's back yard. I tell them the truth: I go there almost daily to stroll and meditate, just as Honoré de Balzac did (he's buried in Division 48). In the 1810s and '20s the sardonic novelist noted that he wandered among the tombs regularly "to cheer myself up". I find nothing bizarre about eating lunch on a bench among the monuments when the weather is nice, for instance. But most people I know recoil at the thought of a picnic at Père-Lachaise.

Innocent picnicking is one thing, I retort. Scavenging for souvenirs is another. Just as visitors to Paris' catacombs sometimes emerge with skulls or tibia tucked into their packs, a certain kind of souvenir-hunter combs Père-Lachaise searching for ceramic wreaths, stone heads, brass ornaments and, of course, bones. One egregious example of mindless souvenir hunting revolves around the cemetery's most problematic resident: James Douglas Morrison, the "Jim" carved on scores of trees and tombs.

Jim is none other than the celebrated lead singer of The Doors, who died in Paris of a drug overdose in 1971. From the start his grave attracted attention, much of it unwelcome. However, not long after the release of Oliver Stone's movie *The Doors*, the numbers of rowdy Jim-worshippers swelled into the thousands. Many vandalized Morrison's and other, nearby tombs. Someone even managed to break off and steal Morrison's stone bust, probably at night.

Why bother? For the same reasons the Grand Tour travelers of the 18th century looted the cemeteries of Rome, Naples and Athens, perhaps. It may well be that for some benighted souls such trinkets represent a means of possessing the past, stopping time or climbing back through it to another age.

"One day these hills with their urns and epitaphs will be all that remains of our present generations and their subtle contrivances," wrote a prescient Etienne Pivert de Senancour in the early 1800s. "They will compose, as Rome was said to do, a city of memories."

In French the word *souvenir* indicates both objects and memories. Despite the eternal ambitions of the *concession à perpetuité*, though, nothing lasts forever, neither urns nor epitaphs nor even the memories associated with them. Who remembers Pivert de Senancour, for that matter, or fellow writer Benjamin Constant? Constant died famous in 1830, drawing 100,000 mourners to his funeral. Who remembers François Gémond, whose obelisk (in Division 25) is the tallest in Père-Lachaise? And what of Félix Beaujour (1765-1836)? His penile stone tower in Division 48 rises from a rusticated stone drum to dizzying heights and is surely one of the world's most astounding funerary monuments. The stones still stand but the men and their deeds have been forgotten, one and all.

Each year dozens of tombs collapse, exposing generations of coffins stacked vertically underneath. The roofs of chapels give way. Trees fall in storms, crushing tombstones and statuary. Iron rusts and stones flake into nothingness. Families, too, disappear. If the city authorities deem a tomb abandoned – usually because it is unsafe to passersby – its owners have three years to respond and make repairs. If they fail, the city revokes the concession, removes what remains of the tomb, and resells the land.

Eternity? The going price for a repossessed plot at Père-Lachaise is about 5,000 euros. That does not include work needed to make the site build-able, or, naturally, the cost of a monument. Private firms or family members must maintain the tombs and plots. The city of Paris merely sweeps and repairs the paved streets and gravel lanes, and plants the petunias or chrysanthemums in the many raised beds that grace the site.

Death goes on, you might say, but then so does life. Among the monuments, oblivious children play. Lovers twine on hidden paths, unwittingly reenacting the passion of Abelard and Héloïse. Old men sit in the sun, reading *Le Parisien*, while widows, always outnumbering them, polish the granite gravestones or feed the stray cats. And of course there are the tourists, most of them clutching maps as they trip from tomb to tomb many, doubtless, wondering why they are here and what it all means in the grand scheme of things. Père-Lachaise is a lively city of the dead indeed and it's likely to remain so, perhaps not for eternity, but for a long, long time.

Louvre Pyramid, 1989

François' Follies

"The idea that Paris in a century or two could become the privileged enclave of Japanese tour operators is a thought that makes Mitterrand bristle."

Luc Tessier, director of the
Coordinating Body of *Les Grands Projets*, 1988

Pharaoh", "emperor" and "king" were favorite titles given former president François Mitterrand. Admirers and detractors alike also called him "Tonton" for his avuncular charisma, or "Le Grenouille", because he looked startlingly like a frog. Mitterrand's presidency lasted from 1981 to 1994. But his heritage as a builder lives on. Like a pharaoh, he commissioned a pyramid (at the Louvre) and a Great Library of Alexandria (the Très Grande Bibliothèque, at Tolbiac). With Napoléonic imperiousness he ordered a triumphal arch (at La Tête Défense) and one-upped Napoléon III with a bigger opera house (at La Bastille). To prove he could subsume his presidential predecessor, he adopted the unfinished projects of Valéry Giscard d'Estaing: La Villette; the Musée d'Orsay; the Institut du Monde Arab.

Anyone who thinks Mitterrand's so-called *Grands Projets* are old news should rethink: the international conference center he planned for the Quai Branly near the Eiffel Tower is only now getting underway (and will house Jacques Chirac's African art museum, instead, as excogitated by star-architect Jean Nouvel).

With something approaching awe and horror I watched Mitterrand's follies coalesce and had the good fortune to scramble through many while interviewing the projects' prime movers. Recently I revisited the president's main offspring. Have they, as Mitterrand hoped, saved Paris from becoming a "museum city" cut off from its suburbs? Have they lastingly boosted the prestige of French architects, while indelibly impressing Mitterrand's name in the history books?

Métro line 1 links the troika of sites that were closest to Mitterrand's heart: Bastille, Louvre, Grand Arch. For the sake of chronology and convenience my first stop was the Louvre. Mitterrand's earliest and most ambitious operation was transplant surgery on what had become a dusty, dreary place whose decline threatened Gallic *gloire* and *histoire*, not to mention tourism revenues. After visiting Washington's National Gallery, Tonton highhandedly hired its designer I. M. Pei to create Le Grand Louvre. No architectural competition was held, a technical illegality. Mitterrand briefed Pei to respect the Louvre's historic components. His solution was the now-familiar 22-meter high pyramid of glass and crisscrossed steel, with an underground entrance, a theater, state-of-the-art restoration labs, a shopping concourse and parking facilities.

Like most Paris denizens Pei's proposal didn't thrill me. But I recall my bafflement when critics claimed the pyramid would "deface" the Napoléon Courtyard's façades. A historicist's hodgepodge, they were as kitsch in their day as the pyramid was in the early '80s. In reality, at issue was the Socialist president's perceived defiling of a royal enclave. As some pundits put it, Mitterrand marked it as a dog might.

Swept by crowds from the métro station into the Louvre's subterranean maw I couldn't help marveling now at Pei's success in hitching high art to consumerism. Where the weary masses of old once deciphered turgid texts or strained their eyes on the museum's badly displayed, unloved and largely looted treasures, here were smiling hordes stuffed with exotic delicacies from the merry-go-round of Louvre restaurants, casting beatific glances at skillfully lit artworks before loading up on reproductions, CDs, designer sportswear and gadgets.

Pei's entrance was conceived to simplify the Louvre's labyrinth. Experts claim it takes less time than ever to reach the Mona Lisa (the goal of 90 percent of visitors). Persnickety regulars at first grumbled about a crass Grand Louvre for beginners, and militated for a reopening of doors in the museum's many wings. But they soon learned to slip in through the Pavillon Flore, thereby skipping the subterranean feeding frenzy. More doors will soon reopen, the Louvre's director now promises. Everyone seems happy enough in any case.

Early on boosters said the pyramid would blend into the cityscape. They were right. As Pei predicted, the glass panes reflect changeable skies. They also collect soot, despite frequent scrubbings. Cosmetic concerns aside, I saw nary a grimace now as I shuffled with thousands from sculpture courts (where cars once parked) through restored Renaissance rooms and lavish Second Empire salons (formerly the Finance Minister's office), to excavated medieval bastions. Back outside, I took a table at Café Marly and watched visitors dance in feathery water sprays or soak their feet in the fountains flanking the pyramid. Attendance has risen from 2.5 million in the early 1980s to nearly 6 million today. What better sign of approval might a monarch desire?

Laid out in 1670 by Louis XIV's royal architect Le Notre, the so-called "Triumphal Way" runs west from the Louvre's Cour Carré through the glass eye of the pyramid and nearby Carrousel Arch, across the Tuileries and up the Champs-Elysées, under the Arc de Triomphe, straight across town to La Tête Défense, crowned by Mitterrand's Grand Arch. My subway train covered the distance in twenty minutes. Even though from La Défense's highest point I couldn't see back into central Paris, I knew the Triumphal Way, alias the "Power Axis", was there, also extending east from the Louvre to the Bastille.

Unexpectedly the Grand Arch is the sole Mitterrand project to have garnered near total support. It actually improves La Défense, a paragon of architectural mediocrity bristling with mirrored-glass skyscrapers and studded with concrete apartment bunkers. The absence of cars, and recent landscaping, are the saving graces of this Moscow-meets-Manhattan satellite city.

As I queued under the Grand Arch in the windy vortex comically termed a "piazza", then rode to the roof in a glass bubble elevator, I recalled watching back in the late '80s as the viewing deck was poured into place at a height of over 100 meters. Building the arch required much engineering wizardry. The vistas from on high aren't nearly as spectacular as those you see from the Eiffel Tower, but if you're into cannon-shot perspectives you won't be disappointed.

Arch designer Johan Otto von Spreckelsen adroitly poised his bobble 6.30 degrees askew, mirroring the skew of the Louvre's Cour Carrée without blocking the Power Axis. In theory a superhuman bowler could roll a ball through the arch's wind-tunnel piazza to the grubby panes of Pei's pyramid. At a distance of twenty years this sounds like manual self-pleasuring, but it long preoccupied Tonton's planners.

A nitpicker might carp about the arch's smog-stained Carrara cladding, the threadbare carpets inside, or the prison-camp aesthetics of the rooftop terrace. Even arch devotees cannot help noting that the suspended canvas windbreaks called "Nuages" look less like the hovering clouds Von Spreckelsen had envisioned than a tattered and stained Bedouin tent. They simply don't work. Wind or not, the arch is standing up to time's weathering, and it seems a pity that Von Spreckelsen died before it was completed.

A lesser archway, this one clad with sparkling dark granite, graces the entrance to the Bastille Opera at the historic axis' eastern end. Of all Tonton's arch-follies it has aged the worst and looks, though still jailbait, like a shabby, overweight old cocotte with a hairnet. The netting is there to keep the shoddily anchored gray granite cladding from falling onto passersby.

In a rush to make a July 13, 1989 bicentennial celebration deadline, but desirous to appear fair this time around, Mitterrand held a "blind" competition for the project. Everyone in Paris soon knew that the president's choice was remote-controlled by associates who mistakenly believed they had identified star-architect Richard Meier's opera house mockup. The fruit of this cock-up is Canadian-Uruguayan Carlos Ott's $350 million behemoth. It measures nearly half a mile (800 meters) around and 150 feet (48 meters) high. "People don't like my opera house because they say it's ugly, it's fat, it doesn't have any gold or red velvet inside, and it looks like a factory," a red-faced Ott told me in 1989. "And all those things to me are compliments!" Ott has received many compliments since *Newsweek* first compared his masterpiece to "the alien mother ship that spawned the public toilets".

However, as I bustled into the behemoth with droves of elegant opera aficionados and enjoyed a tear-jerking performance of "La Bohème", I had to admit that the main auditorium is a formidable resonating chamber (Ott had help designing it). The blue-gray granite walls, oak flooring and black velour seats that seemingly disappear when the lights go down are as handsome and functional today as the building's outside was, is and always will be ridiculous.

A ten-minute walk further east and I came upon Mitterrand's unsung Ministry of Finance complex. It's Europe's longest continuous building, seemingly leftover from Stalin's USSR, and goosesteps in an "L" from the Gare de Lyon to the Seine at Bercy. I remember the spiel co-architects Paul Chemetov and Borja Huidobro gave the press in the late 1980s. The Bercy métro-viaduct, they said, with its double set of white stone arcades, inspired their concept. Too bad the inspiration penetrated only as far as the architects' highly active vocal chords. Detractors dubbed the $500 million trifle "futuristic", "Stalinesque" and "nightmarish". Its defenses include a moat and a cubical citadel of glass (for private ministerial meetings). A hive buzzing with 6,000 pen pushers, honeycombed with identical, modular offices, the color-coded signage is devised to get drones through a synapse-stunning thirty-five kilometers of corridors. That's nearly twenty miles. When I first toured the building in 1989 my embarrassed PR guide lost her way on the sixth floor of Building C, panicked and had to call for help. Little has changed, though nowadays Bercy is smog-stained and seems less futuristic or "intelligent", as it was once called (meaning 100 percent computerized). I walked through it now and was comforted to learn that the air-conditioning still turns off when windows are opened. In-house mail continues to arrive via something called "Teledoc", a ceiling-mounted electronic shuttle system. The minister flies in by helicopter (there's a landing pad on the roof) or splashes in by speedboat (to a high-security dock on the Seine). With synthesized voices the elevators tell visitors what floor they're on. And countless people still get lost.

While tanking up on a restorative dose of caffeine at a café outside the moat, I asked the barkeep how the fortress complex had changed the neighborhood. Local businesses are profiting, he chortled. Real estate values have risen. "And who cares if it could be in Moscow," he asked, jerking his thumb eastwards. "The TGB is worse!"

Upstream I crossed to the Left Bank at Tolbiac and stood before the Incan plinth on which the National Library rises amid a forest of construction cranes. Local redevelopment is still underway. The library's catchy official name is "Bibliothèque de France, Site François Mitterrand". But everyone calls this $1 billion-plus marvel the TGB (Très Grande Bibliothèque).

Can kitsch be dangerous, I wondered? I skittered in the windswept shadows of four, 300-foot towers of glass splayed like open books framing an expanse three football fields long of slippery, buckling tropical planks. A half-hour search among caged holly trees rattling in the wind revealed an entrance – luckily I'd been here before and vaguely remembered the way. The site's hidden heart is a glassed-in subterranean garden the length of two football fields, accessed via a tilted, moving sidewalk. Like the caged hollies, the gardens' handsome red pine trees double as contemporary bondage art, girded by steel cables so they won't crash through the windows.

Wind is not the only problem at the TGB. I still haven't gotten used to genial architect Dominque Perrault's underground reading rooms, or his cleverness in storing books in glass towers, where retrofitted wooden panels block daylight. The original plan was worse: conveyor belts were to cross an open courtyard, exposing books to rain and sun. I stood now in the western atrium and had plenty of time to take in the view of leaking ceilings and plastic buckets extending almost 700 feet east. Hours can go by while you get a computerized pass then summon a book from a tower into a reading room half a mile away. Best of all is trying to exit: if your returned loan hasn't been scanned back into the system, as happened to me, you can't get out. Red lights flashed. The turnstile wouldn't turn. Librarians and security guards leapt into action. Then Big Brother pushed a button somewhere and finally I was free to go.

My explorations of Mitterrand's megalomania had a surprisingly happy ending at La Villette in the 19th arrondissement, four *grands projets* in one. Three times the size of the Pompidou Center, the old meatpacking plant west of the Ourcq Canal has been the world's biggest science museum since it opened in 1986. No beef here, I reflected as I hoofed through this Emerald City of hi-tech. Cast as the Wizard of Oz, Mitterrand hijacked but couldn't ruin the project after drubbing Giscard d'Estaing at the polls, and it is Mitterrand's name that you see writ large on a bronze plaque in the cavernous main hall full of electronic gizmos.

I crossed the canal and found the doors open to the reconverted 1860s glass-and-ironwork cattle auction hall. Now an expo and concert venue, the Grande Halle evokes Baltard's dearly departed Les Halles, and, as with Giscard d'Estaing's equally successful Musée d'Orsay and Institut du Monde Arab, try as he might not even Mitterrand could ruin it.

Not content with surrogate fatherhood at La Villette, Tonton commissioned the Cité de la Musique, a silly name for the national music conservatory and instrument museum. Architect Christian de Portzamparc subsequently won the prestigious Pritzker Prize and is perhaps the sole Frenchman to have fulfilled Mitterrand's hope of global glory. He also designed classy Café Beaubourg; its counterpart here felt like a grand piano turned inside out. Like the other *grand projets* De Portzamparc's compound shows precocious signs of gritty wear. The superfluous metal superstructures that metaphorically "bridge" the abutting Péripherique beltway and the bathroom-tiled facades seem hopelessly mired in a post-modernist aesthetic. Yet the curving indoor "street" playfully evokes an inner ear, and the museum's displays and live music are a harmonious delight.

Before heading home I took a turn around the Parc de la Villette, a deconstructionist's dream its American architect Bernard Tschumi termed "an urban park for the 21st century", meaning it rejects the notion of a refuge. His "discontinuous building" is a sequence of twenty-six whimsical "garden follies" painted fire engine red, set along cobbled footpaths, lawns and the Ourcq Canal. A refuge from the city it isn't: cars thundered by on the beltway, riverboats chuffed past. The follies merge jungle gym, firehouse and lifeguard station. Despite "keep off" signs, kids gleefully scaled the wheel rims of Claes Oldenburg's outsized "Buried Bicycle" sculpture. Others hunted frogs in a bamboo-stippled marsh, unaware of their prey's resemblance to a certain former president. It struck me that few of those happy children had lived through Mitterrand's murky reign, and probably not a one would recognize his name.

Trompe-l'oeil banisters, boulders and trees, 1999

Montsouris and Buttes-Chaumont: the Art of the Faux

"Let us stroll in this décor of desires, this décor filled with mental misdemeanors and with imaginary spasms..."

Louis Aragon at Buttes-Chaumont

The leaves of the horse-chestnut trees hanging over the sidewalk broke into a sudden jig. Smoke and steam shot through them, puffing up over the tops of the hedges along the street where we were strolling, outside the historic park of Montsouris in Paris' 14th arrondissement. My wife poked her head through the hedge and beckoned me to follow. I heard a swish and a chug and saw an old black steam engine dive into a tunnel under the park, on the tracks of the Petite Ceinture – theoretically an abandoned railway. A ghost-train? I'd read somewhere that back in the 19th century those tracks had linked in a loop the outer edge of Paris. I'd also read that they were used occasionally by train buffs to exercise vintage rolling stock.

By the time my wife and I had ambled across the shady, landscaped curves of Montsouris and dug into our picnic on a lakeside bench, we'd forgotten about the train. The quacking ducks and shifting light, the luxuriant greenery and human parade passing by lulled and enchanted us. There were students from the nearby Cité Universitaire campus and the usual selection of au pairs, plaster-spackled workers in blue dungarees and tourists shod with running shoes. The gingerbread Pavillon de Montsouris, a restaurant filled with hoity-toity Parisians in their Sunday best, seemed plucked from the proverbial Impressionist painting. So too the oversized prams, the fancy picnic hampers, and the awkward 1870s statuary dotted around us on freshly mowed lawns and raked gravel paths. Exception made for the tourists and joggers, and the cars parked outside the gates, much was as it might have been when the park was built, almost a century and a half ago, by Napoléon III's planners, atop abandoned quarries.

The quarries of Mont Souris gave the place its name. Mont Souris means "Mouse Mountain" and I couldn't help chuckling at that as we circled the flower-edged knolls covering about forty acres of prime real estate. It seemed an unlikely moniker for the site of an ancient Roman burial ground originally strung along the road leading south from Paris to Orléans. Among the sepulchral monuments once stood the tomb, now lost, of a supposed giant: the gravestone measured about twenty feet long. The giant's name has come down to us twisted from something now forgotten to Ysorre, Issoire or possibly the mousy-sounding Souris. "Issoire" lives on in the avenue de la Tombe-Issoire, a nearby traffic artery.

From the Middle Ages to the late 1860s, windmills rose among the ruined tombs and quarries. Nowadays the modest heights of Montsouris sport the parabolic antennae of Paris' meteorological station. From the park's belvedere we gazed down and saw a flash of steel – a train rattling over the RER express subway tracks. The railway, originally linking Paris to suburban Sceaux, has been there since the inception of Montsouris as a park. The engineers who landscaped the neighborhood used the quarries and the lay of the land to route the trains through almost unnoticed. Those of the Petite Ceinture ran through tunnels even further underground.

It was the thought of those tunnels that reminded me of the steam train we'd spotted earlier that day. A penny dropped in my head, a rusty handle turned and I recalled a similar scene in another of my favorite time-tunnel parks, also built on abandoned quarries: Buttes-Chaumont. The event had taken place ten, maybe fifteen years ago, when I'd first stumbled upon the lush Buttes-Chaumont on the opposite side of town in the 19th arrondissement. There too I'd heard a steam train rumbling below, hidden by trees. Irrationally I now wondered if the ghost train we'd just seen could possibly be circling Paris, and if we could intercept it across town.

I took my wife by the hand and we rushed down Montsouris' snaky paths to the RER station. We transferred at Gare du Nord then trotted from the Ourcq subway station to the northern entrance of Buttes-Chaumont. Panting and sweaty like the droves of joggers on the park's paths, we found the footbridge over the Petite Ceinture. Did we see the old black steam train conveniently chuff by? No, of course not. But as I leaned on the bridge's iron grills catching my breath amid swerving perambulators, swinging picnic baskets and bourgeois families seemingly whisked along behind us from Montsouris, I was glad to have been so impulsive. Though the scene around us was in living color – a riot of blossoms and garish outdoor casual wear – my mind's eye focused on a sepia-tinted image from the Second Empire circa 1865. In it there were brand new boulevards lined by balconied buildings, and as many smokestacks as church towers on the surprisingly familiar horizon. It was an image my brain had clicked on and dragged from the novels of Zola and Balzac, the poetry of Baudelaire, the photography of Charles Marville – Napoléon III and Haussmann's official photographer. Welling up from it I could almost smell the electrifying greed of the Second Empire's new bourgeoisie, a perfume powerful enough to overwhelm the cabbage-scented misery of the hundreds of thousands of peasants pouring into town, seeking their fortune amid the smokestacks. How might it have felt to wake up in Paris one day in the 1860s to discover a new city had mushroomed overnight, with not only new roads and buildings and parks like Montsouris and Buttes-Chaumont, but also a new soul, a new way of living – the birth of the modern?

My wife tugged my hand. It was too hot to stand around waiting for a steam train that might never arrive. We sought shade on the far side of a lake. A graceful suspension bridge spanned the greenish waters. Stone pinnacles shot up from the center of the lake. An airborne colonnaded temple nested atop one of them, at least 100 feet above the groups of rowdy teenagers rowing in leaky boats around us. A waterfall rumbled in a grotto, setting mist adrift through gaps in the cliff face. A colorful kaleidoscope of neighborhood children played in channels of rushing water that spilled from rockeries. Sun-baked codgers pulled big, lazy bottom-feeders from the lake, dangled them in front of goggling toddlers then tossed them back into the water. Swans and geese cruised by, honking and snapping at flotillas of stale bread. We cooled our heels in the shady stream, safely out of the swans' reach, and my wife wondered out loud how many city kids and hot, tired adults like us had sought refuge in the park over the years.

I had a vague notion of the Butte-Chaumont's history, gleaned from park panels, guidebooks and French literature. I knew, for example, that the site had been called Chauve Mont – bald mountain – because the gypsum and clay in the soil kept vegetation from growing, so that when it was turned into a park tons of horse manure and topsoil had to be brought in. I remembered vaguely that the same team of planners, architects and designers who built Buttes-Chaumont worked their magic on the Bois de Boulogne, Bois de Vincennes, Montsouris and about two dozen city squares, at more or less the same time – the 1860s zenith of the Second Empire. Romantic English and exotic Asian gardens were in vogue then, and that would explain the park's sinuous paths, I now reasoned, as well as the strategically positioned copses of trees and rock outcrops. Like anyone who's read any French history, I'd come across stories, most of them inaccurate, of the *Gibet de Montfaucon*, a gallows built on a rise somewhere near here, where countless men and women were hanged from the Middle Ages into the Renaissance. And of course there were the tales of the bloody repression of the Communards, who fought the Emperor's counter-revolutionary Versaillais troops at Buttes-Chaumont in 1870, were slaughtered by them and buried or burned en masse on the Butte's lawns.

But as we sat in the shade and dangled our feet in the stream the violence the park has known was nowhere to be seen, heard or felt. Caged peacocks called from atop a grassy knoll, children squealed, teenagers exchanged bodily fluids, and I thought I caught the hissing of the old steam train echoing out of the cutting below the Rue de la Crimée. But I was too dazed and content to climb the rise and have a look.

The heat, the summery garden scents and the murmuring water lulled me into a state of reverie. That dazed sensation followed me home and, having engendered a powerful curiosity in me about the park, drove me to crack open several reference books on Paris, the Second Empire and Buttes-Chaumont in particular. I soon discovered some curious facts. For instance, the park's pinnacles were created to emulate the cliffs of Étretat, a favorite resort of the Second Empire's upper classes (and of its painters, including Monet). My reference books also confirmed that the pinnacle-top temple is an exact replica of the Temple of Cybele in Tivoli, near Rome, dedicated to a goddess of the hearth. I learned that the suspension bridge stretches 120 feet across and thirty-five feet above the lake, and that the other, shorter bridge linking the temple to the park's upper section is known as the Suicide Bridge. Jilted lovers long favored its tempting seventy-foot free-fall. Another nugget of information I came upon is that Gustave Eiffel built one of the park's least remarkable bridges. As to statistics, various sources agree that amid the twenty-five acres of lawn, the 3.2 miles of paved road and 1.5 miles of winding paths there are approximately 3,200 trees. My estimate would be that there are about thrice that many shrubs, something on the order of 10,000. Among the vegetation sprout many sculptures – some innocuous, some ludicrous – plus a hodgepodge of neo-Gothic, neo-Renaissance, Sino-English and faux-Swiss park buildings typical of late-1800s eclecticism.

Though Baron Haussmann was in charge overall of the remake of Second Empire Paris, the real hero of its parks was Jean-Charles Alphand, an engineer and public works designer, flanked by landscaper Édouard André and architect Gabriel Jean Antoine Davioud. The big parks they created were linked by the ultra-modern Petite Ceinture steam railway, and were conceived as more than mere rehab projects. The depleted quarries of Buttes-Chaumont, for example, had become the garbage dump of Belleville, to which the area then belonged, as well as an open-air slaughterhouse for horse-butchers, and the lair of murderers, robbers and literary heroes like Arsène Lupin, the gentleman thief.

Ostensibly the reason Napoléon III commissioned his men to build Buttes-Chaumont, Montsouris and the city's other green spaces was the International Exposition of 1867. But these "democratic oases" as they were called were first and foremost an experiment in social engineering, what surrealist writer Louis Aragon in his bizarre book *Paris Peasant* called "artificial paradises." The new parks of the brave new Paris were as essential as the *grands boulevards*, the train stations and smokestacks, thought Aragon and others. They were safety valves for the age of patriarchal capitalism, which depended on immigrant labor. Every leaf, every landscaped knoll and babbling watercourse was calculated to outdo Nature. By spending a few hours in the park, went the theory, the worker-bees of the empire, most of them transplanted French provincials or starveling Italians, would better bear the stress of the factory, the overcrowded city, the loss of beloved forests and fields. So, these soothing parklands were in reality tools of exploitation, an anti-revolutionary opiate?

Buttes-Chaumont is a half-hour's walk across the Ménilmontant and Belleville neighborhoods from my office near Père-Lachaise cemetery in northeastern Paris. I go there fairly often. Having satisfied my bookish curiosity about Napoléon III and his diabolical amusement parks, I was eager to have another look at the Buttes – to me the most astonishing, picturesque and alluring of the city's artificial paradises. I wanted to view the place with knowing eyes. Would this proto-

Disneyland dreamed up by a dictatorial emperor be as seductive now as I'd found it on earlier, unknowing visits?

"Let us stroll in this décor of desires, this décor filled with mental misdemeanors and with imaginary spasms," wrote the playfully cryptic surrealist Aragon from the Buttes-Chaumont. *Décor* is the right word: as I stood again in the grotto near the thundering cascade I could see that the stalagmites were poured from cement, like the faux-wooden railings on the faux-stone pathways. But they were covered with fresh moss and seemed so worn and weathered that I couldn't help finding them endearing.

From Cybele's panoramic temple I took in the jumbled view, with Montmartre's kitsch cupolas and the housing projects of Pantin on the northeastern horizon. It was not a view calculated to please tourists, but I found it intriguing nonetheless, another example of social engineering, this one dreamed up by 1960s-70s French president Georges Pompidou. Glancing down at the placid lake around the pinnacles' base, I noticed in its ugly concrete bottom a tangle of water pipes.

Was the curtain being drawn back on the Wizard of Oz, I wondered ruefully?

Down the cast-concrete steps I clambered, through faux-caves, settling eventually on an old green bench near a garrulous group of fishermen.

"No, we do not catch sardines," one of them quipped when I started to make conversation about the fishing. "We catch gudgeon, carp and pike and we know some of them by name, like we know the swan, who's name is Jojo by the way."

The fishermen chuckled at these apparently oft-recited lines. They knew the fish as well as they knew each other, they explained, because they bought them from a fish farm and stocked the lake yearly and were the only anglers legally entitled to wet a line here.

More artifice, I sighed, realizing that the poor dumb fish keep biting the same fishermen's bait day in, day out, hooked and released, until the day they die of old age. But as I circled the lake on carefully plotted paths with temple-topped perspectives engineered to be dazzling whether glimpsed from high or low, and as I sipped a drink at the gimcrack café designed by a dictator's minions, I felt a growing kinship not only with the duped immigrant workers of old who came here to rest up after their slave labors. The fact is I felt like the gudgeon, carp or pike stocked by the fisherman. Maybe, I thought, sipping my coffee, maybe it's precisely because Buttes-Chaumont, Montsouris and the other Second Empire parks I love are so utterly artificial, so wantonly faux, that I'll keep falling for their sepia-tinted charms hook, line and sinker for as long as I live in Paris, the world capital of illusionism.

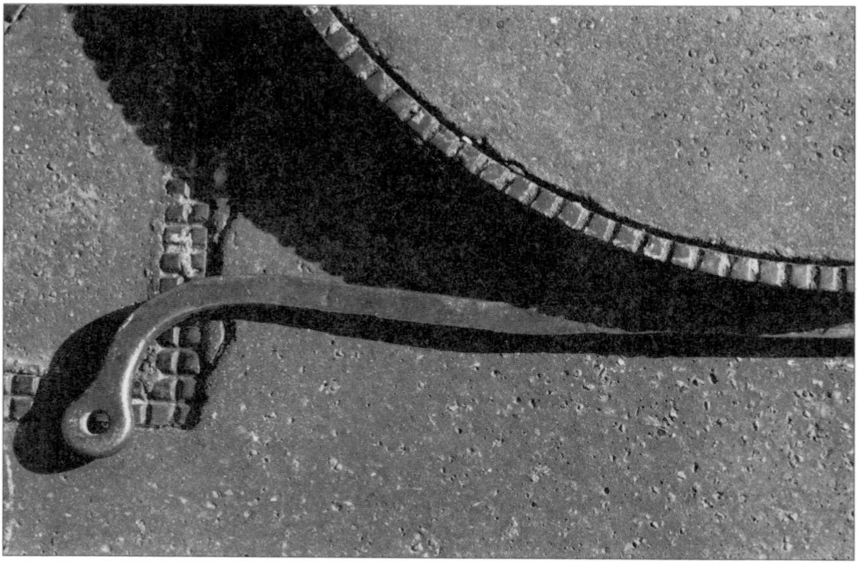

Manhole cover, tool and shadow, 1991

Going Underground

Per me si va nella città dolente/Per me si va in eterno dolore/Per me si va tra la perduta gente… "Through me you enter the city of pain/Through me you enter suffering eternal/Through me you go among lost souls…" – Engraved upon the gateway to Hell.

Dante, *Inferno*

It all started with two apparently unrelated subterranean events. The first was a routine damage-control visit to our basement – the *cave*. Records indicate our Marais building got its façade in a 1784 remake of the neighborhood, near Saint-Paul's, but that the structure dates to about 1630, with foundations and cellar from further back, poised atop the long-demolished priory of Sainte-Catherine-du-Val-des-Ecoliers, founded in the thirteenth century.

You need a chopstick and a key to open our cellar door. Then you wind down a steep, moldering staircase into centuries past, into the chalky, muddy underbelly of Paris – what Victor Hugo called *Lutetia, City of Mud*, a reference to the ancient Gallo-Roman city that stood here. I struck a match, sizzling cobwebs as I went, wrenched open the rotting wooden door to our section of cellar, and dug out a pre-industrial candlestick holder. In the flickering candle flame I spotted a crack in the masonry I'd never noticed before. I could see nothing beyond, of course – the darkness was absolute. But I imagined an infernal world.

The main Roman road from Lutetia to Melun – nowadays the Rue Saint-Antoine – runs a few hundred yards to the south of our building. The priory had stood here five hundred years, from twelve-something until the 1770s. Old-timers in my building had told me of hidden passageways fanning from our cellar to catacombs, quarries and long-gone fortresses.

"There's another Paris under Paris," intoned one neighbor, a paleontologist, echoing Hugo, the bard of buried Lutetia. The paleontologist's words, recalled as I stood in my cellar, sent a pleasurable chill down my spine.

I snuffed my candle and plunged through a time tunnel into the Gallo-Roman city, then burrowed onward and upward to the malodorous Middle Ages, the days of Baron Haussmann and Jean Valjean (fugitive hero of Hugo's *Les Misérables*), slowly resurfacing with Occupation-era French Résistance fighters and their underground networks, before clawing metaphorically back to the comforts of our banal present day. I re-lit the candle and dragged some suitably decomposed junk from the cellar to the garbage.

Not long after this first fantasy voyage, while strolling under the arcades of the Place des Vosges near our building, I decided to step into a cluttered shop I'd passed a thousand times but had only visited twice. The affable owner, Pierre Balmès, a specialist in antique timepieces, reminded me that he'd opened for business in 1949. While moving in he had made a curious discovery. The square's identical pavilions were built, he'd said, between 1605 and 1612 – everyone knew that. But few realized the Place des Vosges' northern flank sits over the cellars of the Maison Royale des Tournelles, erected in 1388, destroyed in 1563 by order of Queen Catherine de Médicis. "I was sweeping the cellar floor," Balmès recounted, "when I noticed what looked like a trap door..." The door led to another vaulted stone *cave* below it, choked with historical debris.

My mind boggled at Balmès' words. Could this cellar be linked to the one under our building, a mere two hundred yards away as the mole burrows?

A kind of feverish curiosity seized me. Wherever I went in following days I peered down, not up. I peered into stairwells, and into churches to see if they had a crypt, into road works, drains and wells. Slowly I began assembling a list of underground sites, a mental mole's map of Paris, including but not limited to classics like the sewers and catacombs.

On that list are nightclubs, supermarkets and shopping centers, a reservoir, the Senate building, movie theaters, the Opéra, swimming pools, crypts, wells, burial grounds, quarries, wine cellars, half a dozen museums, department stores, rivers, subways, secret passageways, a canal, dozens of train lines, a fabulous Art Nouveau public bathroom and more.

Let's get one thing straight: I have never been a devotee of the underworld. But two things continue to fascinate me about subterranean Paris. There's the physical layer cake of civilizations, a millennial *millefeuille* of Gallic, Gallo-Roman, medieval, Renaissance and more or less modern constructions, with associated lore.

Perhaps even more intriguing, though, are the people I've encountered who are obsessed by this buried metropolis. Take, for example, the thousands of (mostly young) Frenchmen and women who spend countless hours on their hands and knees delving into the 175 miles of Paris' abandoned limestone quarries, a subterranean cityscape as porous as the proverbial Swiss (Victor Hugo, better than I at simile, compared it to a sponge). Parisian cave mavericks are known as *cataphiles* – lovers of catacombs. Because the quarries have been off limits since 1955, *les cataphiles* are pursued in an endless game of cat-and-rat by a special police squad, the Brigade de Dispersion et d'Intervention en Carrière, whose members are nicknamed *cataflics* – catacomb cops.

Decked out in survival gear, cataphiles will do just about anything to get into the intestine-like quarry passages and chambers 100 feet or more below the city's surface. They throw drug parties, conduct spooky chthonic rites, play at Phantom of the Opera, or Jean Valjean escaping the gendarmes. Wherever bones have fallen into the light-less tunnels from the cemeteries above – at Père-Lachaise or Montparnasse, for instance – hardcore cataphiles crawl undaunted over mounds of moldering skeletons. Skulls are favorite trophies.

I've long wondered whether the cataphiles are misunderstood Romantics or certifiable loons. Whichever, they're extremists. They often cut through the metal bars installed by cataflics over the 388 known quarry entrances, many of them in abandoned railroad tunnels. They sometimes use dynamite to blow open new access holes. To elude the cataflics, they toss smoke bombs then disappear into the labyrinth. Some get lost for hours or days. Some get hurt. Some have no doubt died underground, like Philibert Aspairt. In 1793 this doorman at the Val-de-Grace convent descended into the cellars to fetch a bottle of liquor, turned the wrong way and was found eleven years later under what's now Rue Henri Barbusse. The spot has been a cataphile pilgrimage site ever since.

Mystery, danger, disobedience, a yearning for things lost, hidden, dead – this is what motivates Paris' peculiar cave people, anomalies in the Internet age, and therefore somehow remarkable if not endearing.

But as the ex-commandant of the Brigade de Dispersion et d'Intervention en Carrière told me one day, those thinking of joining a band of cataphiles for a foray should know that some cynical veterans also use their smoke bombs to frighten and disorient *touristes*, meaning first-time visitors. As in fraternity-style hazings, newcomers are sometimes stripped of their flashlights then left to whimper in the impenetrable darkness. "In case that isn't enough to discourage you," added the new head of the cataflics, Brigadier Févier, when I spoke to him, "there is always Mother Nature." Bona fide claustrophobia is unpleasant, but it's nothing compared to leptospirosis, a potentially lethal illness carried by germs in rat urine. Before venturing into Lutetia's muddy bowels, therefore, savvy cataphiles get immunized against it. "Be warned," say the cataflics, sounding like the soothsaying damned in Dante's *Inferno*.

Most casual underground thrill-seekers – meaning people like you and me – start and end their visit to subterranean Paris at Les Catacombes. You might better spend your time reading a page or two of *Les Misérables*, or looking at Félix Nadar's sublime 1861 photographs of this bizarre realm (Nadar actually invented flash photography to immortalize Paris' sewers and catacombs). A good place to begin an underground itinerary is the unsung Crypte Archeologique, under the square facing Notre-Dame cathedral. This admittedly tame display of ruins, jazzed up with clever spotlighting, nonetheless provides a potted history of Paris from pre-Roman times forward. You see maps and mockups of the city as it spread from the Île-de-la-Cité outward, a history written in rubble. There are Roman roads and the rooms of Roman houses, medieval staircases and wells, and an egg-shaped section of 19th-century drainage tunnel. A hodgepodge, the crypt hints at the true buried treasure of this ancient, palimpsest city: an understanding of the past and a perspective on the present.

You can continue a Roman-to-medieval visit at the Musée de Cluny, built atop Imperial-era baths (the cold, warm and hot rooms are still there, in ruins, plus plenty of archeological finds). Within a few hundred yards of the crypt and Cluny are several centuries-old Left Bank cellars open to the public. The most easily accessible lie under the celebrated (or notorious) Caveau de la Huchette and Caveau des Oubliettes, both nightspots. Here you descend into atmospheric jazz dens, under venerable vaults where unspeakable horrors – torture, imprisonment and execution – were once daily activities. At la Huchette there's even a skeleton on view, and a well-worn chastity belt. A quarter-mile west, another chastity belt lurks in the buttressed basement of Le Relais Louis XIII restaurant, which is built atop the defunct Grands Augustins convent, an institution presumably familiar with such contraptions.

In my desultory pursuit of information relating to Paris' underbelly, I have discovered that many of the Latin Quarter's hundreds of *caves* were formerly linked by secret passages, some leading into abandoned Roman quarries beneath the Montagne Sainte-Geneviève, which is now crowned by the Panthéon. In World War Two both Nazis and

Résistance fighters scurried through these passageways, and in the 1950-60s moviemakers showed their "underground" films here – a dauntingly close ordeal according to friends who participated and lived to tell.

In the hit parade of infra-Paris sites, the Louvre's Carrousel area offers the subterranean spectacle of Charles V's moat and walls – a seductive alignment of round tower bases and inclined ramparts. For aesthetics, however, my favorite Right Bank den is the one underneath the Marais historical society's 16th-century headquarters, the Maison d'Ourscamp, in the Rue François Miron. Its Gothic vaults and elegant columns originally supported the townhouse of a demolished 13th-century abbey. In the cellar's center is a well, a common feature of Paris houses until the arrival of Baron Haussmann and his waterworks engineer, Eugène Belgrand, in the mid-1800s.

To grasp the revolutionary aspects of Belgrand's sewers and water supply try imagining a filthy, disease-ridden Paris where ground and Seine water were contaminated, waste flooded the streets, and thousands died from water-borne diseases. Victor Hugo may have lamented the passing of this soulful, pestilential city, but not Nadar, whose black-and-white photos show Belgrand's spacious conduits in all their stunning symmetry. Today they're much as they were when built in the 1850s – orderly, clean, utterly unromantic yet redolent of a sickly sweetness Hugo would have loved, for the streets of his *Vieux Paris* were legendary for their stench of decomposing cabbage.

Let's be honest, it helps to be a historian or an engineer to enjoy the sewers. Nowadays only a quarter-mile section of them under the Quay d'Orsay is open to the public and only on foot (when I first visited Paris, visitors toured the sewers in rowboats). But your average sewer-goer is too baffled and nauseated to study the museum displays, which range from gumboots to computers, or appreciate the ingeniousness of the gravity-flow tunneling, the tunefulness of the gurgling gutters and 150-year-old devices are still in use, including giant wooden balls that rumble through the system's 1,300 miles, crushing muck as they go. To me this revolting spectacle conjures up images of the big nightmarish ball in the cult TV series *The Prisoner*, and like its star, I long for escape.

Nadar took some of his most ghoulish images not in the sewers but in Les Catacombes, in 1861. They capture that most sublime moment of Haussmann's modernization of the city: the stacking of the bones of some six million dead, many of them transferred here starting in 1786 from the cemetery of the Innocents, near what is now Les Halles.

Unlike those of Rome, Paris' catacombs are an ossuary, created for practical reasons: to empty the Innocents of a decomposing cargo that had burst through walls to poison the surrounding neighborhood.

The catacombs provide proof, if any were needed, that our modern age has no monopoly on perversity. Toward the end of the Ancien Régime the ossuary became a rendezvous of depraved aristocrats. The Comte d'Artois, later King Charles X, held torch-lit *fêtes macabres* here with ladies in waiting from the court in Versailles. The site was officially opened to tourists only in the 1870s, after Haussmann had sanitized it. Nadar's photos show workers sorting and stacking the bones dumped there from a dozen graveyards (all Paris' inner-city cemeteries were eventually cleared), building decorative retaining walls with femurs, tibia and skulls, and tossing smaller bones behind.

Accessing the catacombs is still a daunting experience. A trot down the spiral staircase that worms 100 feet beneath the Place Denfert-Rochereau, the main entrance to the site, is guaranteed to leave you dizzy. Claustrophobics need not apply. You enter a mile-long maze of tunnels that zigzag toward what 19th-century commentators, paraphrasing Dante, dubbed "the realm of the dead". As you march single-file over slippery stones, preceded and followed by hundreds of fellow visitors, it's little comfort to know that sections of these ancient former quarries have collapsed as recently as the mid-1990s. You squelch over mud, wondering when the lights or ventilation might fail, and, if you're like me, asking yourself what you're doing here in the first place, gaping at millions of weirdly displayed age-mottled bones.

Evidently I belong to a squeamish minority. Almost 200,000 tourists a year besiege the catacombs, loving them to death with cameras flashing and boots resounding. If ever there was a time you could quietly contemplate this disconcerting sanctuary's significance – the back-breaking work of underpaid miners, the technical genius of Enlightenment thinkers and engineers, the anonymity of six million forgotten ancestors – that innocent time is long gone. As I clambered out of the caves a security guard was checking backpacks. A stolen skull stared forlornly from a table, and a youngster with a stupid grin was doing his best to talk himself out of trouble. "Happens all the time," sighed a guard when I asked. "You've got to wonder…"

After the catacombs, the life-enhancing qualities of the subterranean Canal Saint-Martin can only come as a relief. You board a riverboat at the Arsenal marina, abutting the Bastille, then putter leisurely toward La Villette under several miles of vaults conceived by

Haussmann – who else? But the first, the great Emperor Napoléon deserves some credit, too. He had the canal built as an open waterway. The relentless Baron covered the canal to thwart riotous Parisians who, he feared (based on the 1830 revolution) might use it again as a defensive moat. Happily, nowadays tour boats and pleasure craft cruise the canal and there is no echo of its bloody past.

Another sublime subterranean spot is the basement of the Bazar de l'Hôtel de Ville – the BHV – an unrivaled Aladdin's cavern of hardware, now equipped with its own subterranean café-restaurant, Bricolò. And under the Place de la Madeleine hide what may just be Paris' most beautiful Art nouveau *toilettes publiques*, with carved wood panels, brass and mirrors, floral frescos and stained glass windows in each *cabinet*. Here, once you've awakened the sleeping *Madame Pipi* (as bathroom attendants are still called) you may tidy up like a real fin-de-siècle lady or gentleman.

Of course the greatest and most useful thing in Paris' underground world is the Métropolitain, opened for business in 1900. Its deepest stations are at Abbesses, halfway up Montmartre, and Cité, on the island of the same name. However, as if to prove that earlier centuries can't claim all the glory, the Météor line running from Madeleine to François Mitterrand's new National Library is a staggering wonder of the subsoil, a postmodern folly, as symbolic of our times as the sewers or catacombs were of theirs. Glass escalators lower you into cavernous halls, then down to the platforms, where glass barriers prevent passengers from falling onto the tracks. Météor is driverless. Its path crosses the Marais, within blocks of where I live. Whenever I ride it, I make a point of sitting in its glass-nosed first car and checking, irrationally, for traces of Paris history buried not far from my dusty, moldy old cellar.

Fishermen on the Seine, 1997

It's the Water

"The time-worn stones were cold and the ever-flowing stream beneath the bridges seemed to have carried away something of their selves..."

Émile Zola, *L'Oeuvre*, 1886

No single element of Paris evokes the city's ambiguous allure more poignantly for me than the Seine. A slow arcing gray-green curve, the river reflects the raked tin rooftops arrayed on its embankments, and the temperamental skies of the Île-de-France overhead. Sea breezes sweep up it bringing fresh Atlantic air into the city. Each day when I step out for my constitutional around the Île-Saint-Louis – a ten-minute walk from where my wife and I live – I ask myself what Paris would be without the Seine. The answer is simple: it wouldn't.

At once source and sewer, lifeline, moat and swelling menace, the Seine gave suck to nascent French civilization. It made the founding of Paris possible, transforming a settlement of mud huts into a capital city whose symbol since the year 1210 is a ship, with the catchy device *Fluctuat nec mergitur* – "It floats without being submerged" (and sounds better in Latin). For centuries this murky waterway has filled Parisians' hearts, minds and nostrils with equal measures of inspiration or despair.

Back in the mid-1970s, the low point of Paris urbanism, I visited the city for the first time and was taken aback by the river's chemical stench and the flying suds from its filthy waves quivering over the cars on the just-built riverside expressways. A decade later I willfully forgot such details when I engineered my move here. I was tantalized by the scenes – of dancers on the Seine's cobbled quays, bridges compressed by a telephoto lens – in what might possibly be the worst movie ever made, *Tangos*. Never able to tango despite lessons, and aware from the start that I'd duped myself into imagining such a place existed, I've been stalking the photogenic quays of Paris ever since. And though I've sometimes felt my passion for Paris ebb, the Seine has flowed along, in its indifference seducing me, a knowing victim, time and again.

Not long ago, after a failed research mission to the National Library on Paris' extreme eastern edge, I glanced down at the river from the Pont de Tolbiac and realized that, despite my wanderings, I'd never actually followed the Seine downstream across the city to the quays of the 15th arrondissement. How long a walk could it be, I wondered? Without real conviction or particularly comfortable shoes I set off to see how far I could get.

Judging by the smokestacks upstream, the glassy National Library towers, and the floating nightclubs moored in front of them, not to mention the cars dueling on the Pompidou Expressway, it struck me as hard to believe the Seine ever was a wild river edged by marshlands, where the area's Celtic inhabitants lived. Five thousand years ago that benign river provided France's mythicized forebears – *Nôs ancetres les Gaulois* – with food, potables and the protection they needed to build their island-city, which the Romans eventually called Lutetia. Until the 1980s no trace of the Seine Basin's early fisher folk had been found, but while reconfiguring the formerly industrial Bercy area's warehouses, workmen turned up several Neolithic canoes. The hallowed site is recalled by Rue des Pirogues de Bercy, a street sandwiched between a multiplex cinema and convention center. City officials quickly latched onto the canoes, seeing in them a symbol of pre-Roman civilization, and the solution to an etymological mystery. The canoes jibe with the Celtic-language hypothesis of the origin of "Lutetia": *luh* (river) + *touez* (in the middle) + *y* (house), meaning "houses midstream", an apparent reference to what is now the Île de la Cité and Île-Saint-Louis. Of course everyone knows the unappetizing alternative, which Victor Hugo pointed out in the mid-1800s: in Latin *lutum* means mud, therefore Lutetia was the "City of Mud". As to the etymology of "Paris", the canoes came in very handy. The ancient Celtic word appears to be composed of *par* (a kind of canoe) + *gw-ys* (boatmen or expert navigators). Therefore the Parisii tribespeople were expert navigators with canoes. The Romans dubbed the muddy settlement *Lutetia Parisiorum*, which later inhabitants shortened to Lutetia then Frenchified to Lutece. Paris' neolithic canoes are evoked by the dozens of paddle-shaped information panels, designed by Philippe Starck, found in many places around town.

If you believe what the conqueror Julius Caesar wrote in *Gallic Wars*, France's expert canoe navigators savored not only Seine trout, but also human flesh. The fearsome Gauls called their river Sequana, meaning "snakelike," presumably because the Seine meanders on its 482-mile course from its source on the 1,500-foot Langres Plateau in

Burgundy to the Atlantic, a torpid yard's tilt per mile. The Romans lost no time humanizing snaky Sequana into a curvaceous water nymph of the same name. In case your mind's eye fails to envision her, a mid-19th-century rendition of Sequana stands in a faux grotto at the Source de la Seine. This watery enclave is near the village of Chanceaux. Sequana's fountainhead was claimed for the city of Paris not by Caesar, but by another emperor, Napoléon III.

By continuing downstream from the National Library on the landscaped left bank, under rows of poplars, past barges, houseboats and homeless people's encampments, you'll eventually catch sight of Notre-Dame's spire. It marks the center-point from which distances in France are measured. Fittingly, not far from Notre-Dame the Romans built their walled citadel or *civitas* (later bastardized as la Cité), ringed by the Seine's natural moat. Then as now the river ran at its narrowest around the Île de la Cité and could be forded when low, which is why Roman engineers first bridged it here.

There was nothing new under the sun in Caesar's day. The Seine's ford lay at the crossroads of older, Bronze Age trade routes, routes that lead south to the Mediterranean and west to the English Channel. In time, Lutetia became the crucible where the south's copper and the west's tin met and melded into bronze weaponry. When Paris was elevated to the capital of the Roman Empire, in the fourth century AD, under Julian the Apostate, the Seine became the new Rome's Tiber. In due course, once the Romans had vacated, upriver paddled medieval missionaries and Norsemen of an equally bloody-minded nature, bent on trading, raiding and proselytizing. And the rest, as they say, is history, a murky tale splayed over centuries and far too slippery to grasp here, with Lutetia becoming "Paris", Sequana morphing into "Seine", and my feet already sore after a mere mile's march downstream.

Except for a short seedy stretch of quay near the Austerlitz train station you can now walk unmolested by cars along the river's left bank for several miles, almost as far as the Musée d'Orsay. I paused on the Pont d'Austerlitz to reconnoiter and rest my bunions. With several specific episodes of city-lore in mind, it struck me that, probably ever since the first Gallic fisherman-cannibal fell afoul of his neighbor hereabouts, the Seine has been the favorite accomplice of murderers, and a convenient channel for the lifeblood of warriors, revolutionaries, royalists and massacre victims. Take, for instance, 18th-century chronicler Jean-Louis Mercier's account of Louis XVI's execution at what is now the Place de la Concorde. Mercier tells of an onlooker who dipped his finger into the sovereign's blood as it ran toward the river, pronouncing it particularly salty. Victor Hugo, no stranger to prose in full flood, preferred the sewers to the Seine for many uplifting scenes in *Les Misérables*, though he did finish off his misguided police inspector, Javert, in the river's maelstrom.

As I ambled downstream, I tried to remember how many times in Georges Simenon's novels Inspector Maigret fished bodies or their parts from the Seine, into whose depths Maigret stared daily from his office on the Quai des Orfevres. The silver screen has certainly upheld the ghoulish-river tradition. People are pushed or fling themselves into Sequana's arms with alarming frequency, most recently in the otherwise forgettable *Paris by Night*.

But I suspect most contemporary visitors to Paris couldn't give a flying buttress about the morbidity of moviemakers, literati and historians. Like me, when I'm in a good mood, they imagine the Seine as a romantic setting, with pairs of lovers twining. That was precisely what I saw ahead, midstream, in the shade of a weeping willow, on the upstream tip of the Île-Saint-Louis. The sight reassured me that, on the river's edge, there's something for everybody. The Tino Rossi sculpture garden has built-in sand pits for insouciant dog-walkers, for instance. There are concrete-lined heat sinks for sun-seeking optimists, amphitheaters for tango enthusiasts, footpaths for red-faced joggers, and many an isolated stretch where anglers wet a line or clochards a wall.

Day and night, the river buzzes with *bateaux-mouches*, speakers blaring and floodlights glaring, gaily conveying some four-and-a-half million merrymakers per year on a magical Paris mystery tour.

But how much of the Seine's glamour is carefully staged illusion? When in a sardonic frame of mind, induced, as was now the case, by the press of bodies around Notre-Dame, I often think of the river's curving sweep as seen from a satellite: an eyebrow raised at all romantic notions of Paris, starting with my own. Romance? Two hundred years ago Napoléon I, ever the poet, dubbed the river "The highway linking Paris and Rouen". Thanks to inspired 20th-century planners, the Seine is still a highway, paved with asphalt on both sides, and commuter train rails tucked underneath the left embankment. Industrial barges and tour boats churn up the dark waters between.

Twenty-five million tons of freight, much of it toxic, transits on the river yearly. The effluent and garbage of the capital and upstream Seine Basin have flowed across Sequana's bosom since the days of Lutetia.

That paragon of romantic bridges, the Pont des Arts, linking the Louvre to the Institut de France, was long where street sweepers dumped their loads. So foul was the Seine by 1970, the statistical baseline for reclamation efforts, that it was pronounced "nearly dead." Of the dozens of fish species pre-industrial anglers once snared in their nets, scientists could find only three remaining. The situation has slowly improved, with bottom-feeders making a comeback, though in the early 1990s then-mayor Jacques Chirac was a trifle premature when he tossed trout and salmon into what was still a sump. The fish promptly went belly up.

Today, with the river's quays and bridges a UNESCO World Heritage site, few Parisians suspect that Sequana is on a respirator: six oxygen-pumping plants hidden along the banks keep floundering fish species alive. Still fewer people notice the submerged garbage-catching barriers discretely emptied by trucks or barges. And hardly anyone thinks of the hundreds of employees working round the clock to keep the river tidy, police it, control its flow and purify its water. This is not done merely to please environmentalists or the tourism board. The fact is eighty percent of Paris' drinking water comes from the Seine. The turgid flow is treated in four plants at the rate of three million cubic meters daily then piped into the homes of unsuspecting residents. I recall the day I heard rumors that, on average, by the time the Seine reaches my kitchen sink it has been through five human bodies. Try telling that to an enraptured visitor at a riverside café.

Parisians shrug off such reports. They seem to acquire a taste for chlorine and kidney-filtered water. With that pleasant thought in mind I gulped an espresso and a glass of Seine then descended a stairway to the riverbank, just downstream of Place Saint Michel. I was in time to see the Brigade Fluvial's firemen, stationed near the Pont des Arts, struggle into wetsuits and brave the waters. I prayed to Sequana that they were inoculated against every known water-borne disease and heavily insured.

Despite the widely reported death of Jacques Chirac's trout and salmon, many Parisians continue to dream of fishing and swimming in the Seine, so much so that Paris' port authority and current mayor Bertrand Delanoë are studying the feasibility of creating inner-city bathing beaches. Delanoë got his toes in the water in summer 2002 with an initiative called *Paris Plage*, as in "beach". He ordered that the right bank expressway be closed temporarily, and had *guingette*-style outdoor cafés, sun umbrellas, and portable swimming pools planted on the tarmac. The initiative is now a regular summertime event. But no one so far has been foolhardy enough to scatter sand on the riverbanks and dive in.

As I shuffled now over the handsome, modern Solferino footbridge to the Right Bank quays flanking the Tuileries, I paused to take in the seductive views, and had to admit that a sandy strand somewhere hereabouts wouldn't be bad. Once the water was clean enough for a swim, however, there would remain the minor detail of the Seine's yearly floods, which tend to wreak havoc and would possibly sweep away the mayor's beaches.

Earthquake-prone California lives in fear of 'the big one'. But Paris dreads a repeat of the 1910 flood, whose height and extent are remembered around town by small plaques. Were it not for the reservoirs, dams, locks and embankments perfected following the 1910 deluge, in the dry season the Seine would be a muddy trickle, while in rainy months it would slosh as far as the Bastille, Odéon and Opéra neighborhoods. A replay of 1910, termed a "Parisian Chernobyl" by police and municipal authorities, would cost billions of euros and shut down the city for months.

Floods would be nightmarish indeed, but occasional high water can be a boon, providing walkers with a blissful respite between marks on the meter stick. Moderately high water means cars can no longer use the expressways, while pedestrians can still pick a path between the puddles. Traditionally, Parisians gauged the river's height by Le Zouave (it rhymes with soave), a giant statue of a soldier. Le Zouave juts from the Pont de l'Alma and when Sequana caresses his neck, the city is in trouble. Happily, the river was barely licking the statue's boots as I crept by on the Pont de l'Alma. I switched back to the Left Bank and sauntered along the stretch of quay in the Eiffel Tower's shadow.

Feet throbbing, I limped onto the Allée des Cygnes, a narrow, half-mile-long island anchored midstream. It joins the tiered bridge of Bir-Hakeim to that of Grenelle, thereby uniting the bridges' respective monuments to hope, pride or self-deception, depending on your interpretation of history, and your world-view. At Bir-Hakeim a 1949 plaque reminds readers that, "France never stopped fighting" in World War Two. Downstream at Grenelle a thirty-foot Statue of Liberty faces west, turning its shapely buttocks to Notre-Dame. On the Allée des Cygnes itself I saw no swans, but spotted many peacocks in designer sportswear. They lazed on benches, and appeared to be enjoying the unusual views of 1950s to 1970s highrise architecture.

Another quarter-mile downstream at Javel (as in *Eau de Javel* or bleach, produced here starting in the 1770s) the Seine flowed melodiously beneath the ironwork Pont Mirabeau. In the rushing mainstream I could hear Guillaume Apollinaire's wistful refrain of time and love slipping by, the one every French high schooler memorizes: *Sous le pont Mirabeau coule la Seine et nos amours faut-il qu'il m'en souvienne la joie venait toujours après la peine*...

But I hadn't walked three hours to weep tears of nostalgia. The goal I had been advancing toward was near: a giant bronze nymph, symbol of the river, affixed to the Pont Mirabeau. On the railing above her head is a crown in the shape of a turreted citadel, and the device *Fluctuat nec mergitur*. The sculpture's décolleté suggests that the sculptor was more interested in his model's bounteous *seins* than in the Seine. I gazed down into her corroded but smiling eyes and recognized Sequana.

Place des Vosges, 1995

The Place des Vosges

"Sitting among old armor, and old tapestry, and old coffers, and grim old chairs and tables, and old canopies of state from old palaces, and old golden lions going to play at skittles with ponderous old golden balls, they made a most romantic show, and looked like a chapter out of one of his own books."

Charles Dickens after meeting Victor Hugo
in his Place des Vosges apartment, 1847

The Marais' centerpiece Place des Vosges isn't the biggest or the grandest of Paris squares, but it seems to me the most alluring. Under its arcades the noise of traffic fades – well, on three of four sides anyway – replaced by the splashing of fountains. Pigeons and sparrows duel over the steep slate roofs of the square's thirty-six identical pavilions. Their brick and stone façades, never shaded by other buildings, catch the shifting light of the Paris sky. People stroll by, peering into shop windows. Waiters weave among café tables set out under the vaults. In the square's center, safe behind iron grillwork, children oblivious to the backdrop play in sandboxes while au pairs chat on double-backed benches.

The Place des Vosges draws me in at least once a day and in all seasons, for the simple reason that my wife and I live about 200 yards west of it. Sometimes, especially on a rainy night, the square feels like our cloister, a place of reflection and meditation. Sit in summer under the scented linden trees as the sun goes down and the street lamps flicker into life and you'll feel not only the linden blossoms' sticky weeping, but also your sensibilities tingling. Or, on a winter's day, wander from shop to well-lit shop under the arches while the rain pours down on the rest of the world, and ponder the ephemera of consumerism.

Architects and art historians will assure you that the Place des Vosges offers France's best example of early 17th-century urbanism. Essentially it's a cross between Italianate Mannerism and late-Renaissance Dutch styles, neatly combining a gracious *piazza* and four sets of row houses. The proportions are on a human scale, with four stories raked skyward, a succession, from ground level up, of arches in rhythmic rows, tall french windows, dormers and *oeils-de-boeuf* windows. Time and the elements have conspired with the foibles and fantasies of man to round the square's hard edges and skew what had been intended as perfect symmetry.

Unlike the bustling, coldly beautiful Place Vendôme or Place de la Concorde, famed for their hotels, clubs and ritzy jewelry shops, people have always lived on and animated the Place des Vosges and ultimately that is what makes it a likeable spot. Madame de Sévigné, the 17th-century queen of epistolary literature and high-society gossip (now read exclusively by French high schoolers), was born on the square's south side. Across the way, Marion de Lorme, the courtesan of kings, distributed her favors, if we must be polite. On the Place des Vosges' northern flank the pious Duc-Maréchal de Richelieu seduced a catalogue of lovers that reportedly included every noble lady then resident in the square's pavilions. Piety and licentiousness walked arm-in-arm, just as it does today.

The duelists, the gamblers, and the glittering *Grand-Siècle* pomp of the place – originally named La Place Royale – inspired Pierre Corneille's now unreadable comic play, also named, somewhat predictably, *La Place Royale*. Even when the square hit its nadir just after World War Two, its badly lit arcades and grubby backcourts provided the setting for Georges Simenon's murder mystery, *L'Ombre Chinoise* (later turned into a cult movie).

"It was Montgomery's lance that created the Place des Vosges," wrote Victor Hugo with typical aplomb (from 1832 to 1848 Hugo lived at number six and his apartment is now an embalmed house-museum). Decrypted, Hugo's line means that Gabriel de Lorges de Montgomery, captain of the French sovereign's Scottish Guards, accidentally killed King Henri II here in 1559. The two were jousting in front of the Hôtel Royal des Tournelles, which stood where the Place des Vosges stands today. Montgomery's lance pierced the king's visor, eye and brain. Understandably, Henri II's widowed queen, Catherine de' Médicis, came to hate the royal residence, so much so that she had it demolished. For decades the former main courtyard did service as a horse market. It was randy King Henri IV (a chicken in every cocotte, a different bed every day), flanked by his minister the Duc de Sully, who in 1605 hit upon the idea of turning the horse market into a piazza – an Italian novelty unknown in Paris at the time. Here the court could stroll and make merry far from the Machiavellian intrigues of the Louvre (or so Henri IV thought). About two centuries later, during the French Revolution, the name was changed from Place Royale to Place des

Vosges, to reward the first administrative *Département* – Les Vosges – that paid taxes, thereby recognizing the revolutionary regime.

Heavy carriage doors, nowadays often locked, hide courtyards, some groomed into pocketsize formal gardens, others dotted with statues. In several there are workshops, art galleries or fashion boutiques, and these are the easiest to breach. Since this is a particularly toney address, you're likely to encounter well-fed movie stars, politicos and other nouveaux on the threshold of L'Amboisie, among France's most expensive restaurants, located at number nine. Starvling models saunter out of Issay Miyake's fief of fashion headquartered nearby at number five.

Like any poor little rich boy, the square has its problems, though none seems life threatening. Locals complain about the rush-hour traffic on the north side, a through street, and the ever-swelling number of tourists on weekends. Some years ago one long-time resident I met, a dealer in antique Japanese art, closed her boutique and retreated to a by-appointment-only showroom in a rear court. Too many visitors were handling her fragile collections, she told me with a shiver of disgust. The square's *bête noire* of the last decade or so is a self-styled antique dealer who spills his ragbag of merchandise under the arcades (but that's nothing new – the first ban on flea market-style displays dates to 1758).

Then there are the itinerant bangle-hawkers, organ grinders and sour mash Dixieland bands that besiege the square daily to the delight of some locals and the horror of most others. Pierre Balmès, an expert on antique timepieces, opened a shop here in 1949 and observed the remake. "Sometimes I miss the old, run-down Place des Vosges," he told me one busy Saturday. "It was so peaceful and quiet."

The one blight against which all residents united back in the 1990s is the tour bus. After many an administrative battle, buses were limited to disgorging their hordes on the north side of the square before moving to less scenic quarters. There's talk every few years of creating a car-free zone here and in the surrounding Marais. That might not be a bad idea, as long as a Montmartre-style elephant train isn't part of the deal, and the pedestrian-only area is big enough to thin merrymakers to acoustically acceptable levels.

"I'd like this to be my kingdom," a thirty-year resident told me several years ago as we stood on his second-floor *étage noble* balcony. The square's original aristocratic residents always lived on the *étage noble*, and my host, perhaps unwittingly, emphasized how privileged I was to enter the hallowed halls of his multi-million euro apartment, and enjoy a glimpse of how the other side lives. "In an ideal world no one else could live here or come in but me," he confessed unselfconsciously, "and that just goes to show you how attached one becomes." He reminisced about how, in the early 1990s, he and other property owners asked the powers-that-be to lock up the park and hand out keys to residents only – a scheme that provoked public outrage (including my own) and much wringing of hands. The square seems to breed such undemocratic sentiments, inspired, perhaps, by the dramatic views from on high. It's as if the architects had drawn their plans with condescension in mind.

There are several public entrances (five to be precise), but only one proper way to approach the Place des Vosges the first time around: take the Rue de Birague. An unremarkable street, narrow by modern standards, it used to be called the Rue Royale. Kings, courtiers and countless red-blooded parvenus have rolled up it in the last four hundred years. What I do to get the right perspective is sidestep the occasional passing car and take regal strides up the middle of the street. Framing its Place des Vosges end is the Pavillon du Roi, built by Henri IV for his own use and therefore considerably larger than the square's other pavilions. Through two of the three arches supporting it (the third was made into a stairwell hundreds of years ago) you get a keyhole view of the square beyond. If, like me, you're shortsighted, as you near the king's pavilion its fluted stone pilasters, lacy ironwork balconies, and the crossed swords, lyre and sculpted "H" of Henri IV will come swimming into focus. Luckless old horny Henri, immortalized in bas-relief, gazes out from the northside of the archway onto the square he didn't live to see completed.

An assassin killed the king as he left the Louvre, in 1610. Two years later the stammering eleven-year-old Louis XIII, a king whose renown rests largely on his subservience to the powerful Cardinal Richelieu, inaugurated the square instead of Henri IV. By then Richelieu had built his own corner pavilion at what is now number twenty-one. Louis XIII promptly retreated to the Louvre and never lived in the Pavillon du Roi. But his court did indeed take over the Place Royale. The Duc de Sully, Henri IV's right-hand minister, saw how the wind was blowing and eventually moved into a stunning residence (known ever since as the Hôtel de Sully) on the Rue Saint-Antoine, with a groomed garden and *orangerie* abutting on 5 Place des Vosges.

Overnight, the Marais mushroomed with townhouses, a vogue that lasted until the end of the 17th century (when the faubourgs Saint-

Germain and Saint-Honoré became the rage). It's for this reason that the Place des Vosges' creation has long been attributed erroneously to Louis XIII. The park in the square's center is named after him, and so too is the architectural style of the square's buildings. Even its centerpiece equestrian statue represents a smiling Louis, his whiskbroom moustaches erect. Poor Henri IV has only a banal boulevard to glorify his name.

Some history-mad locals get worked up about such perceived injustices. Not a few are thankful for the screen of century-old horse chestnut trees that hide the hated Louis XIII's statue. Stendhal, with a slash of his quill, called the king's mount an overgrown mule, not a horse. Truth be told, what enraptured visitors see today is an artless 19th-century copy of the original bronze, which was melted down during the Revolution. If you ask me, the second-rate statue is one of the square's endearing imperfections, like the clunky 19th-century bird-bath fountains, or the weathered "brickwork" that on closer inspection turns out to be cheap trompe-l'oeil plaster applied to wood. A generous admirer might describe this old harlot of a square as a study in layered eclecticism.

Every few years, in the name of architectural purity, some pious perfectionist lobbies the city to get rid of the statue and the fountains, uproot the trees and knock down the Louis Philippe-period grilles and shepherd's-crook street lamps – none was around in the early 1600s after all. These militant purists would restore the square to death in order to bring back its original unimpeded architectural perspectives. They're unlikely to succeed. In Paris, tampering with living layers of history is a tricky business. Here it would involve destroying one remarkable stratum to get at another. Up to now restoration and repair work have been cosmetic. About thirty years ago the park's ailing elms were replaced with linden trees that are carefully pruned to preserve perspectives and views. More recently, the lawns were reshaped and the fountains re-plumbed and equipped for nighttime illumination. Since the early 1960s the French government has paid for two-thirds of the cost of mandatory repairs to façades and roofs. In exchange a few residents have been made to close up unsightly skylights, or remove recent dormers and gables that saw nary a Henri, Louis or Napoléon for that matter. So the pavilions' exteriors now look much as they did in 1612, with only a few not yet fully restored.

Given its age and the number of cataclysmic social events that have occurred around it – the storming of the Bastille, the industrial revolution, two world wars and rampant real estate speculation – it's a minor miracle the Place des Vosges has survived at all. People often say that poverty preserves and prosperity destroys. The postwar building boom threatened not only the square but also the entire Marais neighborhood around it. The bulldozers were stopped a few minutes past the nick of time, in the 1960s, by then Culture Minister André Malraux, who declared the neighborhood a historical monument. But the poverty-prosperity dictum's opposite is also true: the 1789-to-World War Two chapter of Place des Vosges history is a chronicle of corrosive decline. Factories sprang up in courtyards. Pavilions were dismembered, their aristocratic interiors junked (luckily a few were preserved and remounted at the nearby Musée Carnavalet, Paris' city history museum). If vast sums hadn't been spent on the square in recent decades it probably would have collapsed.

Most of the friends I take to visit the square wonder out loud about the people who live behind those handsome, impenetrable façades. If you wander aimlessly along the park's grilles of an evening you can catch tantalizing glimpses of painted ceilings, of rare and valuable pictures hanging high upon a wall. But this is not just a bastion of the wealthy, I discovered some years ago. Henri IV's 1605 building code set the architectural theme and also specified that pavilions had to be owned by single families – presumably very good, old families worthy of the royal square. That unusual law remained in force as late as the 1960s, so there are still about ten single-family pavilions, many purchased in the 1800s or early 1900s when the square was dilapidated. Some pavilions were split long ago into cheap, rent-controlled apartments. Others are occupied to this day by the descendants of once-rich dynasties now living in genteel penury, their cluttered apartments lifted from a Zola novel. I'll never forget the time I visited one, and was led from floor to sagging floor by the pavilion's unwashed, unshaved, ornery owner, who scowled out of the broken windowpanes and cursed his inheritance. "You think it's beautiful," he shouted over and over, "you like the view? I hate it here, I hate it…"

Many impoverished heirs have sold off apartments piecemeal over the last forty years. Properties worth peanuts a few decades ago now fetch staggering sums. *Étage noble* flats are the most valuable at $4 million and up.

Other "nationalized" pavilions have been taken over by an elementary school, the Victor Hugo museum, and an Ashkenazim synagogue, which explains the numbers of small children, the tourists clutching copies of *Les Misérables*, and the more or less constant flow of Jewish wedding parties hamming it up for photographers under the linden trees or in front of the fountains.

In the Place des Vosges' social hierarchy, inhabitants fall into whole-pavilion or single-apartment categories. To some pedigreed clans, former Culture Minister Jack Lang, with his *étage noble* digs, is a *petit arriviste* – a social climber. Toney, trendy denizens abound, though as one self-consciously fortunate resident told me, it's inaccurate to call the square "fashionable." "Fashion is facile, easy to acquire and superficial," he quipped with a regal wag of bejeweled fingers, "the Place des Vosges is complex, expensive – a kind of cloister."

On several occasions I visited the apartment of one of Paris' most successful and controversial art auctioneers, the affable scion of a family that has owned an entire pavilion since the early 1800s. His two-story apartment is littered with priceless antiques and artworks. It is also haunted, he told me, deadpan, by the ghost of the Maréchal d'Ancre, a nobleman murdered somewhere on the property in 1617 by the Baron de Vitry, the pavilion's first owner. The auctioneer leads a resolutely modern lifestyle. He had his beamed ceiling repainted by a Senegalese artist. The dining room looks like something out of Jules Verne, with a curious, curved sheet-metal ceiling. "I like mixtures," he told me.

The auctioneer spoke convincingly of restoration, fashion, purity and eclecticism, and pondered what it means to live today in a monument, dripping with history. "I even like the little 19th-century park there with its slightly worn, old-fashioned look and *bouquet* of chestnut trees," he declared at last, with the easy brashness typical of his trade. He used the word "bouquet" on purpose. "It's a naïf – a sort of Henri Rousseau," he continued, apparently well pleased with his own voice. "But I think it's beautiful all the same." As if echoing his words, a nattily dressed nanny appeared from the arcades below and swerved into the park, her blue baby carriage scattering pigeons and autumn leaves. A charming naïf it was, I agreed, framed by a minor masterpiece.

Les Halles, 1999

Belly Ache: Les Halles

"... the worst of late 20th century Modernity..."
The New York Times, 2005

Les Halles, the historic market district nicknamed "The Belly of Paris" since the mid-1800s heyday of novelist Emile Zola, will evolve in coming years from its gutless 1970s incarnation. Into what, no one is sure. A public architectural competition held in 2004 ostensibly to bring the complex up to European Union safety standards proved unsatisfactory. Fanciful designs by star-architects Jean Nouvel and Rem Koolhaas lost. No one "won." Described by *The New York Times* as a "toothless architectural figurehead" the relatively unknown David Mangin will "supervise" the remake of the subterranean Forum des Halles shopping mall, adjoining park, and RER commuter train station, under the watchful eye of mayor Bertrand Delanoë.

With a budget running into the hundreds of millions of dollars and a timeline of many years, this is no minor urban renewal scheme. Few Paris neighborhoods are freighted with heavier symbolic baggage. Victor Hugo set the riot scenes here in *Les Misérables*, and every French writer or poet worthy of note since has at least nodded in Les Halles' direction. When George Pompidou's Gaullist government brazenly removed Les Halles' wholesale market to suburban Rungis in 1969 then demolished the market's iron-and-glass "Baltard pavilions" two years later, an estimated 300,000 Parisians' livelihoods were turned upside down. From across the political spectrum Frenchmen shouted bloody murder, marching in the streets. Amid accusations of illegal real estate speculation involving Les Halles and other "development" schemes, the Gaullists were defeated at the polls in 1974.

In his broadside *L'Assassinat de Paris*, muckraking historian Louis Chevalier wrote at the time, "Les Halles were Les Halles but then, and even more so, they were Paris itself."

Many Parisians still remember the scandals, dust and chaos to this day. Nostalgia for Baltard's Les Halles and hatred of what replaced them is tangible. That's why Mangin's reputation and Delanoë's political future ride on the project's timing and outcome.

The bland southern suburb of Nogent-sur-Marne may seem an odd place to seek Les Halles' secrets, but the two sites are linked by the RER "A" line, and it is in Nogent, reassembled on a leafy hillside over the Marne River, that stands the only Les Halles pavilion left in France. As I rode the RER to Nogent on a recent visit, I couldn't help noting the irony. Victor Baltard's handsome, airy 1850s structures and their slender fluted iron columns, gingerbread tin roofs, and glass-paned sides, were destroyed in part to make way for what at the time was an ultramodern commuter rail network. Of ten original pavilions eight were sold as scrap metal (and fetched a paltry 395,000 francs). The ninth was bought by the city of Yokohama in Japan. The sole pavilion Pompidou preserved is now a venue for prestigious events such as the World Salsa Dance Championship, the Cat Salon or Miss Europe Contest, and is flanked by cast-iron Belle Époque streetlamps, a Wallace Fountain, a section of Eiffel Tower staircase, and a curbside fire-alarm box. Transplanted and deprived of their original functions, Nogent's tragicomic Belle Époque theme park of architecture is typical of 1960s-70s Paris urbanism.

While riding back into town in a packed RER train I reviewed my own tragicomic experiences with Les Halles starting in 1976, when I watched the high-gloss paintwork being applied to the unfinished Pompidou Center at Beaubourg. In my ignorance I imagined the behemoth was a refinery. Much of the quarter had been bulldozed to accommodate it. A resident set me straight: until a few years earlier a tangle of alleys had converged on the so-called Plateau Beaubourg, a depot for the trucks that hauled fruit, vegetables and meat to the wholesale market.

My curiosity piqued, I walked west from Beaubourg to where the market had been and through clouds of dust watched construction workers lining the celebrated "trou" – the great 25-acre hole of Les Halles – with cement. In 1979 and '83 I was in Paris again, and saw half (then a quarter) of the pit still gaping, and felt the ground still shaking from pneumatic drills. It was only when I'd moved fulltime to the city in 1986 that the hole had finally been filled and the Forum completed (by several teams of architects working at cross-purposes). The once seedy, unmistakably Parisian alleys where Billy Wilder's irreverent 1963 tale of prostitute Irma La Douce was filmed, the streets that had inspired Hugo, Zola, Breton and a hundred others, had disappeared, "renovated" beyond recognition.

Since my first encounter with Les Halles I've probably dashed through the complex a thousand times – usually to change subway trains or buy an otherwise un-findable book at FNAC, among the world's biggest and possibly most claustrophobia-inducing bookstore. Despite goodwill on my part the labyrinthine, five-level underground Forum with its mirrored-glass "corolla" buildings springing from the depths has never won my affection.

Like the 800,000 daily commuters and 41 million annual Forum regulars, I've seen the mall decline from mere architectural hodgepodge to sordid, vandalized sump. The only boosters appear to be restless youths from the distant housing projects the RER was designed to serve. So it was with trepidation that I alighted from my train and talked myself into taking a fresh look.

When still a wholesale market roughshod Les Halles employed upwards of 13,000 round the clock, including hundreds of the famously scurrilous *forts* – bruiser porters who to be certified had to haul 440 pounds of freight on a hand-truck across the hangars – about five football fields in length.

Nowadays, escalators raise you from the dark, joyless RER platforms into a soulless sunken plaza via a laminate of florescent-lit corridors. The plaza and its bulging Plexiglas windows look vaguely like outsized Tupperware. Europe's busiest, with 3,000 employees and 160 commercial spaces, the mall generates nearly $500 million annually for its private leaseholder, Unibail. That might explain the eagerness of '60s-'70s real estate developers, and the pressure still exerted on city hall. Reportedly the only shops that thrive are FNAC (where I stopped to buy a copy of *Le Ventre de Paris*) and those on level minus-3 nearest the RER entrances. Much of the complex is deserted, adding to its gloom.

Despite earnest wishes that it were otherwise, the air proved as caustic as I remembered, perfumed by French fries, disinfectants, and an eye-stinging stench many mistakenly attribute to sewage. "The Belly of Paris aches," pundits quip. Some invoke the supernatural: the Places des Innocents cemetery abutted the site. An RATP municipal transit worker once explained to me that the odor comes not from disgruntled, displaced souls, but rather from decomposing limestone, exposed by the *trou*. Long ago, the district was called *Champeaux – water-field*.

The Forum des Halles has two parts, the more recent and less hideous to the west. Designed by Paul Chemetov (of the notorious Ministry of Finance building at Bercy) it opened in 1985. According to the understandably embittered architect, interviewed in early 2005 by *Le Journal de Paris*, it will cost the city 100 million euros just to tear off the Forum's cement ceiling. How much it would cost (and if it's possible) to eliminate the stench is unknown. Shopping in the supermarket Mangin would install in reconverted car tunnels beneath Les Halles could be interesting.

Spend an hour, as I did, navigating the wilted "corolla" pavilions excogitated by the long-forgotten Jean Willerval then sit in the dog-eared park facing the church of Saint Eustache or the handsome, round 18th-century Bourse de Commerce. You may wind up sharing *The New York Times'* assessment that Les Halles is "the worst of late 20th century Modernity, with its tabula rasa approach to history and its penchant for sterile, inhuman spaces."

The "worst?" To those who suggested in the 1960s that Baltard's pavilions be re-purposed as Pompidou's contemporary art museum, and adjacent areas groomed into a "Central Park", Pompidou retorted, "It would be invaded instantly by 60,000 hippies!"

Pompidou's visionaries dreamed up the Pompidou Center instead, and strove to erect colossi considerably worse than what we now see. They imagined spaghetti bowl freeways and slug-like skyscrapers rearing their spiky heads. Today's "visionaries" seem immune to history's lessons. Jean Nouvel wanted sleek high-rises with rooftop gardens. Rem Koolhaas planned vividly colored "Popsicle" towers poking up from below to broadcast the fermenting mall's "energy." The Dutch firm of MVRDV preferred stained glass expanses judged ludicrous and "un-build-able."

By contrast, Mangin's suggestion to raze the corollas and blaze an esplanade from the Bourse de Commerce to a low, glass-covered subterranean atrium seems downright reassuring. In the end, no matter how the remodel is done, the shopping mall and RER station will remain.

Though eager to slip away, I coaxed myself into exploring the car-free district around Les Halles. It's remarkable how the litter, fast food franchises, down-market souvenir and clothing shops, noise pollution, and aggressiveness decrease the farther from the complex you get. Other than a few pleasing architectural details, and the handsome Fontaine des Innocents, the strongest reminders of the pre-Pompidou era are today's Irma La Douces. They've plied their trade around the Rue Saint-Denis for centuries. A pest-control specialist from rat-infested times, and a handful of cafés did survive the wrecker's ball. Like Baltard's pavilion in Nogent-sur-Marne, most vintage storefronts are bleached bones in a wasteland. Au Père Tranquille on Rue Pierre Lescot facing Les Halles' mirrored facade may be an exception.

Once upon a time market workers and slumming partygoers would sup night and day on the café's "fine, pungent onion soup", as Evelyn Waugh noted in early 1929. Cheap and warming, onion soup was the ideal fast food and hangover cure. Au Père Tranquille still has the requisite broken-tile floors, (faux) cane chairs, and puffing poseurs of market days, and even occasionally the onion soup. From a tiny round table I observed groups of Les Halles adolescents, wondering how much they knew of the site's historical, literary and political significance, and decided that, in fact, they probably knew more than any other segment of society: every French high schooler studies Zola's work inside out, upside down.

It's hard to evoke watery Champeaux, the medieval pilgrimage route of Rue Saint-Denis, or the succession of marketplaces that operated here, starting with King Louis VI's stalls of 1137. There's no trace, either, of Emperor Philippe Auguste's walled market compound from 1183. Of François 1st's Renaissance market arcades (built from 1534 to 1572) only photographic evidence remains. That's because, in keeping with tradition, Emperor Napoléon III toppled them in his seismic Second Empire redesign of the district from 1852 to 1856. Did Parisians protest then, I wondered?

Baltard's much-bereaved pavilions, conceived at the behest of Paris Prefect Rambuteau in 1848, account for little over one-eighth of the market district's 900-year history. But they were – by all accounts, especially Zola's – magnificent not only to look at. Unlike today's neutered Forum the market's energy was dizzying.

How many still read *Le Ventre de Paris* cover to cover, I asked myself, riffling the pages of this 1873 tome, part of the Rougon-Macquart saga. When the shortsighted Zola first stumbled upon Les Halles one sleepless night in 1869, he found "all the blossoming poetry of Paris' streets on the muddy sidewalk amid Les Halles' edibles." But as French school children know, *The Belly of Paris* is no facile ode. The novel's ambivalent hero Florent, mistaken for a revolutionary rioter and incarcerated on Devil's Island during the coup d'état that brought Napoléon III to power in 1851, upon his return in 1856 discovers the then-new Les Halles. Hemmed in by menacing cartloads of carrots, mountains of cabbages and piles of potatoes Florent is swept along by the raucous crowd, slipping on grease and discarded artichoke leaves in a horrifying cornucopia.

Like Zola himself, Florent is fascinated by the architecture and life of Les Halles – "the luminous, polished transparency" of the panes flooded with dawn's light, the "slender herringbone pillars, the elegant curves of the woodwork ceiling, the geometric outlines of the roofs." In the pavilion's vaulted cellars Florent discovers Champeaux's secret waters flowing into giant urns and tanks full of live fish. In the bright, prosperous charcuterie where he works, Florent is mesmerized by the abundance of hams, sausages, salami, lard and other fatty, greasy, slippery delicacies, becoming increasingly obsessed by the corresponding plumpness and carnivorous contentment of the men and women around him – exemplars of a budding consumerist economy.

The smell of the charcuterie, of Les Halles themselves, soon becomes intolerable. Florent develops chronic indigestion from the stench. The book's "belly" is no mere organ – it's a metaphor for the mouth, stomach and burgeoning bowels of the Second Empire's nouveaux riches, for bodily functions, for the disquieting alimentary realities of bourgeois existence. As the novel closes, the tormented Florent battles nightmare images of "giant vats, the vile rendering cauldrons where the fat of a nation was melted down."

I left Au Père Tranquille smoked like a ham and troubled by Zola's words, reflecting that it was perhaps this kind of unsentimental view of Les Halles that had animated Pompidou and his speculator-sanitizers. From the 1940s on, succeeding administrations had threatened to remove the wholesale market, decried as unsanitary, overcrowded, rat-infested, the cause of traffic jams, and a drag on the economy. Some officials openly regretted the fact that central Paris – Les Halles in particular – had not been destroyed in World War Two. The first official eviction notice was issued in 1958. More than a decade later, the lure of potential profits derived from building the new market at Rungis, the RER and the Forum, not to mention the thrill of seeing a bright, new Pompidou Center rise from a remade neighborhood, became irresistible. I realized now why Baltard's pavilions had to go, and why Pompidou exiled the one survivor to a Belle Époque theme park far away. The pavilions were a threat: had they been preserved on site they might indeed have become a rallying point for the "rioters", "communists" and "hippies" Pompidou feared.

A final, comforting thought ushered me home to the pre-modern Marais. Based on past performance, whatever Les Halles' next incarnation is, it will be a long time coming. In the meantime, I will be re-reading Zola diligently. I might even pick up a DVD of *Irma La Douce* – and a gross of popcorn.

Tracks, crane and TGB, 1995

Go East, Young Frenchman!

"The houses were not houses but wine warehouses and the names on the street signs were the familiar names one sees on bottles... There were roads as in a real city, intersections, squares and avenues and, instead of cars, barrels of all sizes that cluttered them."

Georges Simenon, *Maigret s'amuse*

There were two of them, stark naked, two middle-aged men splayed over the riverside walkway's rough cobblestones. The path, sandwiched between the expressway's cement boundary wall and the river, was only four feet wide. Like us about a hundred other strollers, bikers and roller-bladers detoured around the pair of oblivious, glistening guy-sunbathers. Barges and cruise boats buzzed past, their rumblings echoed by the glassy new skyscrapers beyond the expressway. Subway trains traveling in opposite directions met halfway across the circa-1900 iron-and-stone viaduct spanning the river between train stations. Under freshly planted shade trees on cobbled plinths, at barge-cafés and riverside restaurants, other seminude sun-worshippers, hipsters and wannabes sipped cokes, cappuccinos and Cuba Libres, and chatted live or via cellular about their fab lofts in reconverted warehouses nearby.

Where were we – New York, Sydney, London?

Try Paris, eastern Paris, the Quai de la Rapée to be precise, site of the new Seine-side esplanades facing the Gare d'Austerlitz train station and National Library. From here you can glimpse the backside of Notre-Dame a mere twenty-minutes' walk downstream. But the medieval cathedral and its phalanx of tour buses seem a million meters away.

In recent years this edgy eastern part of Paris, long home to freight yards, flour mills, power plants, warehouses and riverside shipyards, has been re-floated by arty dinks riding the tide of French government fiat.

Right up to the city's Boulevard Périphérique beltway whole swaths of town east from Austerlitz on the Left Bank, and the Bastille on the Right Bank, have been remodeled, rebuilt and reconfigured in a frenzy of urbanism unseen since the rape of Paris by Georges Pompidou in the 1960s-70s. In addition to the Seine embankments, the three main targets have been the Tolbiac, Bercy and Daumesnil neighborhoods, each with its own government-funded project. The new driverless Météor subway, line 14, links the three.

The biggest and most notorious of the troika is Tolbiac, site of the new National Library, officially called "Bibliothèque de France, Site François Mitterrand." France's former president commissioned the complex, built between 1988-95 but opened to the public three years late. Parisians call it the TGB (Très Grande Bibliothèque), a play on the acronym for the TGV high-speed train. Whatever you call it, the $1 billion-plus library is *folie de grandeur* incarnate and splendid high-tech kitsch.

Subtle? From our standpoint on the Seine embankment the library's four, 300-foot high towers of glass, designed to mimic open books on end, looked more like flying wedges poised atop a plank-covered plinth almost a thousand feet long. The wonderfully brash crassness of it boggles the mind. The TGB may be the world's defining set piece of post-post-modernism.

Once we'd found it, an escalator about a hundred yards long tilted us down to the library's bank-vault of an entrance. Here we marveled at the celebrated subterranean glassed-in garden the length of two football fields. Dozens of fully-grown red pines transplanted here in 1995 might have been an art installation. Steel cables girded the trees to prevent them from crashing through the surrounding plate-glass windows. Reportedly President Mitterrand fancied this as the 21st-century cloister of a neo-medieval monastery, inspired by Umberto Eco's 1980s bestseller *The Name of the Rose* (later a Hollywood blockbuster starring Sean Connery). Set in a monastery, the tale was still the rage at the time King Mitterrand's courtiers and sycophants came up with the TGB plan. The French government actually contemplated hiring Eco as a consultant.

At length my wife and I entered the library's eastern atrium. The ghostly view looking west extends almost 700 feet down the complex's "cloister." We asked to check out a book – something on the history of eastern Paris. "You'll need to buy a day pass," said a cheerful young librarian. "Go to the cash register, then follow this map…"

She traced a mile-long trajectory to the west atrium, then up to the open stacks on the L2 level, whose location she wasn't sure of. "Press the button in the elevator," she suggested, "you can't go wrong."

An hour later and bingo, we'd located the volume, *Paris s'éveille à l'Est* – Paris awakens in the east. Wasn't this the slogan emblazoned across the many billboards we'd admired in the neighborhood, Alison wondered?

Detractors have had so much fun running the TGB into the ground for the last decade that, standing there with book in hand, I actually felt protective of the library's bigness, coldness and inefficiency. Gone are those early days when TGB employees held strikes against "inhumane working conditions" and a "fundamentally flawed computer system." Certainly, the computerized toy train that fetches books still sometimes goes off the rails, despite several years and millions of dollars' worth of fine-tuning. But huge strides have been made. The library's other minor flaws – leaks, dead trees, cavernous architectural dead-ends, stifling air, dank – are nothing another billion euros won't fix.

Most of all, thousands of French university students seem to love the TGB. It mirrors the spirit of our time, one bright young lady told me as we stood in line together at the snack bar. I bore this glad news to my wife, who was eager to escape the spot lighting in the gloomy, windowless room. There were only a handful of plastic seats allocated to the snack bar area. Apparently the young prefer the floor.

We had further proof of the students' approval of the library once we stepped onto the smoking deck, an outdoor enclosure at treetop level inside the cloister. Future PhDs dressed almost uniformly in black gulped their coffee, posed and puffed, looking much like Jean-Paul Sartre and Simon de Beauvoir might if dressed in 21st-century garb, with piercing.

We resurfaced from the smoking deck into the wind, leaning toward the Seine, and marveled at the score of construction cranes dancing overhead. Since the mid-1990s those cranes have been in action, and for just as long, some Paris newspapers and magazines have been boosting the TGB's nascent surroundings as "the new Marais" or "nouveau Quartier Latin" – meaning they will soon be hip, lively and desirable places to live. Wishful thinking? True, a department of the Sorbonne will eventually move here (promised for over a decade). Some hard-hitting contemporary art galleries have migrated, with their Marais minimalists, to the Rue Louise Weiss, across the tracks from the TGB – but no one else has followed. Office towers, a research institute, additional up-market housing and a greenbelt over the rail yards are being built. When will they be finished?

We asked a jolly construction foreman for the lowdown. He repeated a line I'd heard on my first visit to the library in 1998, and again in 2000. "Tolbiac won't be finished for another thirty years," he cackled. This sounded like lifetime employment in an age of global insecurity. The developers' slogan, confirmed the construction worker, is "Paris

Awakens in the East", exactly the same as the title of the book we'd checked out in the library. Perhaps, I joked, someone should brew stronger coffee.

Still, compared to the empty lots, railroad tracks, 1970s architectural triumphs, abandoned industrial sites and defunct warehouses that formerly stood here, almost anything would be an improvement.

Down on the riverbank, we strolled along the landscaped Allée Arthur Rimbaud, wondering if the tormented poet of *The Drunken Boat* had liked the kinds of weepy, willowy trees planted here, and what he would have made of the TGB.

One bonus of the riverfront re-conversion that Rimbaud, a walk-aholic, would surely have hailed is that you can now hoof it from the promenade to the Latin Quarter on the Seine's banks more or less unmolested by cars. That's no mean achievement in a city as automobile-obsessed as Paris. Rimbaud, also an unrepentant party boy, would doubtless further enjoy the quayside hotspots fronting the TGB. Moored there were half a dozen drunken boats – home to floating cafés, restaurants and nightclubs.

One red-eyed clubber we buttonholed told us the Guingette Pirate (a mock pirate ship disco) is, after half a decade, still among the city's cutting-edge venues. A poster announced the imminent performances of Movement of Jah People (Afro-reggae), Tempo Slavia (Balkan music) and Orchestre de la Lune (free jazz). However, stiff competition comes from the adjacent Blues Café barge (featuring such talents as The Exiles Pop Rock, or TNT Salsa Pura Dynamita) and the celebrated Batofar, a reconverted lighthouse-riverboat. It offers hardcore techno, house and an explosive mix of world music (Negative Stencil, Voo Doo Phunk, 10 Nubians and others). My wife and I assured our talkative acquaintance that we'd return, around midnight, with the appropriate club gear. "Eastern Paris is awake after all," noted Alison. Apparently for some it never goes to sleep.

But we were eager to cross to the Right Bank again and see what progress had been made at Bercy since our last visit. Still waiting to be built is the footbridge – promised for the last fifteen years – linking the TGB to Bercy's spacious park, poetically named Les Jardins de Mémoire (Memory Gardens). Until the footbridge is built you must remember to use the busy Bercy or Tolbiac bridges to get from the Left Bank to Bercy, unless you take the new Météor subway, which is what we opted to do. Unfortunately the subway station is not in or near the library complex. To reach it we mounted an overpass, with railroad tracks below, cars and buses around, a forest of cranes above and the angular towers of the library fleecing flocks of passing clouds. Eventually we found the subway entrance.

If the TGB is high tech, then Météor is hyper-high tech. Glass escalators lowered us into a cavernous, stone-clad hall, then down another level to the platforms. For the time being this station, "Bibliothèque" (library), is the line's terminus. Despite the name it seems more Pharaoh's tomb than library, with granite-clad columns, a vaulted ceiling and a huge amphitheater – for embalming or ritual sacrifice, I wondered? Sacrifice of taxpayers' euros, certainly.

Monitors give read-outs of approaching trains. In the minute and fifteen seconds until ours arrived I peered at a brass plaque set in the granite floor, quoting 20th-century Italian poet Cesare Pavese: *A child went to play in the fields where now the boulevards stretch away.* Change "boulevards" to "rails" or "glass towers" and the quote fits the Tolbiac neighborhood to a tee.

Météor is fully automated. That means there are no drivers. Glass barriers built into a ribbed steel structure have been installed – said the flesh-and-blood ticket seller I queried – to keep passengers from "falling" onto the tracks. Glassy, sleek and open from car to car, our train swooshed in right on time, lined up perfectly with the anti-suicide barrier, opened its inner, then outer doors, bleeped, closed its outer then inner doors, and swooshed off. Beam me up, Jean-Jacques! We tumbled into wrap-around seating in the glass nosecone and blinked into the speed-blurred tunnel ahead.

Unlike Tolbiac and the TGB, as the years go by Bercy and its dreamy park have become increasingly gorgeous. We emerged up more glass escalators from the Cour Saint-Emilion Météor station and strolled the park's half-mile length several times. Kids played soccer on wide lawns. Lovers enlaced *à la Parisienne* under the magnificent old sycamores, or walked arm-in-arm around the romantic lake fed by water pumped in from the Seine. In the walled Potager, a kitchen garden, school children listened to a lecture among the cabbages and rhubarb. Two pocket-sized vineyards flank the exhibition building. They are a Bacchanalian symphony of trellised table-grape vines – Chasselas, Muscat and imported Sopieta – bordered by rosemary and lavender shrubs, and riotous climbing roses. Across a cobbled path we spotted the 400-odd Sauvignon Blanc and Chardonnay vines that Bercy's vintner grows to make the park's annual 200-liter *cuvée*, an undrinkable nod to the site's vinous history.

When I moved to Paris in 1986 I would sometimes buy wine from a wholesaler whose warehouse stood in what are now the park's grounds. The Entrepôts de Bercy, as the place used to be called, operated from the 1700s into the 1980s as Paris' official wine-warehousing district. All alcoholic beverages en route to the capital had to transit through the compound's road, rail or river port facilities.

Parts of the port, and the warehouses' narrow-gauge tracks, have been preserved. So too have a handful of the best 18th-century buildings, plus about 200 horse chestnuts and plane trees, some of them centuries old. A modern rampart several stories high insulates the park from the riverside Georges Pompidou Expressway. The splashing of a monumental granite-clad fountain – a veritable Niagara tumbling down steps from the rampart to the playing fields below – covers traffic noise. Like dozens of other merrymakers, we kicked off our shoes and chilled our feet in the water. It was almost as good as a fire hydrant party.

The Bercy project encompasses more than the 125-acre Memory Gardens, however. On the park's north side rises the former American Center, architect Frank Gehry's whimsical neo-Cubist construction whose teetering, jutting corners are already comfortingly stained and mossy. The center was abandoned in 1995 when funds ran out. Into the breech stepped the French government, with a plan to convert the building into a movie museum, research center and film archives dubbed La Maison du Cinéma. But red-tape experts have brought out their snares. The announced spring-2001 re-inauguration went by and now, years later, the cynics are delightedly wagging fingers and grinning.

The surrounding Bercy neighborhood – once distinguished by its railroad yards and curious 19th-century low-income housing projects – has bubbled back to life as a Bobo enclave. New hotels and fancy restaurants (including posh l'Oulette, a temple of Southwestern French gastronomy) have sprung up among the Gehry-inspired luxury apartment blocks. A glitzy food-and-wine convention center called Zeus stands several hundred yards east of the CinéCité movie multiplex, Paris' biggest, with eighteen screens. Fronting the multiplex is what planners have dubbed Le Village Bercy. It's a Parisian's answer to Disney's Main Street, but happily revolves around a wine theme.

Several dozen warehouses on either side of the village's pedestrian street are now cafés, restaurants and boutiques. They make Le Village Bercy one of Paris' favorite new shop-stroll-and-spend venues. Though tempted by the crowded Café Nicolas (operated by a wine retail chain) and the similarly clogged and foggy Vinéa Café, we opted instead for faux Italian focaccia sandwiches at the CinéCité's sun-sink outdoor café, Toastissimo. The fare was anything but *issimo*, though the self-service proved excellent (we provided it) and the outdoor seating smoke free.

Elegant arching walkways, plus the Seine-side rampart, fly over a road that cuts across the center of Bercy's park. We wove through towering sycamores then climbed the arched footbridges over the flow of traffic for a post-post-modern view.

To get from the park to eastern Paris' other big project, the Avenue Daumesnil and Viaduc des Arts, you can get back on the Météor and ride to the Gare de Lyon train station, or you can take another subway line direct to Daumesnil. But if you take either instead of walking you'll miss two of Paris' strangest specimens of architecture, both at the park's western edge.

The first of these marvels is called the Palais Omnisports, a semi-subterranean 1980 sports stadium with colored tubular metal frames, glass walls and a steeply pitched roof covered with turf. The building is proof that grass can grow at a sixty-degree angle. Parisian kids claw their way up it and slide down. Some graffiti-aficionados are less gentle. As we walked past the stadium we noticed that someone had physically torn chunks of turf out to form the characters "Y" "E" "$", thereby demonstrating a yen for yen (Y), euros (E) and dollars ($). YES! The people most likely to read this cryptic message were of course the bigwigs in the building directly across the street, which just happens to be the Ministry of Economy and Finance.

Another Mitterrand-era mastodon, the ministry is Europe's longest continuous building, an "L" that runs from the Gare de Lyon to Bercy's northern edge, then trudges another thousand feet to the Seine, where it sinks its foundations into the river. It's a modern citadel in glass, cement and steel, complete with a moat, designed by an architect who has vainly denied a purported passion for Stalinist structures. As we stood before the ministry, wondering which square inch our precious tax euros built and maintain, a helicopter thundered into view and landed on the roof. Nearby on the Seine, not far from the naked sunbathers and café crowds we'd seen at the start of our stroll, two armored speedboats tethered to the ministry's foundations started their engines. The minister, or his friends, had arrived.

It takes about twenty minutes to walk the length of the ministry's L, cross the Gare de Lyon and continue north another few blocks to reach the Avenue Daumesnil and its elevated train viaduct from the 1850s.

For many years Alison and I used to go to a gym built into an archway underneath the viaduct. It runs for a mile or so above the tree-lined avenue. But starting in 1987 the occupants of the viaduct's gloomy arches – garages, gyms, fry shops – were evicted as part of a grandiose rehab project that has turned this once down-at-heel neighborhood into yet another moneyed enclave.

Freshly scrubbed and renamed Le Viaduc des Arts, the archways now house over fifty craft workshops, boutiques, cafés and restaurants under graceful, glassed-in spans. The city of Paris, plus a handful of French bureaucracies, bankrolled the eleven-year, multi-multi-million dollar operation. Initially many of the artisans here were to have come from the abutting 11th arrondissement, a traditional craft-workers' district re-jigged by gentrification. In the end, though, prosperous provincial and foreign artisans moved here instead, with a single Parisian family of tooled-leather makers, the Feys, accommodated largely for window dressing.

An unexpected boon to legions of in-line skaters is the extra-wide sidewalk fronting the viaduct. As we walked along, a flying wedge of twenty-somethings clad in neo-medieval roller-blading gear swept past us. The bladers broke formation, slaloming between jog-walkers, cellular telephone bores, octogenarian shufflers, crazed poodles on retractable leashes, young fathers pushing high-tech baby carriages and impeccably dressed French children with posh names like Louis-Amadeus and Marie-Clothilde.

We scrunched up against the plate-glass windows of the workshops, out of harm's way, and once the skaters had passed, watched as a glass blower shaped colored spheres. Next door a decorator painted flowers on porcelain and, as we moved from window to window, we saw a hat-maker make berets, a picture framer frame pictures, and so on. With about a thousand other window-shoppers we wandered from arch to arch among the art and custom furniture galleries, the paper, textile and furniture restorers, the cabinetmakers, a needlepoint shop, an antique doll and music box seller, garden accessories boutiques, stone carvers, copper and silversmiths, an art academy, musical instrument makers and restorers, and half a dozen other arty enterprises.

Pleasantly exhausted we spied a single free table at the trendy Viaduc Café and settled into a comfy booth for a mid-afternoon jolt of coffee. There are a handful of newer restaurants under the viaduct's arches, but this one still seems the most appealing. Fellow customers luxuriated among the potted palms, sipping fresh-squeezed orange juice or nibbling on foie gras. The café is open daily until 4am, our hurried waiter told us. Some of the men at nearby tables cultivating their designer stubble looked as if they'd been up all night – maybe at the Batofar or Guinguette Pirate across the Seine. Perhaps they were gearing up for another sleepless night in eastern Paris? We relinquished our table to a bevy of roller-bladers, amid a chorus of mobile phone conversations muted by dense clouds of nicotine.

Staircases lead from the Avenue Daumesnil to the top of the viaduct, where the train tracks once were. Here an aerial parkway called the Promenade Plantée extends its rose gardens and arbors beyond the artisans' workshops, running a total of about three miles from the Bastille east, over footbridges, into a tunnel and through a sunken railroad bed to the beltway bounding Paris.

We muscled our way up and onto the crowded, narrow promenade and rejoiced at an elevated vision of Paris. Here were red tile or pitched mansard roofs, swaying sycamore tops, architectural details like cupolas and friezes, plus a pigeon's eye-view of lively street scenes. With cars far below we could hear ourselves think – and even smell the roses. "So what's next?" asked my indefatigable wife. "Do we walk to the beltway before doubling back to CinéCité for a movie, or do we have dinner at l'Oulette then the movie, then maybe some dancing at that club in the riverboat near those naked men we saw…"

I sank onto a bench, engulfed by perfumed blossoms, and couldn't help feeling a tinge of nostalgia. Gone were the quiet, cheap old days when eastern Paris meant a sweaty workout in our dingy gym, followed by a bottle of rough red wine from the Entrepôts de Bercy sloshed by a clumsy waiter across the paper-covered table of a now-dead neighborhood joint. "Get me another coffee," I sighed, "this could take all night."

PARIS PEOPLE

Statue and reflections, 1997

Coco Chanel

"Chanel, General De Gaulle and Picasso are the three most important figures of our time."

André Malraux

Haute couture has long struck me as residing somewhere on the scale of human endeavor between useless and obnoxious. Yet I've been fascinated for years by the figure of Coco Chanel, an ambivalent figure if ever there was one, and somehow, for me, the incarnation of a peculiar breed of Parisian. I once had the privilege, usually reserved for VIPs and big spenders, of visiting Coco's private hideaway in the Rue Cambon in Paris. Ever since, certain Paris places associated with Coco have echoed with a special resonance for me: the Rue de Rivoli and its unchanging Angélina tearoom; the Rue Cambon, Place Vendôme and Ritz Hotel. She was not just a denizen of the Golden Triangle for some sixty years, until her death in 1971. She was its archetype and mistress.

Arbiter of unfeminine yet unmistakably female elegance for half a century, lover of men both rich and famous, Coco cut and shaped her past like a suit of clothes. For instance, she fancied herself born in 1893, the daughter of a well-to-do winegrower from Saumur, in the Loire Valley. The truth is her birthday was ten years earlier than that, and her impoverished and unloving father, a street hawker, sent her to be brought up by nuns in a draughty medieval monastery in the Massif Central. Coco's mother Jeanne Devolle died in 1895 of tuberculosis, in utter destitution.

Throughout her long life, Chanel moved between two worlds, one real the other imaginary. Unloved, she lived for love. Despite her countless conquests, from English noblemen to Russian dukes, she spent years alone, work her only solace. Coco knew little about literature, art or music. Yet in Paris her pet celebrities were men the likes of Igor Stravinsky, Pablo Picasso and Jean Cocteau. She never worshipped money but nonetheless made a fortune with her hats, suits and perfumes. A social outcast from the provinces she came to rule Paris society and almost single-handedly revolutionized the way women around the world dressed, smelled and behaved, a feat impossible to contemplate in today's anything-goes world of street fashion and cultural eclecticism. Cocteau described her as at once spiteful, creative, extravagant, loveable, humorous, generous, hateful and excessive, "a unique character." Uniquely Parisian, I would add.

Despite the work of a dozen biographers, several of whose tomes I've read over the years, Chanel remains an enigma. However, she has left behind her in certain Paris places an unmistakable whiff of stale perfume, a fleeting reflection in a wavy mirror, like the one that fills the wall alongside table eleven at Angélina, the time-capsule tearoom on the Rue de Rivoli, facing the Tuileries.

Coco always sat at table eleven and everyone at Angélina knew her. The establishment opened for business in 1903 under the name Rumpelmayer but Coco would've been too poor to go there then. It became her refuge late in life, in the 1950s, when a quiet cup of hot cocoa was a daily ritual. Back then, the faux Louis XVI armchairs in the downstairs salons were covered in green, not brown patent leather as they are today. Otherwise the pleasantly worn décor hasn't changed. Her marble-topped table is still the third from the back in the main room, set against the fifteen-foot mirror. Coco had a thing about looking glasses. She could observe herself in them, certainly, but she could also watch the world in reflection, one step removed. She would sit at table eleven, order her Chocolat Africain and gaze at her wizened reflection, surrounded by the tearoom's sculpted plaster encrustations and faded Belle Époque murals of Mediterranean scenes. Those who knew her well say she was in fact looking into her past, as into a crystal ball that somehow transported her backward in time.

I sat at her table not long ago, a biography in hand, and enjoyed a plump raisin roll and a rich cup of cocoa. The fashion shows, underway in the Tuileries across the street, had not caused an overflow at Angélina. Near me a blue-rinse matron caressed her lapdog. She dug her spoon into a bowl of whipped cream, topped her cocoa and smiled contentedly at the young men and women nearby, escapees, perhaps, from the pages of Henry James. I squinted and imagined she was Coco, slipping through her looking glass.

For the record, Gabrielle Chanel preferred to forget not only her infancy and childhood but also her early years in Moulins, in southern France, before the First World War, when she was a shop assistant and seamstress by day, a café-concert singer by night. From that far-off Belle Époque echoes the nickname given to Gabrielle by the army officers who hung out at Moulin's La Rotonde to hear her sing. She knew only two songs, one of which ran *Qui qu'a vu Coco dan l'Trocadéro* – who's seen Coco at the Trocadero? They shouted *Coco! Coco!* when calling for encores. Etienne Balsan, a French gentleman infantry officer of considerable means, was among them. He was Coco's first famous lover.

Addicted to horseflesh and racy mademoiselles Balsan the bon vivant was smitten. He offered to finance her, first during her short-lived stage career (where she learned about theater costumes and makeup) and later as a milliner. From the nuns, Coco had learned to sew and embroider. From an aunt she had learned to decorate hats. At Royallieu, Etienne Balsan's lavish residence and stud farm near Compiègne, north of Paris, Chanel was installed as official mistress and soon began making hats for society ladies and *irrégulières* – unmarriageable women like herself.

A natural sportswoman, Coco rode horses as well as a man could, and adopted the clothes of the English gentleman rider. Her unusual attire, wit and sharp tongue quickly earned her a reputation as formidable. Balsan's best friend was the star of this horsy set, a rich English polo player named Arthur "Boy" Capel. His infatuation with Coco was matched only by her passion for him.

Edmonde Charles-Roux, Chanel's longtime friend and probably her best hagiographer, once noted that Coco, the model of the modern, independent woman, was "formed, discovered and invented by men." Balsan raised her out of poverty but it was Boy Capel who gave her true happiness – for a time. Chanel liked to say that Boy was the man of her life, the only one who understood her passion and thirst for freedom. Capel introduced her to his society friends and helped her expand from a modest shop at 160 Boulevard Malesherbes in Paris to his own lavish digs at number 138 down the street. He also set her up with a workshop in the Rue Cambon and a stylish boutique in Deauville, the Parisians' seaside retreat, summer headquarters of Europe's great and good. He made it clear she would remain his friend and lover but would never become his wife.

After Boy's marriage, and his sudden death a few months later in a car accident, Coco took to men, and work, the way some people take to drink. Her unstoppable rise began in the Roaring '20s, a decade cast in her image. She bought the luxurious Villa Bel Respiro in Paris' suburbs and began entertaining Stravinsky, Cocteau, the poet Pierre Reverdy, Serge Diaghilev of the Ballets Russes, and the pianist and model Misia Sert, for decades her closest friend. Gone were the social constraints of her youth. Among her artist comrades Coco was no longer an *irrégulière*.

The taste of Angélina chocolate, and the echo of the slender Coco's high heels, followed me the few blocks from the Rue de Rivoli's mosaic-paved arcades north. Swann, the long-established British-American pharmacy in the Rue de Castiglione, evoked Proust. A block east the rare books illustrated by Joan Mirò, Max Ernst and Jean Cocteau displayed in the windows of Librairie les Arcades brought my mind back to Coco. The traffic on Rue du Faubourg Saint Honoré was thick. Still, I was able to smell the perfume wafting out of the historic Chanel boutiques nearby at numbers 27 and 31 of the Rue Cambon. It was on these hallowed premises, during my fortuitous visit to Coco's upstairs apartment, that I heard the story of how "Chanel #5" was born. Shortly after World War One, some Russian friends introduced Chanel to Grand Duke Dmitri Pavlovich Romanov, the murderer of Rasputin, exiled even before the Revolution of 1917. In 1920 Coco took as a lover this penniless aristocrat a decade her junior, keeping him in a style to which he had once been accustomed. In return Dmitri taught her about the heady scents of the Tsar's court, and introduced her to Ernest Beaux, perfumer extraordinaire. A year later, Beaux brought her five phials containing scents intended to express the quintessence of her sartorial styles. Coco sniffed the first four and shook her head. She might've named the last one, marked number five, the sweet smell of success.

Winding upwards one floor from the showroom of the Rue Cambon boutique is the mirrored staircase atop which Coco perched, unseen, to watch models show off her clothes. The private apartment upstairs is off limits, marked with a sign: *Mademoiselle – Privé*. The two immaculate, slightly chilling rooms are not so much a museum as a shrine, dedicated to the memory of Coco – to a certain official version of Coco, I should add. An unrepentant frump troubled by Coco's wartime record, I found myself seated on the vast leather couch where she loved to nap wrapped in a mink blanket. Her eyeglasses sat somewhere nearby and I felt they were staring at me archly, the way insiders say Coco stared at unwelcome critics. Her possessions, displayed for the delight of select reverent visitors, include a pair of Chinese Coromandel screens, plus books, sculptures and *objets d'art,* all of them reflected ad infinitum in the mirrors Coco cherished. Especially egregious are the Venetian Renaissance sculptures of black slaves of which reportedly she felt particularly fond. On a coffee table facing the couch among the gold bobbles lie the heraldic arms of Westminster. I remember asking myself why they were there, and only finding the answer months later, in a biography.

Coco's Slavic period lasted a few years, with Dmitri eventually marrying an American heiress who had means and a more pliable character. Coco continued to mount the social ladder, nonetheless, by moving into a sumptuous two-story apartment at number 29 Rue du Faubourg Saint Honoré, just a few minutes away on foot. As I strolled toward it through bumper-to-bumper BMWs and Mercedes I reflected on the fact that at Coco's lavish digs Stravinsky and Diaghilev had been regulars. Picasso came to stay while working on stage sets for Cocteau's *Antigone*. It's well known that Picasso was a peerless womanizer but hardly anyone remembers that the man-eating Coco snacked on him here between meals. It was at this felicitous juncture that the poet Pierre Reverdy, like Chanel an ambitious product of the provinces, became her third famous lover.

The apartment they shared is in private hands and I've never managed to get closer to it than the unremarkable downstairs entrance hall. Nothing remains from the time of Chanel except the memories the site summons. Reverdy, deep in spiritual crisis, eventually left her in Paris. But Coco was not lonely for long. In Monte Carlo she had caught the eye of Bend'or, nickname of the Duke of Westminster, the richest man in England. He swept her away on his yacht, Flying Cloud, and before the year was out they were inseparable. Their whirlwind romance was to last for half a decade. Despite what appeared to be a never-ending vacation, in 1926 Coco managed to invent *pret-à-porter* fashion with her "little black dress", the revolutionary garment American *Vogue* dubbed "the Ford signed Chanel."

The Duke of Westminster did as dukes do and broke Coco's heart by announcing his engagement to a certain Loelia Mary Ponsonby, whose very name makes anyone without blue blood sneeze. Again, Coco rebounded. In short order Paul Iribe, a flamboyant caricaturist, jewelry designer and magazine editor, took up the flame. It was under Iribe's guidance that Chanel began creating diamond jewelry, spin-offs of which are still sold today. In the spring of 1934, tired of the housekeeping, perhaps, she moved from the Faubourg-Saint-Honoré to a nest at the Ritz Hotel overlooking the Rue Cambon, where she lived on and off for the rest of her life.

A stroll from the Faubourg to the Place Vendôme takes you through several acres of old and, mostly, new money. Leading jewelers such as

Cartier, Bulgari and Van Cleef & Arpels wink at you, the Chanel shop set among them. Fashion boutiques, upscale hotels and Michelin-starred restaurants abound. This was Coco's Paris, the snooty summit, the tip of the tallest peak an impoverished, uneducated provincial climber could reach. Nowadays the Ritz offers clients what's known as the Chanel Suite, though it has little to do with her (for one thing she lived on the opposite side of the hotel). It's certainly not a shrine: you can rent the 1,667-square-foot apartment for 3,500 to 6,600 euros a night. Most mere mortals who ask to see it are directed to ritzparis.com for a virtual tour to the strains of Mozart. However if you ask very politely, dress nicely, and have the good fortune to time your request with a vacancy, you might be able to visit for a fleeting moment without paying. The furniture embraces the styles of Louis XVI, the Directory and the Empire, in other words, it is gilt and gaudy, presumably the way Chanel liked it. The taps in the stone-clad bathroom are gold plated. There are even Coromandel screens like the ones in Coco's Rue Cambon sanctuary. Views from the windows take in the 18th-century architectural gems lining the Place Vendôme and, of course, the celebrated column with its imitation Imperial Roman low-relief sculptures. Like so many symbols of oppression, it was toppled more than once by riffraff and re-erected by the powers that be.

The one time I talked my way into the suite I couldn't help staring out of the window, contemplating the column – and the fact that in 1934, when she first checked into the Ritz, Coco's enterprises boomed despite the worldwide Depression and the violent workers' riots and strikes in which her own employees took part. Business roared for her throughout the grim '30s, in fact.

But money wasn't everything to Chanel. The premature death of her beloved Iribe in 1935 seemed to prove yet again that Coco was as unlucky in love as she had been successful in commerce. A few years later, even that changed: the distant thunder of the Second World War was beginning to shake Coco's comfortable universe. In the summer of 1939 she fled Paris. During the Occupation, however, she quietly moved back into the Ritz. And the darkest period of her life began, a decade in which her name was attached to that of the shadowy "Von D.", a German intelligence officer. It's this period that makes Chanel's business heirs cringe, and is rarely, if ever, mentioned by anyone remotely associated with the Chanel fashion or perfume houses.

How did Coco Chanel escape the punishment meted out after the Occupation to the women who fraternized with the Nazis? As André

Malraux, the celebrated poet, critic, and first-ever French Minister of Culture said, "Chanel, General De Gaulle and Picasso are the three most important figures of our time." She had friends in high places in France and, as the bobbles on her coffee table in the Rue Cambon attest, elsewhere among the war's victors.

Chanel's self-imposed exile to Switzerland after the war lasted until 1954, when she made a comeback. She was seventy years old and had not shown a collection since 1939. Christian Dior was all the rage. Undaunted, Coco revived her Rue Cambon shop and set to work. The show, initially panned by the reigning fashion moguls and called a "fiasco" by London's then-influential *Daily Mail*, was hailed in America. The fame of her youth was revived. *Life* magazine credited her for revolutionizing the industry yet again. Asked whom she dressed, Coco snapped, "Ask me who don't I dress!" Over the next seventeen years, until her last snip of the scissors in 1971, she lived between her suite at the Ritz and her Rue Cambon apartment and shop. "I was a rebellious child, a rebellious lover, a rebellious *couturière* – a real devil," she once confessed. That's not a bad epitaph for the 20th century's greatest mind in fashion, a true Parisienne of the Golden Triangle.

A *bouquiniste* box, 2005

Les Bouquinistes

"They buried him, but all through the night of mourning, in the lighted windows, his books arranged three by three kept watch like angels with outspread wings and seemed, for him who was no more, the symbol of his resurrection."

Marcel Proust, *La Prisonnière*

Coffins. Dilapidated dolls' houses. Treasure chests encrusted with padlocks and bars. The green, battered book boxes of the *bouquinistes*, Paris' quayside secondhand booksellers, slump evocatively along the Seine, anachronistic curiosities clinging to riverside parapets as they have for the last 100-odd years.

A higgledy-piggledy wagon train several miles long loaded with something like 300,000 volumes, the boxes also overflow with posters, engravings, knick-knacks, paintings, soft porn, leather-bound tomes, dusty paperbacks, statuettes, coins, coasters and refrigerator magnets – the sublime, offensive and ridiculous displayed side-by-side.

A city official once confirmed to me that there are about a thousand book boxes all told, each painted the same regulation *vert wagon* – the dark green of old train cars, old buses, old benches and old railings left over from the Second Empire or the Third Republic. Despite the *règlement*, each box is a subtly different shade and shape, frosted here by moss, blackened by smog, rotted by rain and damp, scarred by reckless drivers and the inexorable passing of time, then patched and trussed and slathered with another layer of green paint. In the dark, especially on a wet moonless night, the boxes glistening under 19th-century street lamps take on a sinister, sepulchral cast – the objective correlatives of a dead Paris.

Look again on a sunny morning, though, when the booksellers who preside over the boxes make their way down the stone sidewalks, unlock and prop open their treasure chests following a careful ritual, and the metaphors change. The battered *boîtes* morph into wood-and-tin grasshoppers lifting their legs, or gull-winged vessels carrying precious bundles from the reassuring past toward an uncertain future.

Squint, or use a telephoto lens, to eliminate the traffic, and you can almost see novelist Anatole France – the most famous patron of late

19th-century *bouquinistes* – picking through the swirling crowds, lifting a heavy volume then dickering over the price. It was in France's heyday in fact, in 1891, that the itinerant booksellers of Paris' quaysides were finally given the right to affix their boxes to the parapets, after about 400 years of cat-and-mouse with municipal authorities. That game is now left to the unregistered, largely immigrant groups of bangle-hawkers who pack up and run at the approach of a gendarme.

I'm not sure why but I've always been drawn to the *bouquinistes*. To say I've befriended several would be an exaggeration, but as a regular customer I do know them and their wares. Many are great talkers, and a few know a good deal about the history of their trade. Apparently they take their name from the German *buchen* (books) or the Old Dutch *boeckin* – "little books." In French, therefore, a *bouquiniste* is a seller of *bouquins*. A *bouquineur* is a book-lover, collector or reader like me (and most of us have no room for *bouquins* in our tiny apartments, which is why we do book swaps, to keep down the height of the stacks). It's only logical, then, that the verb *bouquiner* means both "to trawl the quays searching for books" and, more commonly, "to read up" or "study hard" by poring over textbooks.

Funnily no one I've talked to seems to know when these expressions were coined, though city records show that Paris' first printing press was installed in 1470 at the Sorbonne – fourteen years after Gutenberg printed the first *buch* in Mainz. *Bouquins* began to circulate immediately thereafter among the scholars and priests headquartered in the Left Bank's university neighborhoods. By 1500, the city's earliest permanent bookstores had begun to spring up there, and by around 1530, groups of itinerant booksellers were walking the streets of the Cité and the bridges connecting the island to either side of the Seine.

As is their wont, from the start, the powers that be regarded with a baleful eye these motley *bouquinistes* – suspicious, perhaps subversive indigents selling their wares off ground cloths or from trays hanging from straps around their shoulders. A 1577 police document compares them to "fences and thieves" in part because during the wars of religion, many *bouquinistes* sold Protestant pamphlets or "subversive tracts" printed abroad. Routinely the king's men would round up and jail the *bouquinistes* – or do worse.

In 1606, Paris police authorities decided to regulate the trade, limiting business activity to daylight hours, and restricting the sphere of movement to the riverbanks "in the vicinity of the Pont Neuf." These early booksellers were allowed to display their goods on the parapets and roadsides (there were no sidewalks back then except on the Pont Neuf itself). The number of vendors skyrocketed during the French Revolution, when the collections of countless noble families were confiscated and auctioned, or stolen by angry mobs, as patrician heads tumbled into bloody baskets in what's now the Place de la Concorde. Eventually many of the aristocracy's books made their way into the hands of the *bouquinistes*, and in the course of the last 200 years these valuable volumes have been sold and resold many times on the quays.

Order and symmetry have long been national obsessions among France's administrators, and they are regularly subverted by institutionalized revolution. The dimensions and distribution of the *bouquinistes'* boxes go back to the Third Republic, when enlightened municipal officials decided to give the families of wounded veterans and war widows the right to leave their *boîtes* clamped to the riverside walls. A few minor reforms were made to the *règlement* in the 1940s (establishing the total length – exactly eight meters – of parapet allotted per bouquiniste) and in the 1950s (the uniform application of *vert wagon* as a color). In 1993, the City of Paris began requiring bouquinistes to open at least four days a week, buy a business license (about thirty-five euros a year), and pay social security and income taxes (usually about thirty percent of declared gross revenues). Licenses now go to individuals from all walks of life, not just to needy families.

Predictably the *règlement* isn't always respected, but it has kept the worst abusers at bay. Of the four regulation green boxes each bookseller may exploit, at least three must now contain only books. In the fourth, the *bouquiniste* can display "souvenirs related to Paris," which explains the proliferation of miniature Eiffel Towers, Notre-Dame gargoyle paperweights, postcards and faux-Hermès bandannas showing the Arc de Triomphe or other monuments.

One day I buttonholed a youngish woman named Laurence Alsina, who turned out to be a fourth-generation *bouquiniste*. Her boxes face number 65 on the Left Bank's Quai de la Tournelle kitty-corner to the Rue de Bièvre. "I was born on this sidewalk," she told me with understandable pride. "But we can no longer survive selling only books."

With Notre-Dame as a backdrop, Laurence has an ideal location, yet there are days, she noted, when she doesn't sell a single *bouquin*. Carefully wrapped in cellophane, her classics of literature, history and travel are flanked by the usual selection of postcards and posters – the moneymakers. "In summer, tourists want secondhand classics like *Madame Bovary*," she sighed. "Off season, Parisian collectors, quayside regulars and journalists buy out-of-print or rare books, but people just don't read as much anymore..."

The Internet, CDs and DVDs, videos and computer games have squeezed the *bouquinistes'* market share. Still, Laurence's family runs three sets of boxes and shows no signs of giving up. Her father, Marcel Baudon, hails from the Quai de Montebello facing Shakespeare & Company. Her sister, Véronique le Goff, is on the Quai Saint-Michel near the RER station entrance, facing number three. Like most *bouquinistes,* the whole family is driven by an obsessive passion for books – quayside lifers call it *la maladie des livres*. It's also what keeps them going despite meager takings: city officials estimate average monthly earnings per licensee at $1,000-$2,000.

For a long time I wondered where the *bouquinistes* got their books. From regulars like me, certainly, but small-time, occasional swap-traders are notoriously unreliable. It turns out that several days a week most *bouquinistes* rise before dawn's fingers start tickling the Seine, and drive to the scruffy suburbs or distant provinces to scour flea markets, attend auctions or hit village yard sales – the best sources for books. Sometimes middlemen arrive with a truckload jumble rescued from an attic somewhere. Occasionally, burglars try to peddle stolen tomes, but street-smart sellers usually spot hucksters before they get a chance to finish their spiel. Or so it's said.

Competition comes not only from the Web and high-tech, or other secondhand bookstores. Every weekend year-round the Georges-Brassens book market is held under a 19th-century glass-and-iron structure at the Parc Georges-Brassens in the far-flung 15th arrondissement. It has become another favorite of serious collectors, though it lacks the charm – and convenience – of the quays.

Of Paris' nearly 250 *bouquinistes*, perhaps two dozen are specialized – in crime novels, music books, military history, fine art, old magazines, incunabula and so forth. When I'm looking for thrillers or jazz-related books, I go to bearded, affable Jacques Bisceglia, whose boxes face 31 Quai de la Tournelle. He has the biggest jazz-book collection in town, about 800 volumes, plus thousands of crime novels and detective stories – his second passion.

Across the Seine from Jacques, facing 48 Quai de l'Hôtel de Ville, a vigorous fellow named Michel Vigouroux, originally from Brittany, sells every book, magazine or poster imaginable relating to his windswept native region. Down the same quay, Katia Lachnowicz, across from number seventy-two, deals in movie and theater books. Agnès Talec, facing 21 Quai des Grands-Augustins, displays almost every leaf of high-minded literature published by La Pléiade, while Jean-Claude Picon (across from 2 Quai de Gesvres) boasts a nearly complete collection of *Paris Match* – ah, for those weighty words and punchy photos! Some of the finest engravings and rare vintage books in town (and among the most expensive – up to $1,000) are the specialty of Left-Bank institution Michelle Huchet-Nordmann (facing 35 Quai de Conti).

For most other *bouquinistes*, however, variety is the key to survival, so they sell a mixed bag. That means a dedicated *bouquineur* can spend entire days doing the hundred Right-Bank *emplacements* between the Pont Marie and Rue de l'Amiral-de-Coligny before crossing the Seine to the remaining 150 between the Pont Sully and Pont Royal. It's a workout but the views aren't bad and the characters you meet are often salty specimens of *homo parisiana*.

Fiercely independent, sometimes extroverted, sometimes surly, the *bouquinistes* are a caste apart. Solidarity is essential to survival. It takes about forty-five minutes to open or close a stall, for instance, so neighbors usually help each other. They share bottles of wine and stories, passing information along the quayside jungle *téléphone*. They all know each other. They know who's selling what and for how much, and they refer clients back and forth. Among themselves, they use only first names – "Go see Robert for that," they might tell you, giving an "address" as people once did before the days of street signs, "in front of Le Montebello..."

Robert, it turns out, is Paris' oldest working *bouquiniste*, a big man still at eighty-something years old, with luxuriant moustaches and a beard. He sells collectors' books and cheap paperbacks too, from a spot facing Le Montebello, a restaurant on the quay of the same name. Another celebrated sidewalk character is Jean-Jacques, whose *emplacement* faces thirty-one Quai de Conti. His nickname is *le Jacques Prévert des bouquinistes,* apparently because he's an expansive rhetorician. His passions are film, theater and dance, and he doesn't have much time for uninitiated browsers. One hundred yards east of Jean-Jacques, facing 55 Quai des Grands-Augustins, an eccentric newcomer to the business is a retired communications consultant named Guy. He sells a wide variety of books, but his true interest lies in exhibiting his own original oil or pastel paintings, which range from the figurative to the abstract. Purists scoff at Guy, seeing in his unconventional "gallery" the narrow edge of a Montmartre-style wedge. But it's hard to label his paintings as any more tasteless than the hundreds of pseudo-Sigmund Freud posters ("What's on a Man's Mind? – A Naked Woman!") on offer at dozens of other stands, and I have a feeling that Montmartre and its elephant train will never catch on here.

I once conducted an informal survey, asking *bouquinistes* if they enjoyed their life. Most waxed lyrical about the freedom of being independent, the wonders of the book world, the magic of the quays, and the stimulation of daily encounters with people from around the world. But if pressed they often sighed or confessed. Weather is the *bouquinistes'* main worry. Rain, especially, makes business difficult. Snow, high wind, cold or burning sun can keep people off the quays for days at a time. And the elements take their toll on the booksellers themselves. "We're the peasants of Paris," said one wizened old-timer I queried near Notre-Dame. "We listen to the weather reports like fishermen or farmers, then we come out anyway and get soaked, frozen or sun burned."

You can account for the surliness of some *bouquinistes* by the combination of weathering and wear. They're stone-washed by the incessant tides of curious tourists who pick up books, unwrap them, put them back in the wrong place and seem more interested in rummaging than buying. Then there are the city authorities and the tax inspectors – always eager to check on strictly cash-in-hand businesses.

Most annoying and dangerous of all, however, is the car, truck and bus traffic that thunders by, ever faster and thicker and more poisonous as the years go by. In the early 1990s, UNESCO declared the quays of the Seine a World Heritage Site, yet at the same time the city of Paris turned them into "Axe Rouge" expressways. Every stoplight is the start of a drag race. By afternoon, if there's no breeze, the air can be black with smog. The *bouquinistes* shake their heads at this and mutter words like "nightmarish," "idiotic" and "incomprehensible." A modicum of relief has come of late in the form of the bike and bus lanes on the Left Bank and, in some places, wider sidewalks, but not all *bouquinistes* have benefited.

Despite the difficulties, the average age of the men and women on the quays has dropped from sixty (in the 1960s) to forty – proof of the profession's stubborn vitality or, perhaps, an indication of a desperate economic situation that drives the young toward marginal businesses. One thing is certain, there's never a shortage of applicants vying for a license or a spot. The waiting list usually stretches about eighty names long. It takes up to four years to get your first *emplacement* – always in a lousy location – and it might take you decades of hopscotch to wind up near Notre-Dame or the Pont Neuf.

"You start in Purgatory," lifelong bouquiniste Laurence, near the cathedral, explained to me. "Purgatory is what we call the bad spots on the extreme ends of the quays – like the one my grandmother got in 1920 and I got twenty years ago. From Purgatory you work your way to a better life." She smiled, pointing to the buttresses of Notre-Dame soaring above the Seine's leafy banks. When the traffic had subsided, for a blissful moment, it did indeed seem like we were in Paradise.

Place du Tertre, 2005

Midnight, Montmartre and Modigliani

"It is a strange gray study in nature, this midnight Montmartre… Artists with hope before them, poets with the appreciation of some girl only, and side by side with these the hurried anxious faces of unkempt women and tired-eyed men…"

H. P. Hugh, 1899

Charles *The-Flowers-of-Evil* Baudelaire was 19th-century Paris' archetypal *artiste maudit* – the tortured, sensitive, cursed poet of a dead city that had crossed in a single generation from the Middle Ages into the modern age. He lived intensely and died young, his work imbued with a deep melancholy that resonates to this day. In many ways, the Franco-Italian painter and sculptor Amedeo Modigliani picked up in the early 1900s where Baudelaire had left off. It was a dubious honor, perhaps, but Modigliani's soulful artwork, like Baudelaire's poetry, is more coveted than ever, and the story of his tumultuous, debauched, tragically short life in Paris is as moving today as it was a century ago.

A puritanical biographer of our current age might describe Modigliani as macho, womanizing, obsessive and demonic, a substance-abusing madman too handsome and talented for his own good, at once self-destructive and murderous, a kind of proto-Jim Morrison of *The Doors,* a rebel without a cause, the last of the great Bohemian Romantics of the Belle Époque.

Like Jim Morrison, Modigliani is buried at Père-Lachaise cemetery, the graveyard of France's great and good. I often think of the tragic pair as I take my daily constitutional among the tombs – my office is practically in the cemetery's backyard. So when a few years ago, at the behest of an Italian friend, my wife Alison and I set about mapping the places where Modigliani had lived, worked and died, Père-Lachaise seemed the logical place to start. Division 96, Avenue Transversale number three is Modigliani's address, in theory for perpetuity. It corresponds to a simple sandstone tomb in an otherwise uninteresting section of the cemetery. Nearly always covered with flowers, the gravestone bears the inscription: "Amedeo Modigliani, born in Leghorn July

12, 1884, died in Paris January 24, 1920. Death snatched him from the brink of glory." Modigliani died a pauper. But, as Alison, an art historian by training, reminded me, he had a hero's funeral, attended by Picasso, Soutine, Léger, Ortiz de Zarate, Lipchitz, Derain, Severini, Foujita, Utrillo, Valadon, Vlaminck and the poets Max Jacob and André Salmon, as well as dozens of now-forgotten friends and admirers. He'd found glory, certainly in terms of peer recognition, but it came too late.

Further down Modigliani's tombstone is a second, cryptic epitaph. It was added some years after the first and reads: "Jeanne Hébuterne, born in Paris April 6, 1898, died in Paris January 25, 1920. Devoted companion of Amedeo Modigliani till the moment of extreme sacrifice."

Extreme sacrifice? I wondered now who Jeanne Hébuterne had been and why she'd died just a day after the artist. Alison had only a vague recollection, so before setting out to find the places Modigliani knew, we cracked open the art history books and were fascinated and horrified in equal measure by what we found.

Amedeo Modigliani's mother was French, from Marseille, his father Italian. Both descended from solid, middle-class Jewish families. Amedeo grew up on the Tuscan coast and moved to Paris when twenty-one to study art. A freethinker, he abjured the family faith and declared to his fellow students that he wanted "a short but full life." Dashing, charming, witty and perfectly bilingual Modigliani got his "full life" off to a galloping start – he drank heavily, smoked hashish, partied and painted round the clock, changing addresses and lovers about as often as his clothes. It's unclear what stage his consumption, a deadly lung disease, had reached before he arrived in Paris. It's irrefutable, though, that Modigliani was obsessed by fears of the congenital insanity that had plagued his family for generations. He dwelled morbidly on his own impending death, and as his physical and mental health declined he began flitting around the cemeteries of Montmartre and Montparnasse reciting lines from Dante's *Inferno* and *Les Chants de Maldoror* by le Comte de Lautréamont, the notorious adept of De Sade. Tellingly, the nickname his fellow artists gave him was Modì – short for Modigliani, of course, but pronounced exactly like *maudit*, meaning damned, accursed, the spiritual heir of Baudelaire.

While the wine and absinthe flowed no one in his Bohemian circle really believed Modì would insure for himself that "short but full life" by committing suicide. No one, that is, except Jeanne Hébuterne. She was the last of his many lovers, the mother-to-be of his child, and it was with her, some historians think, that Modì swore a death pact. He drank and smoked himself to death and though nine months pregnant, Jeanne Hébuterne threw herself from the fifth-floor window of her parents' apartment the day after Modì died in an unheated garret in Montparnasse.

But we were getting ahead of ourselves. Modigliani may have lived his last years and died in Montparnasse, though you won't find his spirit there today, despite the "Terrasse Modigliani", a dreary parking lot next to the Montparnasse train station, or the "Atelier Modigliani", his garret, marked by a plaque at number 8 Rue de la Grande Chaumière. It's when you wander the streets of Montmartre that the tragic artist's presence seems to flit past you down the zigzag staircases and atmospheric alleys of this hallowed hill capped by Sacré Coeur. We decided to rewind to 1906, the year Modì arrived from Italy by train and headed straight for what people called back then La Butte. At the time Montmartre's hilly sprawl took in vacant lots, scruffy, unpaved streets lined by crumbling two-story buildings, windmills, vineyards and orchards on the city's northern edge. Sundown on a drizzly fall weekday seemed like a good time to me to hit the streets of the Butte – when the light begins to fade the tourist crowds thin but the parks, shops and cafés remain open. We took the Métro to the Anvers station and, swept along by a crowd of Franco-African locals, made our way up the narrow Rue Steinkerque, a straight shot to the Square Willette at the base of the staircase leading to Sacré Coeur. A merry-go-round spun to sour-sounding music. Amid the primly dressed children and their minders sat clutches of placid winos. Modì and his painter pal Maurice Utrillo often sat in this square and sketched the city and the passersby while guzzling cheap wine. Then they would hike up the hill on steep, plaited staircases, past the white hulk of Sacré Coeur basilica, pausing, perhaps, to stare at the skeletal silhouette of the teenage Tour Eiffel before following the dog's-leg streets to the Place du Tertre where Modì lived.

We dodged an elephant train carrying weary tourists and poked around the souvenir stands looking for Modì. Among the Sacré Coeur snow-shower paperweights, pot metal Eiffel Tower replicas and Amelie Poulain posters, we spotted several T-shirts emblazoned with the stylized, elongated, sad-eyed women Modì preferred. I reflected on the fact that a hundred years ago, for the current price of a T-shirt – around $10 – I could have bought several original Modigliani canvasses. He disdained money. The cost of living in his day was only a fraction of what it is now but even that doesn't alter the equation: Modì wanted only enough for daily survival with something left over to buy his artist's materials.

We decided to have a drink at La Bohème du Tertre and do some mental burrowing backwards, down an imaginary time tunnel, to the days when Modì lived in a cheap furnished room above this venerable café, now a tourist trap. Back then the square was the center of an artists' colony – most of them authentic, serious, academy-trained artists. They chose the Butte because rents were low yet it was within walking distance of central Paris. In those dying days of the Belle Époque there were already tourists a-plenty on the hill. Some were drawn by Sacré Coeur others by the cabarets, cafés and restaurants. As Alison and I sipped our overpriced beers I was torn by conflicting emotions, at once troubled by the tour-bus hordes yet conscious of being part of them, repelled yet fascinated by the Butte's world-class kitsch. Accordions wheezed. Yellow pennants fluttered by as tour group leaders gave directions through bullhorns. I wondered if there were an undiscovered Modì, Picasso or Foujita among the caricaturists and other self-styled artists, most of them non-French, soliciting in the square. Modì was Italian, after all, Picasso Spanish, and Foujita Japanese. Each had made his fortune on the Butte's scuffed and littered pavements while others had fallen by the wayside.

During the months Modì lodged above the café where we now sat he had been a tired-eyed regular in the square's troughs but especially at the Clarion des Chasseurs (in business since 1790) and La Mère Catherine, where a full meal cost under a franc – the equivalent in purchasing power of a few dollars today. Naturally both spots charge many times that now, and do a lively trade indoors among bric-a-brac and on shaded terraces using their long-dead, famous artist-patrons to create a faux Bohemian setting.

Modì ranged over the Butte for three years, camping in at least five different places. The first was a ramshackle studio in a shantytown area called Le Maquis – a reference to the wild and wooly Corsican outback where thieves, murderers and renegades hid out. An elderly local woman I buttonholed in a street north of the Place du Tertre seemed to think she'd heard of Le Maquis. She pointed that away, down the Rue Norvins. We explored until we came to the evocatively named Allée des Brouillards – meaning, literally, fog alley – whose pocketsize front yards were overgrown with Art Nouveau shrubs. From it we crossed a small square into a park with another evocative name, Le Hameau des Artistes or Artists' Hamlet. A group of neighborhood seniors polished their steel balls and tossed them down the gravel-and-dirt lanes of none other than Le Maquis, which is now a *boulodrome*, the French answer to a lawn-bowling alley. They glanced over but apparently could not be troubled to acknowledge our presence. I understood. The Butte's inhabitants live in parallel to the tourist flows.

The current incarnation of Le Maquis struck me as something the rebellious, left-leaning Modì might have liked (he often wore a red handkerchief around his neck in the style of the Italian revolutionary hero Giuseppe Garibaldi). The artists' studios of old had been razed, but at least no high-rise apartment buildings had taken their place. The *boule* players appeared to be from the working class, and in the corners of the park sat more of the Butte's winos and outcasts.

Behind the walls of what is now number 11 Rue Norvins is a garden fronting the centuries-old house in which Modì lived briefly with English journalist Beatrice Hastings. She famously described him as "at once pearl and swine." Like her swinish lover, the man-eating Beatrice was no stranger to the bottle. She and Modì often fought and on one occasion he reportedly heaved her out of the window into the shrubbery. She was too drunk to notice, however, and the affair continued on and off for years, even after Modì moved to Montparnasse.

Another hundred yards away in a sloping residential square called the Place Jean-Baptiste Clément, Modì worked in a studio at number seven (it has since been transformed into a handsome residence with an ivy-clad garden wall). In the early 1900s the neighborhood was edgy, so Modì often carried a pistol – at least, that is, when he was dressed. Apparently he enjoyed dancing naked at night in this lopsided square with his demimonde models, most of them prostitutes whom he somehow managed to transform in his paintings into ethereal, Madonna-like beings.

To indulge the growing sense of yesteryear enfolding us, we decided to walk a few blocks back to the Rue Cortot and peek into the Musée de Montmartre before it shut. With old-fashioned streetlights flickering and a sheen on the cobbles, the set of weathered 1600s buildings separated by a garden exuded a crepuscular charm. This was where Renoir lived in the 1870s, followed, in the early 1900s, by the self-taught Utrillo (and his mother Susanne Valadon, a better painter than he). Modì is sure to have known the museum's mossy yard and creaking wooden floors. I imagined him now on the window sill, taking in the sweeping views, cluttered today by apartment towers. Though scrubbed and refitted to handle mass-market tourism, the museum nonetheless manages to transport visitors back in time. One room replicates the interior of Utrillo and Modì's much-loved Café de l'Abreuvoir, complete with bentwood chairs, wooden tables and period posters. Staring out from the dusty memorabilia was the treasure I'd been looking for, a 1918 Modigliani portrait of a swan-necked, almond-eyed woman he doubtless loved, if only for a moment.

Up the Rue des Saules a block or so away is Montmartre's last vineyard, a terraced reminder of the neighborhood's vinous past, and kitty corner to it spreads the small cemetery among whose toppled tombstones Modì liked to wander at night. But this street corner is best known for Au Lapin Agile, a *café-concert* open only at night. If you're an adept of kitsch, it's a fine place to experience Old Montmartre song-and-dance routines performed in roistering, smoky surroundings. The establishment started out as Le Cabaret des Assassins but became known as "Le Lapin à Gill" when in 1880 a painter named André Gill created its now-famous sign showing a rabbit in a red bowtie springing from a copper cauldron. The name eventually morphed to "the agile rabbit." It was already an old standby in Modì's day famed for its absinthe and anything-goes atmosphere. Modigliani went there once in 1909 with the Italian Futurist painter Gino Severini, who was carrying with him Filippo Tommaso Marinetti's "Futurist Manifesto" calling for the destruction of Venice – the Lagoon City had to be flattened, according to Marinetti, because it was ancient, rotten and an impediment to progress. Ever cordial, Modì shared a bottle or three with Severini but refused to sign. In his memoirs Severini described the evening, and the walls of Le Lapin Agile, which were covered with paintings, including a Picasso rose-period *Harlequin* self-portrait titled *Au Lapin Agile*. Artists, including Modigliani, routinely paid their bills here with artworks. The owner Frédéric Gérard, alias Frédé, had a donkey named Lolo and when it was cold outside he'd bring Lolo in and let him wander among the penurious painters and intellectuals, sometimes with a paintbrush attached to his tail. Nowadays the cabaret's historic sign and the street corner itself are outwardly much the same as they were in the Belle Époque but the clientele couldn't be more different.

Relieved that the cabaret was not yet open and thus preserved from temptation, we strolled back down the Rue des Saules, found the tilting Rue Ravignan and zigzagged into the pocketsize Place Goudeau. A green Wallace fountain from the 1860s splashed the cobbles under horse-chestnut trees so old that Modì surely knew them. On the square's right flank was the display case of the once-infamous Bateau Lavoir, an artist's residence. A vintage photograph showed a bare-bones turn-of-the-century studio. Inside we were pleasantly surprised to discover a hive of art students, many apparently convinced of their budding genius. Though completely rebuilt as a nondescript dormitory after a fire in 1970, thanks to that period photo it's easy enough to picture in the mind's eye what the Bateau Lavoir, a converted piano factory clinging to the hillside, must have been like in its heyday, around 1908. That's when Modì got himself a room, a noisy, messy cubbyhole separated by thin panels and hanging fabric from other cubbyholes occupied by the likes of Derain, Juan Gris and Picasso. Modì disliked Picasso, the inventor of Cubism, and hated Picasso's aggressive angular art. After several violent altercations Modigliani moved across the street to a seedy rooming house (in a building which no longer exists).

Like the crown of Montmartre, the Bateau Lavoir is tame these days, an enclave of distinctly bourgeois Bohemians. Despite widespread gentrification, it would be wrong to assume that the Butte's edgy quality has entirely disappeared. The last dive Modì rented was at the base of the hill, an address in the Rue André Antoine, which, at its Pigalle end, is as malodorous, filthy and populated with marginal fauna today as it was a hundred years ago. To get there we coasted downhill to the packed cafés of the Rue des Abbesses, where Modì and his barfly friend Utrillo would drink themselves silly. A staircase flanks the Café Saint-Jean, a distinctly local hangout with a zinc-topped bar. We tossed back a *ballon* of red then clattered down the slippery, uneven stairs. Several hundred yards along the crooked alley we found ourselves among Pigalle's creatures of the night – Brazilian transvestites, nervy drug dealers and their disconcertingly normal-looking clients. As we reached the neon-lit Boulevard de Clichy I paused for a final glance back at the Butte and couldn't help wondering if, with his capacity to empathize and his painterly talents, Modì would be able to elevate Pigalle's modern-day denizens from gutter to empyrean. It was a vain thought, perhaps, but it buoyed me nonetheless.

Bollard and lines, 2005

The Boat People of the Seine

"The rear of the riverboat coughed out black smoke... the propeller started to spin... Jules Naud had caught something with his boathook... it was a man's arm, the whole arm from the shoulder to the hand. Soaking in the water it had acquired a bloodless color and had the consistency of dead fish..."

Georges Simenon, *Maigret et le corps sans tête,* 1949

One spring night as I sipped a glass of white wine with friends on their houseboat near the Eiffel Tower I watched an old riverboat labor upstream loaded with sand. "What a life," I said to no one in particular. My hosts, successful middle-aged professionals, shrugged their shoulders.

"I wouldn't know," said one of them as he fed the barbecue. "They live in a world apart..."

It struck me as strange to share a river in the center of Paris yet know nothing about the people who depend upon your watery home for their livelihood. But it wasn't until several years after this incident that I attempted to find out how the other half – the *bateliers* or freight-boat people of the Seine – live and work.

Upstream a few hundred yards from the Pont d'Austerlitz in the 13th arrondissement laundry fluttered from the riverboats moored to the sun-baked banks. I walked by them slowly, trying to catch someone's eye. Ruddy-cheeked children romped on the iron decks, scrambling among the potted geraniums, bicycles and coiled rope. What I gathered were the children's parents patiently swabbed or scraped the family *péniche*, a vintage vessel locked in a losing battle against rust. But, as I learned, battle the boat people must: their source of livelihood is also their home, a universe measuring about 120 feet long by fifteen feet wide. These craft, most of them Freycinet-type *péniches* from the 1920s and '30s, weren't at all like the luxury houseboats I'd visited near the Eiffel Tower or Notre-Dame, and the people on them proved to be shy, distrustful even. As it turned out, they had reason to be.

Like many children, I once dreamed of lazy days on a riverboat.

When I first moved to Paris I would often pause to watch the brightly painted, snub-nosed *péniches* gliding past the Pont des Arts, the tip of the Île-Saint-Louis or the Île de la Grande Jatte. To outsiders like me the lifestyle of Paris' *bateliers* looks footloose and fancy-free, a never-ending vacation spent sailing through Impressionist landscapes. When finally I got on board and talked to working boat owners, I discovered the truth: the river wears you down and exposes you daily to the danger of drowning and collision, or being injured by machinery and loads. Earnings are minimal, hardships abundant. Since the best spots on the quays of central Paris are taken these days by luxury houseboats, the mooring points that are left for industrial craft are often in noisy, seedy areas populated by fauna lifted from the pages of Simenon. If ever it was one, the vacation is now over for the nomad riverboat people of the Seine, transporters of sand, gravel, flour, potatoes, fuel oil and other unglamorous commodities. As Jean and Elianne, the sixty-something couple I got to know best, told me, they and their antiquated craft are struggling against the flow of history.

In the age of the TGV and container truck, riverboats haul bulk goods at a sea snail's pace. They are not only slow but inflexible, bound by the rivers and canals they ply. Largely because of this, the *bateliers* themselves are an anachronism, a vaguely suspect people – waterborne gypsies in a sedentary world. Traditionally they work in husband-and-wife or tightly knit family teams, rarely receive higher education, and often marry among themselves. Their living quarters, like those of Jean and Elianne, may appear cozy when viewed from the quayside but are in reality cramped and primitively equipped, with whole families crowded into cabins the size of a landlubber's modest living room. In summer the *bateliers* roast; in winter they freeze. Year round they're exposed to the elements, so that by adulthood they often look like ancient mariners.

At the age of six, riverboat children are placed in state-run boarding schools, where they don't mix easily with terrestrial tykes. Once they've done their mandatory schooling, they move home to the boat, some of them eventually taking over from their parents. A flotilla of specialized doctors, lawyers, and priests, strategically established in riverside centers in and around Paris, caters to the needs of these nomads, further isolating them, perhaps without intention, from the general populace. Endlessly cruising the nearly 5,000 miles of navigable waterways that vein France, and sometimes sailing on to Belgium,

Holland, Switzerland or Germany, their floating villages band together and break apart.

Until January 1, 2000 several times a week Paris' boat people crowded into the *bourse d'affrétement,* the local freight exchange on the Quai d'Austerlitz, with the hope of being assigned a cargo. By law, all river- and canal-traffic in the country had to be channeled through government-run freight exchanges. They set tariffs and regulated many of the boat people's day-to-day activities. An administrative relic of the 1930s, the exchange operated on a first-in, first-out basis. As soon as they'd unloaded their corn or coal or gravel, the boat people had to sign the roll and wait to be called. And wait they did. On a typical day back in the 1990s, a hundred empty boats bobbed side-by-side on the rough-'n-ready Quai d'Austerlitz with only a handful of shipments slated to go. Most foreign boats that unloaded in Paris sailed home empty. Together with a variety of evolving technological and social factors, this roll-call system almost killed off France's boat people. Their numbers fell from over 5,000 in the 1970s to under 3,000 today; only a few hundred currently live and work in and around Paris.

But the *bateliers* are unlikely to disappear and may even make a comeback.

Both of them bespectacled, bent and bronzed, Jean and Elianne invited me one day onto their 350-ton Freycinet riverboat named Gondole, a rare honor. Descended from Alsatian boat families whose roots run as deep as the rivers they were born on, the couple lived their halcyon days on the Seine, Moselle and Rhine in the 1960s, when French river and canal shipping peaked at over 100 million tons per year. By the mid-1990s that figure had shrunk dramatically and the distances covered by riverboats had regressed to pre-1930s levels. The reasons for the decline are many. Mining has all but disappeared in France, explained Jean. Coal has been phased out as a fuel. Heavy industry and manufacturing have given way to high technology, and new factories have sprung up near highways, not canals or rivers. Smaller shipments, delivered directly by truck or train, are easier to handle and more economical to stock than bulk loads. To make matters worse, the aging riverside silos and warehouses of yesteryear have rusted and crumbled, and many smaller canals are now encumbered by debris. The cost of restoring waterway infrastructure is high, on the order of several hundreds of millions of dollars.

Though in excellent condition, Gondole was slated for demolition, part of the government's restructuring program for the industry, itself scrapped a few years ago in favor of a kinder, gentler approach. As we sat in the boat's main room, shaded by lace curtains through which I glimpsed eastern Paris' glassy new skyscrapers, Jean told me about the now-defunct plan that almost sent the *bateliers* to the bottom. Early retirement was offered to boat owners willing to decommission and destroy their craft. No new Freycinet-type boats could be built, only larger-capacity industrial boats and modern riverboats able theoretically to compete with trains and trucks. All retirees' craft, no matter how worthy, had to be junked. Thousands were in the 1980s and '90s in what many *bateliers* termed a government-sponsored genocide.

Scrapping their boats proved a heart-rending experience for *bateliers* such as Jean and Elianne. And as several other prospective retirees told me, the government's golden handshake was less than 24-karat. The standard compensation was approximately $80 for every ton of a boat's cargo capacity, worth, all told, about $35,000 for a typical Freycinet. "A lot of boat owners are bitter," said Jean softly. "But we have no regrets. We had a good life, and we were free to go wherever we wanted, whenever we wanted, though it's all over now."

A red-faced boatman probably in his late thirties joined us and voiced his disagreement. "It may be over for you, but I've just bought another boat, and when my son is old enough he's going to take it over."

A clutch of sullen mariners gathered around and began to debate the relative merits of the government's restructuring programs. As one realist put it, only massive intervention by the Ministry of Transportation to revamp infrastructure, and a concerted campaign to convince industry to reintegrate boats and barges into new distribution networks, could reverse the tide.

That is precisely what is currently going on, under the direction of a new agency, the VNF (Voies Navigables de France). Its revised "multiuse" waterway management philosophy, explained a spokesman I met in his no-nonsense office on the Quai d'Austerlitz, is to continue to exploit the country's main canals and rivers for commercial traffic, while slowly repairing a select few secondary waterways. Many have already been converted for pleasure craft or to power small hydroelectric generating plants, however, and it would be uneconomical to convert them back for freight. Younger boatmen are still being encouraged to transform their families' antiquated craft into tour boats, floating restaurants or container carriers, or to increase their cargo capacity to a potentially competitive 1,000 tons or more – an expensive and risky move.

Bad news is always good for someone. As the roads and freeways of France, especially those in Paris, come to a standstill with traffic, and air pollution reaches record peaks, the demand for river-based freight transportation is increasing. The upswing also comes thanks to construction work on longterm projects such as the Austerlitz Rive-Gauche redevelopment, Quai Branly museum complex, and A86 highway encircling Paris. Whether this is a bubble or a tidal shift remains to be seen, but medium-term prospects appear good.

The VNF publishes impressive statistics proving why waterway transport is both economical and environmentally friendly. According to official reports one 12,000-ton push-tug convoy, for example, represents the equivalent of 342 35-ton trucks, which if strung bumper-to-bumper would clog and choke about fourteen miles of Paris roadway. Boats consume less fuel, pollute less, and have fewer accidents on average than other forms of transport. And it still costs less per ton per mile to ship cement, landfill or wheat in an industrial push-tug or 1,000-ton riverboat than in a freight train or truck.

That's great, say the boat people I've talked to, but it doesn't ensure smooth sailing ahead. Industrial push-tugs are beyond the reach of most individual owners and represent the antithesis of the traditional boat person's way of life, with its emphasis on freedom of movement. Because of their length and tonnage, push-tugs are able to ply only the deep-water channels of the Seine, Saône, Rhine and Rhone, a phenomenon known in the trade as being "a prisoner of a river basin." Their routes are fixed. Working hours are regulated. Crews rarely own their craft and almost never live aboard – there is no purpose-built family cabin on such ships. So there are no husband-and-wife or family teams on them, either. Much the same applies to the huge 1,000-ton riverboats, which do not fit in standard locks and are unable to use the 4,000 miles or so of small waterways open only to the old Freycinet-type *péniche*. Ironically, because of their relative versatility, converted Freycinets may prove to be the way forward.

Having talked to scores of boatmen over a period of weeks, I could not refuse their invitation to take part in the big annual Pardon de la Batellerie, the blessing of the fleet, held each June in a town called Conflans-Sainte-Honorine. Twenty miles downstream from Paris and still in its suburbs, with regular commuter trains, Conflans nonetheless felt a thousand leagues from the Quai d'Austerlitz. Fish were jumping at the wide, murky confluence of the Seine and the Oise rivers where the town is sited. Boys and old men baited their hooks in silence and watched the boats slip by. Lashed to the wharves were row upon row of Freycinets, block-long riverboats, tugs and push-tugs – just about every kind of inland watercraft I could imagine. Some were half submerged with their heavy loads of gravel or grain. Others, bearded with moss, had been transformed into the houseboats of retirees.

Conflans, population 30,000, is not only the Mecca of the boat people of the Seine. It's also an important shipping center for Belgians, Dutchmen and Germans. Popular cafés boast names like *Le Batelier.* There are floating time-tunnel dance halls festooned with flowers where boat people play accordions and sing folksy songs from decades past. On a hill overlooking the Seine is the Chateau du Prieuré. It houses the Musée de la Batellerie, the repository of boat people's history. And rising near the now-defunct freight exchange is a huge winged Statue of Liberty holding high a wreath to commemorate the boat people who fell in the two World Wars. Mariners salute her as they pass.

But the town's center of gravity, it turned out, is an old white riverboat named *Je Sers* – I serve. Its captain is the spiritual guide of the boat people's community, an ageing priest named Père Arthur. Most French boatmen are practicing Catholics, and the big moments of their lives from cradle to grave are played out in Père Arthur's company. The blessing of the fleet is the summer season's signal event in both Conflans and nearby Longueil, a placid backwater upstream on the Oise River. I joined Père Arthur on a garlanded old Freycinet with a makeshift alter and glided into Longueil where hundreds of boat families, their craft streaming with banners, processed to the riverbank to receive their blessing. It was a moving sight, even for a freethinker. But the festive air was tinged with solemnity. Some of the boats present were receiving their last rites. They would soon become floating clubhouses or cafés, noted the priest as we motored back to Conflans. This was preferable to the fate suffered by others in the bad old days of the 1990s: they were sent to what locals call the "boat cemetery", in reality a scrap yard in a dead branch of the Seine directly opposite Conflans. Though now closed the scrap yard is a constant reminder to *bateliers* of the precariousness of their situation.

As I stared across the river at the cemetery a young boatman stood next to me and defiantly swore he would survive against the odds. "I'll get a bigger boat if I have to," he said. "I'll work on someone else's boat if I have to. But I'll never leave the river." They were hard words spoken with passionate determination. I would remember them the next time I sat sipping white wine with our friends on their houseboat near the Eiffel Tower.

Coiffure pour âmes (Hairdresser for souls), 1994

Meeting Moreau

"He paints dreams... sophisticated, complicated, enigmatic dreams."
Émile Zola

I once met a dead man in Paris named Gustave Moreau. It happened one rainy morning in the 1980s when I had nothing particular to do. I was drawn to the Passage Verdeau, a 19th-century, glass-and-ironwork covered gallery just north of the Boulevard Montmartre in the dowdy 9th arrondissement. A thin coat of dust hung on old storefronts such as Pascal Entremont – Chasseur de Pierres, a rock collector's shop, and Photo Verdeau, with its array of early cameras in worn leather cases. The doors of some of the Passage Verdeau's establishments seemed to have rusted shut. Yet there were the clerks and salesmen bent behind their desks, waiting patiently for the rare customer.

At a bookseller and curio shop appropriately called La France Ancienne I was delighted to discover a box of old postcards marked *sculpture, peinture, beaux-arts.* Looking out at me from among the fountains of Rome and the statuary of Versailles was the portrait of a man with a bushy white beard and the eyes of a seer or a maniac. The card was postmarked 1908. In faded black ink the sender had scrawled "A bizarre and disappointing place."

The postcard had come from the Musée Gustave Moreau. It represented a self-portrait of the artist. The name rang a bell. Where had I seen the work of Gustave Moreau? Wasn't he the crazy symbolist, the enigmatic recluse who'd lived during the heyday of Impressionism?

Intrigued, I bought the postcard. The museum, if it still existed, was only a few blocks north of the Passage Verdeau, beyond the Folies Bergère and the cheap clothes shops and eateries of the unfashionable Rue du Faubourg-Montmartre. Around here and in the nearby Rue Notre-Dame-de-Lorette, I recalled, were the brasseries and cafés Émile Zola described in his bleakly evocative novels of 19th-century Paris life. This was "the last bright and animated corner of nocturnal Paris" where Zola's notorious lady of the night, Nana, and swarms of others in the trade did their business "as though along the open corridor of a brothel."

Could this be where Gustave Moreau had lived, I wondered?

Though most of the prostitutes had moved out, the neighborhood was not that different in feel – rundown, tired, soulful, seedy, a rare slice of un-gentrified inner city. I walked north past the church of Notre-Dame-de-Lorette, remarkable only for its gracelessness, then got turned around in the Place Saint-Georges. It was more a traffic circle than a proper square but it had character. No one I asked had heard of the Musée Gustave Moreau – try the Marais, suggested one helpful resident. "The Marais is where all the museums are…"

I was about to give up when I came across the Rue de la Rochefoucauld. That was the address on the postcard. Wedged between the faded, staid apartment buildings of vaguely Second Empire style was number fourteen, an ungainly neo-Renaissance brick palazzo. On it was a plaque and an old-fashioned brass doorbell. Museum visitors were to ring and enter.

"A bizarre and disappointing place" – the words came back to me as I climbed the stairs to the ticket desk. I surprised the woman dozing there. No one else was around. At the foot of the worn and poorly lit staircase I spotted a handwritten biographical sketch of the artist. Gustave Moreau was born April 6, 1826 in Paris, the son of a successful architect. He dearly loved his mother, with whom he lived for decades, until her death. He never married. A student at the École Royale des Beaux-Arts, he traveled extensively in Italy and later showed his work in various salons. Finally, in 1883, at the height of his unusual career, he was named Officer of the Legion of Honor.

Moreau died in this house in 1898, where he had lived and worked for nearly fifty years. He willed the house-atelier's entire contents to the state with the proviso that it be maintained as is. The museum was created a few years later and, when I first visited, had remained virtually unchanged. In it are some 1,200 paintings, watercolors and cartoons, and 5,000 drawings. Moreau threw nothing away. For the record, only Turner and Picasso have left a greater body of work to posterity.

On the first-floor landing of the house hangs a large drawing of a Persian poet riding a unicorn. Beside it is a sketch of an effeminate Oedipus apparently being seduced or raped by a lascivious Sphinx.

But nothing could prepare me for what I found on the second floor. In a huge hall, scores of oil paintings hang floor-to-ceiling on three sides. The fourth wall of large windows illuminates the room in any weather. Here was the Virgin Mary, depicted as a jewel-encrusted pistil protruding from a giant lily. The artist called the work *The Mystical Flower*. In *The Chimerae*, a hundred or more female creatures make love to dragonflies, snakes and turtles. Behind them rises a fairytale medieval city at the foot of a rocky precipice surmounted by a tiny cross. This overtly misogynistic work the painter described cryptically as "a satanic *Decameron*" (presumably referring to Giovanni Boccaccio's 14th-century tales, many of them prurient) and "an island of fantastic dreams enclosing every form of passion, fantasy and caprice of Woman" (the capitalized "W" is the artist's).

I scanned my memory for an explanation. Did it lie, perhaps, in the fact that during Moreau's adult life, which coincided with what we now call the Belle Époque, relations between men and women stood at a critical juncture? The first assault on patriarchal society had been mounted – a kind of proto-Women's Liberation was underway. A favorite theme of many male artists of the time, especially symbolists such as Moreau, was the tale of Salomé – the devilish temptress – usually shown dancing or lustily holding Saint John the Baptist's head on a platter.

I glanced around. There she was, among the unicorns and swans, lilies and acanthus leaves. Winged horses pranced and swayed with the reinterpreted mythological or biblical figures in *The Return of the Argonauts, The Daughters of Thespius,* and many other larger-than-life-size canvases, some of them only half finished, all of them stylistically very different. What could this hodgepodge of symbols ultimately mean, I wondered? Was Moreau insane or had he, like many artists of his day, been an opium addict?

I sat in the center of the room feeling dizzy. A lone museum guard paced back and forth in front of the wall of windows where a gray, glary light poured in from the equally gray, unappealing neighborhood beyond. I wondered where the crowds of the Louvre or Picasso museum were. A bizarre place this was, as my old postcard suggested, but not disappointing.

Unable to make sense of the paintings, I decided to go back down to the entrance area and see if there was a catalogue for sale. When I stood the guard approached me. "Aren't you going to look at the third floor?" she asked. How could there possibly be more of this, I asked without thinking. "But you've only started, monsieur," she retorted, pointing to an unusual spiral staircase – a double helix, in fact. "The best is on the third floor!"

I assured her politely that I would return then dashed down the stairs.

On the way out of the building I bought a catalogue and began to read it as I walked. The bells of Notre-Dame-de-Lorette and La Trinité, another nearby temple of architectural gracelessness, were tolling noon. The streets, though as outwardly drab as before, started to take on a new meaning for me. Here, said the catalogue, in the Rue de la Rochefoucauld, Nana had kept a room. Zola himself had lived a few blocks away in the Rue Ballu. This was where Charles Dickens had had his disappointing encounter with Frédéric Chopin's celebrated lover George Sand, "the kind of woman in appearance whom you might suppose to be the Queen's monthly nurse." Turgenev and Thackery and a dozen other writers and painters had lived in the area, within a few hundred yards of Moreau's house. The ateliers and galleries had apparently been as thick here then as they are now on the Left Bank or in the Marais. The streets had been alive. During Moreau's day the neighborhood was known as The New Athens, and even spawned its own architectural style, heavy with Hellenistic, classical references. Moreau in his youth frequented the salons, restaurants and cafés with his great friend and fellow painter Théodore Chassériau, who was also among the 19th century's most successful artists, at least from the commercial standpoint.

But as I walked by, on the Place Saint-Georges there was only one modest café. Cars swerved around the statue of a now-obscure lithographer named Gavarni, also famous in his day. Locals sifted through bric-a-brac at a tumbledown shop that advertised *antiquités et curiosités* – yard-sale castoffs and oddments rescued from attics and cellars. The neighborhood was quiet, with a few small public gardens flanked by tidy, uninteresting streets. The red-light district of Zola's day apparently had split in two, shifting north to Pigalle and south to Les Halles.

I decided to backtrack to the Rue du Faubourg-Montmartre and have lunch at Chartier, a workingman's restaurant that has been in business since Moreau's final days. Perhaps the painter had been a habitué I fantasized. Given the elaborately decorative, eclectic nature of his work, Moreau surely would have liked the décor. Brass racks run over wooden booths. Customers eye each other in mirrored panels. Waiters arrive, carrying in a single load eight plates and three bottles of *vin de pays* (the menu warns that the management declines responsibility for stains caused by reckless waiters).

It was here at Chartier, over pepper steak and a carafe of very ordinary red wine, that I read the catalogue cover to cover and began to learn the details of Moreau's life and career. For some mysterious reason – possibly the death of his intimate friend Chassériau – Moreau stopped attending the salons of the Countess Greffulhe (later immortalized by Proust) and the Princess Mathilde, Emperor Napoléon III's cousin. Over the years Moreau became, as the novelist and critic J.K. Huysmans wrote, "the mystic shut away in the center of Paris." He was thought to be homosexual or bisexual but there is nothing to corroborate such speculation. Highly secretive, only a handful of his friends knew of his 25-year liaison with a certain Adélaide-Alexandrine Dureux, a "spiritual companion" whom he maintained in an apartment in the Rue Notre-Dame-de-Lorette.

Moreau was uncommunicative. Often he refused to explain the meaning of his hermetic artworks. To one collector who bought a picture and requested a written key to decipher it, Moreau replied that he had simply to "love to dream." Zola, reviewing Moreau's pictures at a salon in the 1880s wrote, "He paints dreams… sophisticated, complicated, enigmatic dreams."

Zola also said that Moreau had had no master and would have no disciples. But Zola was wrong. Rouault, Matisse, Marquet and many others were his pupils at the École Nationale des Beaux-Arts. Odilon Redon, better known nowadays than Moreau himself, was heavily influenced by the mystic's work, as were Picasso, Dalì and Matta.

With a well-to-do family behind him, a secure job and regular patrons, Moreau was the antithesis of the starving artist. Only once did he deign to show his work in a commercial gallery. The real motive for his reticence was a morbid fear of criticism. In the last years of his life he worked frantically to give titles to his pictures and to write notes about them so that future critics – and museumgoers like me – would not misinterpret them.

Eventually, several years after my first visit, I returned to the Moreau museum. I was not alone this time. The doorbell had been disconnected and the dust removed. Somehow the mystery was gone, and with it a good deal of the magic. As the guard had said, the best pictures were on the third floor – gemlike canvases sparkling with cobalt and gold that Moreau had labored over for months or years.

The hundreds of watercolors and drawings mounted on ingenious wooden stands revealed another Moreau. Here were gentle landscapes and fine sketches with all the mystical power of the oils, but none of the tortured anguish. Here too was the self-portrait I had first seen on that old postcard, which I had lost in the meantime. Moreau had been commissioned to draw it by the Uffizi Gallery in Florence. It was to have hung in the Vasari Corridor, among the self-portraits of history's greatest painters. But Moreau, believing himself unworthy, had never delivered it. He wished to disappear as a man, and live on in his works, at his museum.

At the Montmartre Cemetery later that day I asked a caretaker where I could find Moreau's tomb. No one had ever asked for it before, said the caretaker, and he had never heard of the man. I gave the full name and the year Moreau died. The caretaker dug out an enormous leather-bound ledger marked *sépultures des célèbres* and looked for an entry. He was as surprised as I to hit upon it. The tomb, registered in a meticulous Belle Époque hand, was in section twenty-two, row seven, at gravestone number two. But I was never quite sure that I'd found it. The headstone of that tomb had fallen over, the name worn off.

Concierge à Droite (Concierge to the right), 1989

The Perils of Pompidou

"We learn from example that cities, too, can die."
Rutilius Namatiamus, Roman Emperor, *De reditu, I,* AD 413

Few cities can claim a tradition of urban vandalism nobler than Paris'. Perhaps it's genetic: archeologists insist the Gauls burned their Seine-side settlements before going to battle, thus depriving rivals of the pleasure. Caesar and his descendants endlessly reconfigured their fledgling city, as did generation upon generation of kings, French Revolutionaries and emperors, who continued vandalizing Paris right into the modern age. When a ruler wanted something new he merrily tore down everything in his way.

But Parisians have not been immune to progressive sentiments. For the last 200 years or so those in command have usually prefaced their assaults by citing public safety, sanitation or, that magic word, "modernity." Many Paris connoisseurs think Emperor Napoléon III and his prefect Baron Haussmann were the archetypal modernizers: they flattened thousands of buildings for a variety of reasons, from bona fide health concerns to crowd control and rampant greed. Decried as a rape by sensitive souls such as poet Charles Baudelaire or Victor Hugo, "Haussmannization" was nonetheless carried out by visionary planners and skilled architects. Whatever they built was built to last.

What is less well publicized is that the vandal heritage, slowed occasionally by recession or war, has been the driving force behind each of the various French republics that followed the Second Empire. It peaked under the current "Fifth Republic", which began in 1958. Predictably the orgy of state-sponsored speculation the new republic ushered in was dressed up as Haussmann-style modernization. This time it was not an emperor and a baron directing the show but an aging general and a little gray technocrat named Georges Pompidou.

Pompidou rose to power as De Gaulle's right-hand man, moving in smooth succession from a 1958 advisory position to that of prime minister, before becoming president in 1969. A statesman, De Gaulle didn't like cluttering his mind with minor concerns such as the economy, environment or urbanism. So he delegated. "Ask Pompidou," he would say with a vague gesture.

Pompidou's reign ended with his sudden death in 1974, meaning that he presided over France and the capital's fortunes for sixteen years (Paris had no mayoral authority from 1871 to 1977). This was the height of *les trente glorieuses* – thirty glorious years of bull market.

When I hear someone say "Pompidou" I lift my eyes to Paris' skyline and see the name writ large. Pompidou lives on in the opaque, sixty-story silhouette of the Tour Montparnasse and the nervy university complex of Jussieu that's about half as tall. Look west and there's Pompidou again, mastermind of the mock-Manhattan towers of La Défense. Of course, there are the multi-colored pipes and Plexiglas tubes of the Pompidou Center at Beaubourg, a prime example of what was formerly (and without irony) called Brutalism, from the French word "brut", as in raw or unfinished. That meant deconstructed structures with their guts exposed. Lower your eyes and you'll see many minor examples of the Pompidou era, from unremarkable administrative carbuncles and low-income housing to the mirrored squalor of Le Forum des Halles.

But there's more to Pompidou's Paris than most people realize. The Pompidou Expressway snakes along the Seine where leafy river ports once stood. The Boulevard Péripherique, originally the no-man's land outside the 1848 city walls, was slated to become a greenbelt until Pompidou had it transformed into an eight-lane cement moat that separates Paris from its surroundings. Facing La Défense alongside the Péripherique is the Porte Maillot hotel, shopping and convention center so dear to Pompidou. Though only a few decades old, it was judged ugly enough to deserve a multi-million dollar facelift not long ago, and it's still an eyesore.

The list of Pompidou-inspired marvels goes on. It includes much of the damage done to the Marais and other historic districts (where streets were systematically widened by destroying rows of townhouses). And don't forget the Place d'Italie apartment blocks on Paris' south side, seemingly lifted from outer Moscow, or the Front de Seine high-rise pseudo-Cubist clusters and garish shopping center at Beaugrenelle in the 15th arrondissement, not to mention the "nouvelle" but already crumbling Belleville, and much of what is now the blighted, high-crime suburban ring around Paris.

Actually, the city got off lightly. Many of Pompidou's most outlandish schemes were abandoned because of public outcry, or because the great modernizer died while still in office, and his successor, Valéry Giscard d'Estaing, refused to carry them out. Here are a handful of examples: a spaghetti bowl of expressways with skyscrapers in their midst, from Les Halles to the Seine; a freeway atop the Canal Saint-Martin; a Left-Bank expressway from Tolbiac to the Pont Mirabeau; a bridge across the tip of the Île-de-la-Cité that would've obliterated the Square du Vert Gallant; the demolition of the entire Marais except for two churches and one townhouse; and, in 1966, Pompidou planned to build "Paris II", a residential city conceived so that what was left of the real Paris could be gutted and refitted.

"It is up to the city to make way for the automobile," Pompidou pronounced midway through his reign, "and not the other way around." He spoke of "surgical themes" and "necessary transformations", promising Parisians a modern metropolis to rival New York and London, made to the measure not of man, but the machine.

To this day some people actually admire Pompidou's heritage. So let's be fair: he bequeathed the city the RER commuter-train system and lovely La Défense. He created the Nouvelles Villes satellite cities and a network of freeways any sprawling megalopolis would be proud of. He was a man of his mixed up, paradoxical times, the days of atonal "classical" music, hard rock and "free jazz", free love, Pop Art, Agent Orange, LSD and the domino theory. Pompidou may have resided on the historic Île-Saint-Louis in a luxury townhouse but he earnestly wanted a freeway in front of his picture windows – and almost got one. The automobile was his God.

Small and swarthy, with a perennial, wolfish grin wrapped around a smouldering cigarette, Georges Pompidou was in fact a provincial from the Massif Central. A lifelong overachiever, he graduated summa cum laude in Greek then fought alongside De Gaulle. After the war he proved his quiet brilliance by rising to CEO of the Banque Rothschild. Hard to pigeonhole or place on the political spectrum, he was backed by some of the great French intellectuals. Literary icon André Malraux, the country's first Minister of Culture, worked cheek-by-jowl with the little gray man whose real personality screamed in primary colors. Incredibly, Malraux's celebrated urban conservation laws helped save the Marais, but he nonetheless signed the permits for many of Pompidou's catastrophes, including the Tour Montparnasse.

"Pompidou said little and wrote nothing while Malraux talked too much and wrote too much," noted historian and Pompidou-confidant

Louis Chevalier in his still-controversial exposé *L'Assassinat de Paris,* first published in 1977. A chronicle of how the De Gaulle-Malraux-Pompidou troika massacred the city, the book points out that Pompidou was at heart a banker. The banks owned real estate and were cozy with building contractors. The rest of the riddle is easy.

Another intellectual bigwig of the postwar period who came to despise Pompidou was author Georges Pillement. In *Paris Poubelle (Garbage-Can Paris)* Pillement asserts that Pompidou was aware of – and possibly the source of – the systematic vandalism occurring in central Paris. The aim of that vandalism, theoretically, was to get neighborhoods declared unsafe so they could be bulldozed. In this scenario, Pompidou's long-term plan was to transform Paris into *the* European business center, studded with Le Corbusier-style high-rises and veined by highways. He "seduced" Malraux with visions not of banal skyscrapers for businessmen but of neo-medieval towers.

If De Gaulle was king and Pompidou his white knight then Malraux was the court decorator and savant, writes Chevalier in *l'Assassinat de Paris.* In any case, Pompidou was firmly in control, pressing the right buttons: with De Gaulle he spoke of France's renascent glory and with Malraux, who could've thwarted him, he wrapped his visions in the fluff of whimsy. Thirty years on the results – now cracking, rusting and peeling – are plain to see.

A bad Chicago skyscraper set in what used to be an artists' quarter of two-story workshops, the Tour Montparnasse is so brutally banal and clearly out of place that I've become almost protective of it. That familiar brownish hulk is an ever-visible reminder of what not to do in a historic European city. Several years ago rumors began spreading about the tower's possible demolition. It is universally loathed and, worse from the city's standpoint, has not been profitable. With this peril in mind I spent an hour recently wandering through the could-be-anywhere shopping center at the tower's base, pondering what might replace it. Then I rode an elevator to the top floor.

Inaugurated in 1973, the tower feels like it's about to deconstruct itself. No one appears to have celebrated its 30th birthday. Several windows were missing, replaced by plywood panels. The fingerprints of the project's Chicago-based developers were everywhere: this was a piece of '60s-'70s Americana owned by the French, a typical De Gaulle-Pompidou act of defiance vis-à-vis the postwar period's new global,

English-speaking power.

Soon after the Eiffel Tower was built, novelist Guy de Maupassant began lunching in the panoramic restaurant there because, as he put it, it was the only place in town from which you could not see the Eiffel Tower. The same could be said for panoramic Montparnasse: the view is splendid and there's no Montparnasse tower to be seen. Unhappily, amid the centuries-old mix of inner Paris spread below, you're treated to a pigeon's-eye view of Pompidou's other creations. There is simply no escaping them. The 1965 Jussieu university complex, for example, almost obscures the handsome tree-lined alleys of the Jardin des Plantes behind it. And unless you're as shortsighted as Pompidou himself, you can't help staring at the paint-box innards of the Pompidou Center, whose construction entailed the demolition of the historic Beaubourg neighborhood.

As I crossed town along "Haussmannized" yet appealing boulevards toward the Pompidou Center I recalled the time I interviewed Renzo Piano, the center's co-architect. "It was a joke," Piano had snorted, stroking his bushy beard. "A parody of technology... a great, insolent, irreverent provocation."

Were Piano and fellow architect Richard Rogers really thumbing their noses at Pompidou and his technocrats? Maybe. Piano, I reflected, is an affable guy, and has had years to develop a convincing patter. His idea, he now says, was to create a place where the arts and other disciplines would mix and match – a culture factory. When people said that his building looked like a refinery Piano was delighted. As to the destruction of historic Beaubourg, Piano pointed out that Pompidou's men had already wiped the slate.

Love it or hate it, the giant culture-refinery of Beaubourg has been a surprise success. Six to seven million people visit it annually, loving it to death. French taxpayers like me spent tens of millions of dollars to restore it a few years ago, even though the building was barely into its twenties. Gaining admission to the Pompidou these days is a feat: typically the lines snake for a quarter mile through the sloping "piazza" out front, among the caricature artists, fire-eaters and mimes. The high culture starts inside.

This time around I skipped the world-class museum displays and the vast library to look again at the building itself. Light streamed in through the thirty-foot windows. People floated by on escalators in Plexiglas tubes. Transparent elevators bobbed up and down. The color-coded pipes and ducts, another mock-industrial provocation, shone bright. For a moment I thought I'd stepped back into the caustic, gutsy, colorful '70s.

Luckily I hadn't. I poked around the trendy, panoramic restaurant called Georges (a reference, perhaps, to Monsieur Pompidou?) but could not afford to sit down. From the viewing terrace, lower than that of Montparnasse, I could see the roofs of old Paris. Georges had disdained them and tried, with a large measure of success, to bring them down. Sadly, he never lived to see his namesake center completed (it opened in 1977). As I exited through the lobby I looked up at the round, deconstructed black-and-white Op Art portrait of Pompidou hanging there for all to see. His wolfish grin shifted as I passed.

In retrospect Pompidou's most impressive achievement was not the building of the Tour Montparnasse or the Pompidou Center at Beaubourg; it was the eviction of the messy old general markets from Les Halles. Planners had been trying to get rid of them for decades. Mysteriously, once the market was gone, the area became a slum in short order. Soon thereafter the 19th-century glass-and-ironwork Baltard pavilions that had housed the market were flattened. Another decade went by before a five-story subterranean RER train and metro station – the world's biggest underground station – and a shopping center with a sunken "forum" filled the "hole of Les Halles."

I thought of Émile Zola as I rode a steeply raked escalator into the Forum's pit. In his 1873 Rougon-Macquart series of novels Zola dubbed the old market *le ventre de Paris* – the guts or stomach of Paris. Apparently the site has permanent indigestion: it emanates an acrid stench. Some say it's the disgruntled spirits of place. Others believe it's the smell of oozing sewage, scented by disinfectants and bubbling fast-food fryers. Experts claim it's the scent of decomposing limestone. In any case, at least the suburban adolescents, hucksters and drug dealers surrounding me among the stained and broken cladding seemed to be enjoying the Forum.

I headed as fast as I could out of the area, the words of the Roman emperor Rutilius Namatiamus, written in 413 AD as Rome collapsed, ringing in my ears: "Cities, too, can die."

In the '70s, critics of Pompidou pronounced Paris dead. But as I sipped a beer in a building that would have been destroyed had Pompidou's plans been carried out, another thought came to mind. Like the proverbial phoenix rising from the ashes, cities can also be reborn.

Despite Les Halles, Montparnasse and many a blighted suburb, it seemed to me that Paris was alive and ready to box its way through the 21st century. Now, if only the authorities would follow Pompidou's precepts and dynamite his towers and shopping malls, then close the Seine-side expressways and transform the Péripherique into that mythical greenbelt, we'd really be talking modernity.

11th arrondissement workshop, 1989

Past Masters: Keepers of the Craft

"Gold is for the mistress – silver for the maid – Copper for the craftsman cunning at his trade. 'Good!' said the Baron, sitting in his hall, 'But Iron – Cold Iron – is master of them all.'"

Rudyard Kipling, *Cold Iron*

I walked one day not too long ago down the picturesquely named Rue du Pont aux Choux – the street of the bridge of cabbages – near where I live in the Marais. As if in a dream I stepped through a set of steamed-up doors and witnessed a scene from Dante's *Inferno*: a blazing-hot furnace showered sparks into a dark workshop where leather-gloved men molded sheets of what I came to recognize as molten glass. Around the corner from the glassworks, in a 17th-century townhouse near the Place des Vosges, I paused to watch a craftsman tap-tap-tapping with an old hammer, finishing a tooled-leather box. About half a mile east, still in the Marais, a solitary woman quietly carved antique wooden panels in an Alice-in-Wonderland workshop with sawdust reposing on wounded collectibles, yellowing plaster busts and cupids suspended on rusty wires.

To me, the word "artisan" evokes just such sepia-tinted images of yesteryear, of atmospheric ateliers where master craftsmen and eager apprentices toil into the night to create or restore goods at once useful and beautiful to behold. This is not the throwaway junk we're used to, but the solid, desirable stuff of our forebears. Happily in Paris by some small miracle the craft tradition has survived not only the fall of the *Ancien Régime* and the advent of industrialization, but also the myriad manifestations of contemporary mass consumerism.

The French language is ambiguous when it comes to defining the term "artisan." It can stand for anyone from a plumber to a baker or a taxi driver. Often it simply means "independent contractor." But when I use it I'm thinking of crafts people who fashion one-of-a-kind items, shunning large-scale production methods, and catering to clients directly in their workshops.

Over the last two decades I have been lucky enough to meet several dozen skilled artisans in Paris: glassworkers, silver and coppersmiths, bronze founders, ceramists, enamelers, painters of miniatures, cabinet-makers, leather workers, book binders, stained glass window makers, hatters, fan-makers, engravers, gilders, ivory sculptors, violin and lute-makers, saddle-makers, jewelers, goldsmiths, printers and others still.

There are an estimated 4,000 artisans working today in central Paris, living proof of the superiority in many fields of man over machine.

One reason the craft tradition remains encouragingly resilient here is apprenticeship. It continues in many workshops, though not in the 19th-century sense of indentured servitude. Parisian youngsters wouldn't buy that. Almost anyone can learn at any age to be an adequate artisan. The key word is "adequate." For many crafts – inlay and cabinet-making, for example – the experts are unanimous in saying that budding craftsmen really must begin when very young in order to develop the muscles and reactions needed to mature into a master. So, in this laser-guided world of ours, apprenticeship is still the most vital means for training young talents and passing craft secrets down the generations.

Apprenticeship is what the Compagnons du Devoir du Tour de France is all about. This extraordinary, 400-year-old association has always fascinated me, in part because of its quirky window displays of roof beams, stones or furniture at its headquarters behind the church of Saint-Gervais, a hundred yards east of city hall. Mostly, I've been drawn to the Compagnons because they resemble a medieval crafts guild. Only adepts, and I use the word intentionally, aged 15-25, may join. They must agree to spend up to ten years traveling around France learning their chosen trade from masters – bakers, tapestry makers, carriage builders, stone masons, locksmiths, roofers, carpenters, saddle-makers, plasterers and so forth. Reportedly, there is no such thing as an unemployed Compagnon. After their tour of duty, once they have set up shop, they must agree to train other Compagnons.

There's another reason the craft tradition survives in France, and especially in Paris: the handful of world-class technical institutions scattered around the country, with four in the capital alone. The most famous is l'Ecole Boulle, named after Louis XIV's court cabinetmaker André Charles Boulle (1642-1732). The school was founded in 1886 to train cabinetmakers and workers in related trades. Today Boulle graduates might work in cabinetry or inlay, or venture into the fine arts, jewelry or industrial design. One graduate I met works for Cartier, another was a member of the TGV high-speed train design team.

Other Paris crafts schools include the 140-year-old EPSAA (graphic arts and architecture); the century-old Ecole Duperré (fashion, textile design or printing, interior decoration, tapestry, ceramics); and the equally venerable Ecole Supérieure Estienne (engraving, book binding and gilding, printing, illustration and graphic arts). Both Duperré and Estienne offer adult education courses, and if I weren't so hopelessly incapable of working with my hands I would be tempted to retrain and recycle myself through one of them, perhaps as a bookbinder, or something equally out of step with the times.

Of course luxury goods are yet another reason – perhaps the main reason – French artisans continue to thrive. They work for companies such as Hermès, Cartier or Louis Vuitton. Fashion designers, too, though a pernicious breed in my book, do their part to keep alive a variety of unlikely specialties such as *plumassiers* (feather decoration makers), leather workers, silk dyers, hat-makers and, yes, fan-makers.

There is usually a flipside to a happy story and in this case it is one of numbers: a mere twenty years ago there were almost 20,000 crafts workers in Paris' two main crafts districts alone, the Marais (comprising the 3rd and 4th arrondissement) and abutting Faubourg Saint-Antoine (the 11th arrondissement) east of the Bastille. If 4,000 remain, where have the other 16,000 gone?

To find out, I decided to talk to Gilbert Sommier of the government-funded SEMA (Société d'Encouragement aux Métiers d'Art). Sommier, it transpires, is in charge of developing local assistance programs for artisans all over France. "Where have they gone?" he repeated my question rhetorically. "To the suburbs, the provinces or out of business!" An affable, middle-aged man, Monsieur Sommier confirmed that only a handful of Paris artisans actually create new, original goods, mostly for luxury manufacturers or fashion houses. Everyone else now earns his living by making replicas of antiques or doing restoration work for individual clients or the French government.

Sommier gave me a few examples. Paris spends millions of dollars annually to restore the roofs and wooden structures of the city's churches, it seems, and further millions remodeling townhouses like the Hôtel de Saint-Aignan in the Marais. It now houses the Musée d'art et d'histoire du Judaisme (the Jewish Art and History Museum). Additionally the city commonly spends about half a million dollars annually restoring works of art, furniture, books, woodwork and so on, mainly in municipal museums and warehouses, those dusty repositories of microhistory rarely visited and most often unloved. The Museum of the History of Hospitals isn't exactly the Musée d'Orsay, but it and others like it keep dozens of crafts workers busy.

"From the historical perspective, the number of artisans plummeted early in the 20th century," Sommier explained to me, "and again after World War Two because of industrialization and standardization. Handmade or custom goods couldn't compete or simply went out of fashion." The French crafts industry seems to have bottomed out in the 1990s. Supply-and-demand is in balance now.

Despite the loss of thousands of ateliers, the Marais and Faubourg Saint-Antoine are still Paris' main craft districts, though you might not think so upon casual inspection. Both have undergone profound changes in recent decades. That's a polite way of saying they've been gentrified almost beyond recognition. Redevelopment, real estate speculation and the restoration of landmark properties in the Marais led from the 1970s onward to the destruction or conversion of scores of workshops that in the 19th or early 20th century had been dropped into palatial courtyards, or added between wings of *hôtels particuliers* (townhouses). Ever poetic, local architects and building authorities now call these drop-in structures "pustules." The add-ons go instead by the name "parasites." By shedding their pustules, parasites and – unfortunately – the artisans who worked in them, many townhouses have come full circle, reclaiming their pre-Revolutionary architectural beauty while losing their souls.

The story is somewhat different I discovered in the Faubourg Saint Antoine, still the city's woodworking and furniture district. Blanket gentrification over the last fifteen years has led to the demolition of entire city blocks, where many a workshop lurked in a dingy back courtyard. Take a walk from the Bastille north along the Rue de la Roquette then down the Rue du Basfroid and you'll get a glimpse of how much has been reconfigured.

Even in neighborhoods spared by developers, though, the usual combination of rising rents, stricter anti-pollution laws and lack of parking and warehouse space began squeezing out crafts workers in the 1980s. Most of them migrated east, to places such as Vincennes, Saint-Mandé, Saint-Maur and Montreuil. Many moved even further into the suburbs, so far out that it's unfair to count them as Parisians.

In the too-little, too-late department, government officials have tried various means to stem the flow or lure some crafts workers back. Particularly desirable are sculptors, cabinetmakers and decorators, whose activities are judged less "polluting." That means they're less noisy or dangerous than other crafts in a crowded inner-city context. About twenty years ago Paris began re-housing its beleaguered artisans in new, light-industrial buildings, most of them sited in the 11th arrondissement. A handful of other complexes were tossed up in the 13th arrondissement (the Vincent Auriol and Tolbiac quarters) and the 20th.

As you might expect these modern workshops lack the charm of yesteryear, and some nostalgic artisans I have spoken to lambaste the city for having created sterile environments while allowing speculators to destroy historical properties. Others point out, though, that these new ateliers are better lit, warmer and safer than many of the funky, vintage sites they replaced, and that, generally speaking, the artisans lucky enough to have found a place in them are satisfied.

Why not judge for yourself, I often ask friends who enquire about Paris' craftsmen. You can get an idea of what these new complexes are like by visiting the Cité Artisanale de l'Allée Verte, built in the 1980s. My wife gets her banged up old cameras fixed there. One day while she talked shutters and flash cords I wandered around and met a fifth-generation engraver named Gérard Desquand.

One moment Desquand was stooped over his cluttered workbench like Albrecht Dürer, magnifying lens and antique engraver's point in hand. The next he was designing a family crest on his computer. He smiled and shrugged in one telling gesture, unused to talking about himself. His workshop is called G4 Gravure. He set it up in 1986 with three partners. Like his father before him, Desquand won the Meilleur Ouvrier de France award, the country's highest craft recognition. He might miss the cozy old family workshop but he did not say so to me. His clients have included fashion houses like Yves Saint-Laurent and Dior; and famous Paris stationers or genealogists such as Stern, Agry or Benneton. Private clients, he said, making sure I took note, need only provide drawings or a description to commission an engraving from him. Many aristocratic families rely on Desquand, for he specializes in heraldry and, he boasted, once engraved the royal devices of the Comte de Paris, the now deceased pretender to the throne of France. Yes, there is a throne of France, he assured me. It lodges in the minds of passionate Royalists, of whom there are several hundred thousand, whom detractors consider a royal pain in the Republic.

City officials may have re-housed dozens of artisans like Desquand, but you can't help feeling that the enthusiasm of the penpusher-and-bulldozer set lies elsewhere. Specifically, it abides in a visibly impressive and publicly accessible urban project that was initiated in 1987: the Viaduc des Arts. It took ten years to reconvert the arches of the mid-

19th-century former railroad viaduct on Avenue Daumesnil east of the Bastille into a showcase for the city's upscale arts and crafts. The official inauguration took place in October 1998. The Viaduc des Arts stretches about half a mile with perhaps sixty shops tucked under its arches. This being Paris, several cafés and restaurants are at hand to slake shoppers' thirst. This being France, there is also a good deal of state-sponsored money being spent by organizations that hide behind acronyms, including the V.I.A., a contemporary furniture and design showroom.

The eye-catching activities of the artisans, and the attractively landscaped Promenade Plantée linear-garden that runs on top of the viaduct, have turned the Avenue Daumesnil into a favorite walking, roller-blading and window-shopping area. You could, I suppose, spend several days visiting the workshops and boutiques here, though most passersby simply pause and peer into the huge plate-glass windows. Behind them ceramists paint plates, puppet makers make puppets, glass blowers blow bobbles, and so forth, all of them doing their tricks in public view. The artisans double as performers. Luckily some of them obviously enjoy hamming it up and the others manage to forget they're the monkeys at the zoo.

Here's a curious fact to consider: while the Viaduc des Arts has had an enthusiastic reception by Parisians, and appears to be a commercial success, most of the artisans working there came from the provinces, not from Paris workshops. I once chatted with the only family of artisans from town that I could find, the affable Michel Fey et al, a clan of tooled-leatherworkers whose great grandfather André created Maison Fey in 1900. Until recently, said Michel as he stretched a hide, the family workshop occupied two dank, cluttered ground-floor spaces in the Faubourg Saint Antoine a few blocks away. Michel added that though he and his son Christophe continue to use century-old tools to craft or restore leather desks or tabletops and blotting pads, the family is thoroughly delighted to have moved into their light, airy, modern space. Not only can they see trees and passersby as they toil. They also have easy parking and freight loading areas, and three times as much space as before to boot. They pay more rent but that's offset by higher turnover because of increased visibility. So everyone is delighted.

Fey confirmed that he is just about the only craftsman who moved from the 11th arrondissement to the Viaduc. I asked him why other Parisians hadn't followed. "Because," he whispered, "most Paris artisans are secretive, conservative, traditional, ornery and obsessively independent." As if that weren't enough, he added, many old-timers simply couldn't afford the move, or were discouraged from making it by the commission responsible for allotting space. As the project's name suggests, the emphasis at the Viaduc des Arts is *l'artisanat d'art,* meaning arty things that are pretty, quiet, clean and good for the city's image.

I was pleased for Fey, just as I was for the artisans of the modern, soul-less complexes I'd visited earlier. Still, it was as surprising as it was gratifying for me to revisit three of the city's premier artisans in the atmospheric old Marais workshops I'd seen when I first moved to the neighborhood in the mid-1980s. I started my artisan hunt with Patrick Desserme, the glass-molder on the Rue du Pont aux Choux.

When the Bastille was stormed and dismantled in 1789 some of the stones were used to build the glassworks where Desserme, a third-generation *bombeur de verre,* molds magnificent globes, camber-windows, clock crystals and lantern panes. Wearing T-shirts even in winter, the feisty Desserme and his assistant were working in the infernal heat of half a dozen furnaces (one, a wood-burner from the 18th century, has since been retired).

Wiping away sweat, Desserme confirmed to me in short vocal blasts that he is among a handful of European glass molders still using artisan techniques. With over 5,000 new and antique molds strewn and stacked around his workshop, he boasted that he is able to replace glass elements of everything from Louis XV lanterns to postmodern furniture. His grandfather worked with Lalique, he said, his father with Max Ingrand. He himself teams up with contemporary design gurus the likes of Philippe Starck, Andrée Putman, Jean-Michel Wilmotte or Garouste and Bonetti. The reclusive Desserme is a rarity among glass-molders in that he also creates pieces for collectors, one-of-a-kind glass consoles, for instance, or tables and *objets d'art,* though he does not advertize this fact, and indeed prefers to be left alone.

A five-minute walk from Desserme's furnaces is Gilbert Rotival's cupboard-sized atelier. Like his father and grandfather before him, Rotival, a tooled-leather craftsman and case-maker, was named Meilleur Ouvrier de France. He carries on the family tradition in an utterly impractical but magical workshop wedged into the ground floor of a 1637 townhouse. Rotival's buttery-soft wallets are worth more than the money in them, unless you're carrying large bills. His jewelry cases are as precious as the stones they hold – more precious, if you ask me. Quiet, kind and shy, Rotival showed me again the vintage tools and century-old sewing machine he uses to transform dyed and gilded leather into attaché cases, hand bags and steamer trunks for the lucky few, or for companies like Cartier and Morabito. I asked him what his most memorable job had been. He thought then spoke quietly. "An elaborate leather-covered treasure chest for Saudi King Fahd's collection of priceless gold objects," he said at last. "It took me and five assistants over 200 man-hours to make."

I reflected on that number: 200 man-hours for a treasure chest. I wondered if King Fahd had appreciated it. By the time I'd thought that through, and considered its geopolitical ramifications, I'd walked up the Rue des Franc-Bourgeois and turned north on a side street, the Rue Elzevir. Here, over fifty years ago, a wood sculptor named Jean Renouvel began his working life as a humble apprentice. He carved his way to the top. About twenty-five years ago Renouvel began training a young, timid apprentice named Anne Nicolle. In the early '90s when I first met them, Jean and Anne were working together to recreate wood panels for Marie Antoinette's boudoir at the Petit Trianon in Versailles. Nicolle, as shy as ever, eventually took over the workshop. But nothing in or about it has changed. Ancient sculpted wood and plaster casts – used as models – hang from the ceiling above cupids and Corinthian capitals, festoons and friezes. When I met Renouvel for the first time he told me he absolutely refused to use new chisels and gouges for the simple reason that they were no better, and usually considerably less good, than the heavy, cumbersome tools he'd inherited in the 1950s. Nicolle, now a middle-aged woman and herself a crafts master, has inherited Renouvel's 1,200 antique tools and is quietly following his example.

View from cemetery, Auvers sur l'Oise 1999

Dear Dead Vincent van Gogh

"Some day or other, I believe I will find a way to have my own exhibition in a café."

Vincent van Gogh to his brother Theo, June 10, 1890

The commuter train from Paris' Gare du Nord took about an hour and a quarter to cover the twenty miles to Auvers-sur-Oise, via a bedroom community called Saint-Ouen-l'Aumone. "That's a quarter of an hour more than it took Vincent back in 1890," scoffed the man at the café facing Auvers' vintage train station. He sipped his coffee and spread his arms. "When Vincent came out here from Montmartre the train was direct and we were in the countryside – farms, the Oise River, thatched houses, it was beautiful, beautiful..."

Beyond the blue clouds of cigarette smoke curling through the café I could make out heavy car traffic. Suburbs hedged in the south side of town. Auvers is now part of Greater Paris, a city Vincent Van Gogh hated and loved in equal measure, like so many of its denizens.

Two essential things emerged from what this loquacious local had told me. First, he called Van Gogh "Vincent," as if he knew him. Second, he was obviously suffering from acute nostalgia for a period he couldn't possibly have known. I judged him to be around fifty years old. Van Gogh came to Auvers on May 21, 1890. He died here at the Auberge Ravoux, at the time a cheap lodging house, seventy days later, on July 29th, having shot himself in the chest during a fit of the intermittent insanity that came over him throughout his tumultuous thirty-seven-year life. It might have been a form of epilepsy or possibly porphyria, a hereditary nervous disorder. Theo Van Gogh is thought to have succumbed to it, too: he died six months after his brother, aged thirty-four.

Vincent and Theo Van Gogh were buried in Auvers' otherwise unremarkable cemetery. Since then the village's fame has increased many fold. It draws about 400,000 Van Gogh pilgrims yearly. After living in the capital for over fifteen years I thought it high time I join them. Most beeline to the graveyard, the Auberge Ravoux and the locales Van Gogh painted. I decided to do the same.

Boosters call Auvers the "cradle of Impressionism." Before Van Gogh arrived, painters the likes of Pissarro, Guillaumin, Monet, Daubigny (of the Barbizon School) and Cézanne lived or worked here from the mid-1800s onwards. Vincent remains the star of the show, however, because of his tragic end and the notoriety (and astronomical prices for his paintings) that followed.

Having finished our coffees and said goodbye to the chatty man in the café facing the train station, my wife Alison and I marched a few hundred yards north to the village church. You can't help recognizing if from Vincent's painting.

Notre-Dame-d'Auvers started life at about the time the Normans conquered England, that is, in 1066 (and all that). But the Romanesque tower and buttressed backside that Vincent loved were built in 1170. Or so said the friendly woman volunteer at the table inside the church. She was eager to show us around, though in truth there wasn't much to see. Apparently we were the only visitors so far on this winter weekday, early in the morning. The cold, musty, echoing sanctuary instilled in us poignant thoughts, however, propitious for Van Gogh-hunting.

It was Alison who noticed the panel outside the church, flanking the road to the cemetery. The panel showed a full-color reproduction of Van Gogh's painting of l'Eglise d'Auvers. As we stood bemused before it, a group of tourists trudged up the hill from their bus and paused. Several framed the panel and the church on the LCD screens of their digital cameras. Bzzz, bzzz, bzzz went the cameras. There was a good deal of jostling. Everyone gave suggestions on how to reproduce the mad genius' framing while also including the panel.

A raw-boned white horse roamed freely in a field between the church and the cemetery, which sits on an elevated plateau. This part of Auvers hasn't been developed and looks pretty much the way it would have in 1890, to judge from period photographs. The horse led us toward another panel. It showed Van Gogh's summertime painting of a wheat field with crows and curling unpaved roads. The crows and muddy roads were still there. Caw, caw, caw croaked the crows as we tramped in the icy mud.

In Vincent's day, the view from up here reportedly took in the Oise River, endless farmland and thatched houses (though they were disappearing already in 1890, noted the artist). Now you can't help noticing the inevitable spread of apartment buildings, small industry and commerce.

Somehow we managed to miss the maps indicating the whereabouts in the cemetery of the Van Gogh brothers' twin-tomb. A smiling local showed us to it. He turned out to be the gravedigger and was disarmingly friendly, like the woman in the church and the man in the café by the station. Chilly Paris, rising just across the fields, seemed distant.

We hurried over to have a look at the grave before the busload of fellow visitors arrived. To me, the tomb evoked old-fashioned twin beds, except that here the headboards were lichen-frosted stone knotted with ivy. The gravedigger removed a few decomposed offerings left by Vincent's admirers, said farewell to us and disappeared.

I couldn't help feeling queasy. Here we were, two unwitting pilgrims sighing and looking forlorn, already calling Van Gogh by his first name. "Vincent."

We failed to find the resting place of Dr. Gachet (the art collector-doctor who ministered to Van Gogh is in fact buried at Père-Lachaise cemetery in eastern Paris). We could not find a single historic personage whose name we recognized, and soon squelched back across the plateau to the wheat field panel. On it was a quote from one of Vincent's many letters to Theo: "Immense expanses of wheat under troubled skies, and I don't mind trying to convey the sadness, the extreme solitude..."

Apparently it was a few hundred yards from this spot, behind the chateau, that Vincent shot himself. I couldn't help wondering how many visitors to Auvers overlook the fact that something about this place drove the mad Dutchman to kill himself. Here.

The muddy road led us from the plateau down to the edge of another part of town. Long and narrow, Auvers straggles along for about three miles, wrapping around the plateau. Soon we stumbled upon the workshop of landscape painter Charles François Daubigny (1817-78). Stumbled? Well, not really: there were several signs pointing to it. In fact there are signs on just about every street corner in Auvers pointing to one attraction or another. You can't get lost for long.

Daubigny was an illustrious member of the Barbizon School of painters who worked primarily around Fontainebleau. Nonetheless he spent much of his life in and near Auvers. Thirty years before Van Gogh arrived, Daubigny was here to welcome the aged master Camille Corot, sometimes called a "pre-Impressionist," and the young Claude Monet.

Although Daubigny's atelier wasn't supposed to be open in winter we weren't aware of that and boorishly rang the bell. Instead of snarling, the owner smiled winningly and let us in. He turned out to be Daubigny's great great-grandson. A small, soft-spoken man in his sixties or seventies, Daniel Raskin Daubigny was wearing worn leather slippers and a woodsman's shirt open at the collar. His wife shook our hands then returned to the kitchen where she was cooking up something that smelled delicious.

"Delicious" was the word that kept dancing in my mind as Monsieur Raskin Daubigny showed us from room to room. It was a humble family house and workshop, built in 1861 and decorated by Corot, Daumier, Oudinot, Daubigny *père* and his son Charles (alias Karl). The plank floors creaked. The heady smells of beeswax, dust and old paper mixed with those of Madame's slow-simmering stew. Wintry light slanted in through high windows. On the walls hung lovely landscapes and seascapes, or light, joyful renditions of bundled wheat, roosters, the Four Seasons.

As we shuffled along, Monsieur Raskin Daubigny told us how he'd spent years and a small fortune restoring the place then decided to open it to the public in 1990. The convoluted tale of the inheritance and the travails of his relatives seemed straight out of Balzac or Zola. To top it all, once he'd fixed the atelier and thrown open its doors, the French tax inspectors tripled his taxes, or so he claimed with disgust. But he was a cheerful man nonetheless and proud of his heritage.

"Oh yes, this was my room, too," he announced, showing us the children's room, called la Chambre de Cécile. "I was terribly afraid of the big bad wolf," he added. In 1863 Daubigny, his daughter Cécile and son Charles had painted the walls with fanciful scenes from the tales and fables of Perrault, Grimm and La Fontaine. Little Red Riding Hood was there, and the wolf. I, too, would've been afraid of him, staring out at my crib, licking his chops.

The best was yet to come. The atelier itself, now furnished like a living room, has a cathedral ceiling and a wall of windows. Enormous landscape canvases showing Italy's lake district, herons, and French country scenes cover the other three walls. "Corot conceived them," said our host. "Daubigny father and son painted them, with Oudinot. Some parts may have been done by Corot himself..."

Whoever painted them, they remain perfect for the site, a true, unselfconscious work of installation art. We stared at the landscapes long and rapturously as Monsieur Raskin Daubigny told us in fascinating detail about his great great-grandfather's friendship with Corot and

Monet. And about how an unscrupulous art dealer tried in the 1980s to buy the whole house and atelier from him planning to dismantle and ship it to America. "I don't care about money," he said, eyes twinkling. "I care about this." Happily the atelier is now a registered landmark and no one can touch it.

By the time we'd studied the clutter of Daubigny souvenirs in a glass case (medals from painting salons, a Daguerreotype, plaster casts...) and stepped out into the garden, it was nearly lunchtime. Monsieur and Madame showed us a last oddity: the floating painting workshop that Monet used. It was a small riverboat with a studio-cabin (for painting, cooking and sleeping). "Actually this is a replica Monet built of the boat my great great-grandfather used when he drifted down the Oise to the Seine, painting as he went, all the way to Normandy and the sea..."

It was this delicious image that accompanied us as we followed the signs back to Auvers' church and a lunch spot called Les Roses Ecossaises, recommended by Monsieur Raskin Daubigny. Though the interior was pink and twee, it was a good choice: the ham and cheese omelets were the size of Frisbees, and the homemade pear-and-chocolate pie was worth the trip from Paris to Auvers. Visitors like us talked in hushed voices of "poor, sad Vincent." A table of locals, instead, noisily applauded a freshly coiffed white poodle that yapped on command and sneezed at its owner's cigarette smoke. "Is he called Vincent?" I asked. "Vincent? No, his name is Event," answered his owner. "Because he was such an important event in my life..."

The Daubigny Museum and Museum of Absinthe were both closed. But the inevitable signs pointed to Dr. Gachet's house. We recognized it immediately from the full-color panel near the front gate showing Van Gogh's *Portrait du Docteur Gachet.* A soulful little man with a crinkly white hat and blue coat, Gachet clutched in his hand a spray of foxglove, also known as medicinal digitalis.

Some of the same trees Van Gogh shows in another Auvers picture, *Le Jardin du Docteur Gachet,* appear to be still alive well over a century since he painted them. The tall white house (also painted by Cézanne, another of Gachet's artist friends) once held many priceless paintings. Closed for decades, to locals it became a haunted house whose reopening as a "Place of Memory" only partly dissipated the ghoulish feel. The red window frames are no longer peeling as they once were, and the green shutters that flapped in the wind like the gills of a dying fish have been restored. The Maison du Dr. Gachet is ostensibly a house-museum, but as I wandered around its echoing, somber rooms I felt a chill. There isn't a lot to see – some vintage photos, a reproduction of Vincent's only eau-forte showing Dr. Gachet. I have never been fond of shrines, especially when they're associated with commercial enterprises, and a commercial shrine is precisely what the house appears to be, for it is managed by the same people who own the Auberge Ravoux, the hallowed place where Vincent drew his last breath.

At Auvers' 17th-18th-century chateau we discovered one of the town's most popular family attractions, a multimedia extravaganza called "Voyage to the Time of the Impressionists." We hesitated. It sounded like high kitsch. But the weather was foul and we soon tired of sloshing around in the chateau's muddy grounds, unable because of the rain to see from the panoramic terrace.

Inside the chateau we were issued with outsized headphones and pointed at the first room, the Portrait Gallery. There were the usual suspects: Renoir, Monet, Pissarro, Caillebotte, Sisley, Boudin and the sole woman Impressionist, Berthe Morisot.

Suddenly we were whisked by voices and images into the dark, dank Paris of the 1860s, among the riff-raff of the Rue de la Tuerie (Slaughter Street) and other charming addresses wiped out by Baron Georges Eugène Haussmann in his colossal Second Empire remake of the city. Period photos showed Haussmann's destruction of medieval Paris – about 25,000 buildings razed – and the birth of the modern capital the Impressionists painted.

As we walked from room to room in the chateau the tableaux and voices changed with eerie ease. Here were Haussmann's comfortable new buildings aligned on wide boulevards, with new train stations, grand cafés, legally registered whorehouses, iron bridges, bourgeois families out for a stroll.... Here, too, were dozens of wonderful political cartoons hanging on the walls or projected on a screen. All focused on the works of the Impressionists. In one a disgruntled viewer comments: *These paintings need to be seen from afar!* Another retorts: *I know, that's why I'm leaving.* Other rooms faithfully reproduced historic Paris interiors where 19th-century music hall songs played, the period's charm and seediness evoked side-by-side.

By the time we'd learned about ghastly green absinthe (the LSD of the 19th century) in a replica Impressionist Café-Thèatre; waited in a mock-1870s Paris train station; then ridden the steam train out through beautiful countryside to Auvers the way the Impressionists did; we were both thoroughly taken in. Having already eaten our giant omelets earlier at les Roses Ecossaisses, we resisted the temptation to lunch at the chateau's Impressionist *Guinguette* – a popular eatery as depicted in the paintings of Renoir et al.

This may be Auvers' answer to Paris Disneyland, I thought, but it's cleverly and intelligently done, the best evocation of the City of Light in its heyday I have yet to encounter. Even the silly, computer-modified image of Monet's self-portrait blinking its eyes at you is irresistibly funny.

There was just enough time to get to the Auberge Ravoux before it closed. We raced a mile or so back through town and squeezed in. The auberge is from 1855. It faces the town hall on one side, a cobbled courtyard on the other. In Vincent's day its owners sold wine and wood, served meals and rented out three rooms upstairs. Authur Gustave Ravoux took it over not long before Van Gogh arrived. For 3.50 francs a day the Dutchman got a tiny room and three squares: meat and vegetables, salad and bread.

Theo Van Gogh had probably hoped that his ailing brother could stay at Dr. Gachet's house and get treatment there, but that proved impossible. So he arranged for another young Dutch painter named Anton Hirschig to move into the room next door to Vincent's at the auberge and keep an eye on him. No one really knows precisely where or with what kind of gun Vincent shot himself. He managed to get back to the auberge, though, drag himself upstairs and hang onto life for a painful day and a half. After he died, no one wanted to sleep in the room of an insane suicide victim, so it was used for storage and somehow escaped alteration.

We climbed up to the room via a well-stocked, luxurious bookstore-boutique on the second floor. The Auberge Ravoux is no longer a quaint little inn: shortly after Van Gogh's paintings became the most valuable in the world, in 1987, a businessman named Dominique-Charles Janssens bought the place, created the Institut Van Gogh, restored the building to its original configuration and in the early 1990s reopened it as the Maison Van Gogh, a tourist attraction. Janssens did a consummate job.

From the bookshop you open an old door and hike up the final flight of steps. Anton Hirschig's room has been restored to its 1890s simplicity: period wallpaper, a single box-spring bed, a washbasin and chest of drawers. Vincent's even smaller room next door is barren: no furniture or wallpaper. You can taste the raw plaster in the air. On one side of the room is an empty plate-glass display case with an extract from a June 10, 1890 letter Vincent wrote his brother Theo: "Some day or other, I believe I will find a way to have my own exhibition in a café."

Starting in the mid-1990s Janssens' institute began lobbying France's museum bureaucracy for permission to decorate the room with *Landscape of Auvers After the Rain* (owned by Russia's Pushkin Museum). The bulletproof display case clashes somewhat with the garret's evocative bare walls and somber mood, which generate the same shrine-like quality as the Maison du Dr. Gachet. But it's understandable that Janssens wanted to exhibit a real Van Gogh. The auberge in its first decade of operation drew about 80,000 paying pilgrims a year. With a multi-million-dollar original in Vincent's room that number was destined to soar.

In the third upstairs room we watched a twelve-minute video about Vincent's seventy days in Auvers. Skillfully made, with music by Richard Strauss, it presses all the right buttons. I blew my nose and dried my cheeks as we walked downstairs and dropped $30 for a short book on Vincent's Paris-Auvers life. I resisted the temptation to buy the Van Gogh-inspired cookbook.

The last stop was the ground-floor restaurant, an authentic recreation of something a bourgeois traveler may have experienced hereabouts a century ago, with wooden tables, period settings, and carafes and glasses designed to look like those in the Van Gogh painting *l'Absinthe*. The restaurant is a favorite among Paris' glitterati. Hanging on a wall was a sketch by the celebrated French political cartoonist Sempé. It shows a throng trying to get into the Grand Palais for a Van Gogh exhibition. The caption says: "This is the guy who wanted to have a show in a café..."

Beaumarchais and Gay Pride Parade, 2002

Beaumarchais' Marais

"Je me presse de rire de tout, de peur d'être obligé d'en pleurer (I make myself laugh at everything, for fear of having to weep)."
Pierre-Augustin Caron de Beaumarchais, *The Barber of Seville*

You can walk across the Marais in half an hour or, like me, spend a lifetime exploring the leafy squares, alleys and mossy courtyards of one of Paris' more atmospheric neighborhoods. They're woven along imperfectly traced arteries between the Bastille and Beaubourg, the Seine and Temple, in the third and fourth arrondissements. Nowadays *le shopping* may well be what draws most visitors to this self-consciously chic theme park for what Parisians call *Bobos* – Bohemian bourgeois. Boutiques, art galleries and faux-bistros are shoehorned wall-to-wall between museums and administrative offices in landmark Louis-something townhouses.

But behind the scrubbed façades and under the cobbles lurk layers of history. Since the mid-1980s I've lived near the Place des Vosges, the neighborhood's centerpiece, and when it comes to understanding and appreciating the Marais I've barely scraped the icing off this luscious layer-cake.

Despite its inauspicious name – *marais* is French for swamp or marsh – and equally murky proto-historical days as a floodplain, the neighborhood has long lured an impressive roster of humanity. Some contemporary admirers like to hark back thousands of years, but in my wanderings I've never heard the rumble of chariots on the Rue Saint Antoine (the neighborhood's ancient Roman backbone) or the clatter of medieval knights en route to their fortresses at the Bastille, La Force or Temple. Some echoes from the Marais' past, especially those from the 17th and 18th centuries' Golden Age, do still resonate, though, above the white noise of cell phones and sour-sounding street-corner jazz ensembles. One voice in particular often calls out to me, the voice of Pierre-Augustin Caron, better known as Beaumarchais. "I make myself laugh at everything," Beaumarchais' Figaro famously quipped, "for fear of having to weep."

Clockmaker, musician, playwright, pamphleteer, arms dealer and spy, Beaumarchais was born in 1732 on the Rue Saint Denis, a few blocks west of the Marais, and later lived in a Rue Vieille du Temple mansion in what's now the Marais' gay district. He died in 1799, having made and lost several fortunes, in an extravagant palace he'd built on the Boulevard Beaumarchais, abutting the Place de la Bastille and Boulevard Richard Lenoir. Beaumarchais certainly loved the Marais. Would he love it today?

A bronze statue on the Rue Saint Antoine in a small square on the corner of the Rue des Tournelles shows a handsome, vigorous Beaumarchais. His walking stick is bent: for the last 100 years people have been hanging bouquets from its tip, during the protest marches that start at the Bastille and, traditionally, move up the Rue Saint Antoine to city hall or along Boulevard Beaumarchais to the Place de la République. Also, there's a hotel just off the Rue de Rivoli, and plaques on walls scattered here and there, bearing Beaumarchais' name. They remind the Marais' window-shoppers that Beaumarchais was the author of the plays *The Barber of Seville* and *The Marriage of Figaro*. Like the neighborhood's façades and cobbled recesses, these physical testimonials to the man's passing open the doors of speculative fancy. To my mind what makes Beaumarchais ever present amid the Marais' bumper-to-bumper trendies is his eerily contemporary, disconcertingly ambiguous character. It merged in a single person the brutal contradictions and wild paradoxes of an age more like our own than many might think. If such a thing as "spirit of place" exists then Beaumarchais' might very well have been – and still be – the spirit of the Marais and that of many of its residents: ambitious, litigious, subversive, licentious, arrogant, nostalgic, progressive, enlightened, opportunistic, self-important, at once aristocratic and thoroughly parvenu. Sound like the designers, architects, statesmen, fashion models and starlets who call the Marais home today?

If he were alive the contrarian Beaumarchais would probably be director of the Opéra de la Bastille, receiving a salary plus subsidies (as a librettist, musician and playwright) from the Ministry of Culture while simultaneously trying to dismantle the old-boy bureaucracy sustaining him. Since the Boulevard Beaumarchais is traffic-clogged and undistinguished nowadays, he might choose instead to live in, say, the quietly posh Place des Vosges, perhaps in the same restored townhouse as former Socialist minister Jack Lang. Or maybe he'd gut and reconvert a historic property in the Rue des Francs-Bourgeois, like celebrity architect Jean Nouvel, whose bald pate and flashy black designer-wear are a neighborhood curiosity. More likely, Beaumarchais would knock down a landmark mansion or two and build something new, vast and provocative – after all he was a passionate innovator, and he did help bring down the sclerotic Ancien Régime despite his closeness to Louis XVI and Marie-Antoinette. Doubtless a modern Beaumarchais would dine regularly at such Michelin-starred Marais perennials as l'Amboisie or Benôit, breaking bread with politicos from left and right, needling and wheedling both, soliciting and dispensing kickbacks, making and breaking allies and enemies alike. Perhaps he would lobby the Greens to turn the Marais into a car-free zone, as some misguided inhabitants are currently trying to do, while ensuring that he could still drive his SUV or Ferrari to his sumptuous digs (and those of his many mistresses).

"Drinking when we're not thirsty and making love year round, Madame, that's all that distinguishes us from other animals," sang Figaro. And, as Beaumarchais' biographers agree, Figaro and his creator were one and the same.

It was among the clocks, jewels and musical instruments with which his father was entrusted that Beaumarchais, barely out of his teens, invented a spring mechanism that made watches run more accurately. And it was in defending his invention from Lepaute, the royal watchmaker who stole his idea, that Beaumarchais demonstrated his preternatural talents as writer and orator. He won his case before the Academy of Sciences and soon replaced Lepaute at Louis XV's Versailles court, quickly becoming among other things, harp instructor to the king's daughters, the associate of the kingdom's biggest arms dealer, and protégé of the king's official mistress, Madame de Pompadour.

The young Beaumarchais craved respectability, and while the city's best addresses at the end of Louis XV's reign were being built in the Left Bank's Saint Germain neighborhood, the Marais was still a fashionable enclave, just as it is now, for bluebloods and professionals at the top of their careers. Only after years of social climbing, court intrigue, spying on the king's behalf, gun-running, and two marriages (the first to a rich widow with a property named "Beaumarchais", whence his title) did the watchmaker-become-nobleman manage to move from Versailles via London to a Marais townhouse. That townhouse was the luxurious Hôtel Amelot de Bisseuil, often called the

Hôtel des Ambassadeurs de Hollande, in the Rue Vieille du Temple.

If you stroll up this café-lined street from the Rue de Rivoli you'll see immediately on your right the three-star Hotel Caron de Beaumarchais. It liberally derives its name and theme décor – a 1792 Erard pianoforte in the lobby and cozily faux-Ancien Régime style rooms – from the proximity of Beaumarchais' residence, two blocks north. Hidden among the bookshops, fashion accessory and specialty food boutiques, you'll recognize the mansion at number forty-seven. Its exterior is grimy, its heavy carriage doors elaborately carved with writhing Medusa heads.

Rebuilt in the 1650s atop medieval foundations, and repeatedly remodeled by the time Beaumarchais rented it in 1776, the townhouse was more than merely the budding playwright's dream residence. It was here, in the gilded, frescoed salons frequented by emissaries and artists, that Beaumarchais headquartered Rodriguez, Hortalez et Cie, a cover worthy of a modern spy novel. The company was at the heart of an intricate clandestine operation to supply American revolutionaries with ships, arms and gunpowder. With one adroit hand Beaumarchais brought Figaro to life in this townhouse, while with the other he spent over six million *livres* of French and Spanish gold to help the Insurgents beat the British. Without Beaumarchais, historians say, the decisive Battle of Saratoga couldn't have been won and America might never have gained its independence. Without Figaro, add others, the Bastille might never have fallen.

It shouldn't detract from his achievements that Beaumarchais undertook both his arms dealing and playwriting to turn a profit – his motto ran, roughly, "Do the public good while lining your own pockets." He was prototypically modern, with eyes firmly on the bottom line. That explains why, in the salons of this mansion in the heat of July 1777, he also created the Société des Auteurs Dramatiques, paving the way for the first laws on intellectual property and royalty payments. It was here too that Beaumarchais became publisher of Voltaire's collected works. This ruinous venture heightened suspicions among hereditary divine-right Ancien Régime aristocrats and plutocrats terrified by Beaumarchais' subversive atheism and beliefs in meritocracy. "You made the effort to be born," says Figaro to Count Almaviva, "but nothing more than that."

Ring the bell on the right of the carriage door and push past the carved medusas into the mansion's outer courtyard. The concierge will intercept you – this is still private property. By a series of flukes the building has changed little since Beaumarchais' day. Even the low-relief sculptures surrounding the court have survived (they show Romulus and Remus nursed by the She-wolf; and allegories of Strength, Truth, Peace and War; plus the goddesses Ceres and Flora). You can only peer through the vaulted passageway at the tantalizing main courtyard, freshly restored, with more sculptures, masks and garlands. If you're lucky, you might glimpse through parted drapes the dazzling ceilings the playwright-spy knew so well.

Imagine Beaumarchais' gold-encrusted carriage rattling down the Rue des Francs-Bourgeois, past the sumptuous Hôtel Carnavalet, now the History of Paris Museum, across the Place des Vosges, to the wide boulevard that today bears his name. For several hundred yards along the boulevard's east side stretch the landscaped grounds of the estate Beaumarchais and his third wife have been building since the late 1780s for the phenomenal sum of 1.6 million *livres*. Inheritances and settlements, plus real estate speculation and a controlling interest in Paris' first-ever water utility, have made Beaumarchais fabulously rich. Known as the "Mansion of the Two Hundred Windows", Beaumarchais' estate is a parvenu's paradise, with a semi-circular colonnade, temples to Bacchus and Voltaire, a Chinese humpback bridge and a waterfall. The Bastille rises to the south, its towers and bastions an ominous theatrical backdrop. The main house is not yet finished when, in April 1789, Beaumarchais and a party of aristocratic friends, including the future king Louis Philippe, watch with horror as rioters ransack a nearby mansion then assault royal guards, with a loss of some 200 lives. Have Figaro's spiritual heirs gone mad? Beaumarchais can't help wondering. A few months later, on July fourteenth, Beaumarchais again watches from his terrace as rioters from the blue-collar Faubourg Saint Antoine neighborhood storm the Bastille. And the rest is history.

"If we were to allow that play to be performed," remarked the otherwise unperceptive Louis XVI in 1784 about *The Marriage of Figaro,* "we would have to demolish the Bastille." Fittingly, when the demolition began on July fifteenth, Beaumarchais, as president of the Marais' Blancs-Manteaux district, was sent with other dignitaries to supervise. With his typical pragmatism and aplomb he bought – or requisitioned – some of the Bastille's stones and sent them trundling to the worksite of his personal theater under construction at number eleven, Rue de

Sévigné, between Saint Paul and the Carnavalet – the heart of the Marais.

Demolished in the mid-1800s, there's nothing left but the façade of the Théâtre Beaumarchais (sometimes referred to as the Théâtre du Marais). In 1791-92 the chameleon citizen-playwright staged here the third of his Figaro series, the little-known *La Mère Coupable*. More recently, starting in about 1960, for forty years a Hungarian delicatessen ensconced in what was the theater's foyer sold some of the best salami in Paris. An elegant, could-be-anywhere boutique has now moved in to replace it. Like dozens of unglamorous shoe repair, grocery and hardware shops, the deli was one of those Marais touchstones from the blue-collar age that have given way to gentrification. When I look up at the former-theater's pilasters, my mind's eye sees a slice of the Marais' layer-cake. First there was a swamp here, then came Philippe-Auguste's medieval city wall, followed by part of the La Force prison, then a theater built with the stones of the Bastille, a Hungarian deli, and now a trendy boutique.

Rewind to Beaumarchais' speeding carriage – by now a nondescript vehicle sans glittering gold, in keeping with Revolutionary etiquette. Who knows how many times it rumbled from the theater to the Mansion of Two Hundred Windows, racing past carts loaded with prisoners on the way to the guillotine? Ironically, the Committee of Public Safety together with Robespierre almost managed to execute the subversive author of Figaro. True to character, he had reinvented himself as gunrunner for France's new Revolutionary despots. Only by luck, chance and intrigue did Beaumarchais, declared a "counter-revolutionary" and exiled, keep his head on his shoulders. During his absence, troops stormed his Marais estate expecting to uncover weapons. All they found were thousands of unsold volumes of Voltaire's collected works.

There's nothing left of the Mansion of Two Hundred Windows and its grounds, where Citizen Beaumarchais spent the final years of his life, still rich and full of fire but no longer a hero. He died in the last year of the 18th century, on the cusp of the modern age, and was buried in his garden near Voltaire's temple, on the edge of the Marais. The final irony, a postscript to this extraordinary life, is that, before the estate was demolished to make way for the Canal Saint Martin and Boulevard Richard Lenoir, King Louis XVIII's men dug up the free-thinking playwright's bones, in 1822, and moved them to Père-

Lachaise, a cemetery named for a Jesuit priest. Even in death the itinerant iconoclast knew no rest. Over the rumble of traffic on his boulevard I sometimes hear Beaumarchais chuckling, reminding me that if you don't laugh you're destined to cry.

Couple and graffiti face, 1993

Madame X's Seduction School

"Frenchmen aren't seducers the way they were..."

Madame X

A small black sheepdog darts over the lawns of Paris' fashionable Bois de Boulogne parklands, among coiffed pooches and Catherine De Neuve look-alikes. The middle-aged man at the other end of the retractable leash eases over to a chic Parisienne with a poodle. "Ah, you must be Madame Fifi," he splutters, taking cues from another woman standing nearby. "Perhaps you could advise me on how to help my dog adapt to Paris life – I've just moved here you see and..."

Cut to the outdoor terrace of a crowded Paris café. Another man, this one a frump in his mid-30s, has been eyeing the young woman at the next table but hasn't screwed up the courage to talk to her. On cue from a half-hidden figure seated at the table behind him, the man clears his throat, leans toward the object of his desire and smiles winningly. "*Pardonez-moi,* I know this is going to sound strange, and I don't usually do such things, but I have to say there's something really interesting on the back page of your newspaper. Could I take a look at it?"

At an upscale boutique in the Rue Saint Honoré, a cute sales woman shows a pair of expensive shoes to a 40ish man dressed like someone from Federico Fellini's *La Dolce Vita.* The man is exquisitely polite and charming, though he's obviously shy, and after paying for his shoes returns a few minutes later with a single white rose. "Your eyes are so beautiful I just wanted to thank you," he says. The sales woman – used to dealing with gruff or blasé types – is speechless. He hands her his card. "Next time I'm in Paris can I take you to lunch?"

"But my boyfriend..." the woman begins to object.

"It's just lunch, I assure you, your boyfriend has nothing to fear, but there's something about you, your eyes..."

What do these corny pick-up scenes have in common?

A shadowy puppeteer I'll call Madame X, the feisty founder of Paris' first École de Séduction – a school where you learn the fine art of seduction. Madame X and her crack team of Latin Lover "seduction coaches" accompany advanced students into the field for hands-on sessions. Dogs in parks, newspapers in cafés, and roses in boutiques are just a few of the tricks Madame X uses to push her tongue-tied French males to take the plunge, to make the move and try to pick up the femme fatale of their dreams.

A seduction school in Paris – land of adultery and philandering, the fountainhead of De Sade? Yes indeed. The operation got started in the mid-1990s and was such an immediate success that other Madame X Seduction School campuses may be coming soon to a town near you, possibly even in puritanical middle America. Madame X featured heavily in the French press for a time. American TV stations then interviewed her. Why?

The answer is straightforward: it's difficult for anyone to believe that Parisian men need to be taught how to pick up women. What has happened to the Jean-Paul Belmondos, the Jean Gabins, the Alain Delons of the country? Most people consider France to be a paradise of the senses – fabulous food, an excess of culture, and sex a-go-go.

"Frenchmen aren't seducers the way they were up to the mid-1980s," Madame X told me in rapid-fire French, flinging her arms around for emphasis. "The relationship between men and women began to go downhill starting then. The reason is fifty years of feminist revolution. At a certain point it had to backfire for women. We've become victims of the war we've waged."

A tall, muscular forty-something, Madame X is an ex-Club Med staff member, a former sales team manager and business consultant, matchmaking agency director, and dancer. She has the imposing presence of a permanently bronzed Alpha Female, with large mobile features, big brown eyes, serious hair, lavish gestures and canon-shot exclamations. Her body language shouts out conflicting words – randy, bossy, tough, pushy, single-minded, saucy, outspoken, physical. To hear her speak of French women as "victims" of feminism struck me as comical.

In my two decades in Paris I have encountered French women like her, though none wearing, as she was, a loose white shift paired with red basketball shoes, her hair crowned by a pair of sunglasses (despite the fact that we were inside an office building). Most of the Parisian Alpha Females I have known sport smart Chanel suits and flirt dangerously with the executives come to cut deals with them.

High-strung, impatient, guarded, Madame X moved around her small office in Paris' Opéra neighborhood like a caged lioness – or a Puerto Rican dancer in *West Side Story*. She plucked the sunglasses off her Medusa curls, twirled them, dropped them on her cluttered desk by her shrilling cellular phone, replaced them, scratched her stress-martyred hands then answered the mobile with a sigh.

If previously I had doubts about her qualifications as a seductress – she certainly had not conquered me – this telephone conversation dispelled them. Her face and voice altered as she purred into the cellular phone, cajoling the woman at the other end in several languages. If nothing else, I sensed, Madame X was a good actress.

"Seventy percent of my clients are men," she confirmed once off the phone, "thirty percent women." Almost all her women clients, it turned out, come not to learn how to seduce men. Some want to master more effective business communications techniques. But, in a country with a thirty-three percent divorce rate, where bed-hopping is the national pastime, most of them simply want to learn how to keep the men they have.

"Between you and me," she said, getting colloquial and chummy, "we French women are spoiled. We've got full rights, we can have an abortion, we can take the pill, we can cheat on our husband – no one busts your ass anymore if you commit adultery and it sure wasn't like that once upon a time. We work, we're independent – I just don't understand why we complain. My grandmother always told me, 'you're so damn lucky!' I've got to say, I'm very happy to have been born and to live now."

The main problem with Frenchmen, it seems, and therefore the raison d'être for Madame X's school, is the very power of French women today – women who don't have time for men, families, love or courtship.

Madame X's men – most of them engineers, computer programmers, professionals or business executives aged thirty to fifty – don't know how to behave with these superwomen, have difficulty communicating with them, and have come to fear them. Madame X's school is the last resort, the Last Chance Saloon for many who've already been to shrinks, matchmakers and a variety of singles clubs. So her clients spend several thousand dollars and two to nine months learning how to overcome their fears – of rejection, ridicule, or psychic castration.

"For a while there, I wasn't exactly cuddly with men myself," she said, fixing me with a razor-sharp gaze. "I was one of those *castratrixes*. Yes, a ball-cutter. Yes, we are ball-cutters, but Frenchmen have become pretty wimpy, too, pretty weak. It's like, 'We were victims, now the men are victims – everyone gets his turn'. But that's not going to fix anyone's problems."

A similar set of problems, related to post-feminist psychic castration, arose at about the same time in Italy, long believed to be the true heartland of the Latin Lover. I mentioned this to Madame X and told her how in the late 1980s I attended and reported on a similar school run by a certain Dr. Giuseppe Cirillo, alias the Prince of Seduction (in real life, a Neapolitan lawyer-turned-psychologist-sexual therapist). With increasing social mobility and waning family values in Italy as in France, starting in the 1980s Italian men were suddenly finding themselves washed by their careers onto the shores of strange cities, surrounded by unfamiliar and demanding women. Liberated Italian feminists of the day dreamed up the slogan "Bread but also roses", a baffling refrain to many Italian men and one which spawned countless then unheard of lonely hearts clubs, as well as Cirillo's seduction school (it is still in operation, with branches in Naples, Rome and Milan).

The colorful Cirillo Method, as I experienced it, involved individual and group activities that ranged from the banal – matching facial expressions with Cirillo's so-called "75 primary emotions", gauging "gait and body language", using "voice modulation, eye and hand techniques" – to the outlandish. Not only did we engage in thigh-to-thigh role-playing (in one session I had to explain my way out of being caught sleeping with my girlfriend's best friend, in another I had to try to sell seminude ballerina figurines to the Salesian Brothers' Oratory). We were also introduced to Cirillo's secret weapon, the *tavola delle esclusioni,* a painted wood silhouette of a woman, with strategically placed slots at head, shoulder, and waist level. Out went the lights. In came a female presence. After sliding the silhouette's panels back and forth, allowing us to see the mystery woman's eyes, lips or waistline, Cirillo ordered us to step up and knead and stroke her. This was one of the most extravagantly embarrassing episodes of my adult life, but my fellow students, some of whom hadn't touched a flesh-and-blood woman in years, were delighted.

Being French, and a woman, Madame X did not offer her clients anything remotely like Dr. Cirillo's silhouette contraption. When I finished telling her about it she became pyrotechnic. "He must have a bunch of basket cases as clients, guys in death throes, morbidly shy guys," she said, referring to Cirillo and his men. "I don't have morbidly shy types, I have normal guys." As proof she showed me a few photographs. Her clients did look normal. The first thing she does, she said, when she meets a potential client, is interview him, then send him to a clinical psychologist she works with. After he's been profiled, she and the psychologist consult with the client and set up a strictly personal course of instruction. It can include everything from role-playing to field trips (pick-up practice in clubs, cafés, parks), to dance classes or visits to a sexual therapist. "Some of my clients are virgins," she admitted, "others say they don't know how to put on a condom."

Often the beginning of a typically Parisian course with Madame X involves the sartorial and hygienic remake of a client. She showed me a series of photos demonstrating how she and her crew have transformed one client from a hopeless slob – mismatched tie and shirt, baggy outdoorsy pants and raingear, unkempt hair – to a snazzy hunk. In the photos the remade man wears a gray suit and dark turtleneck and his hair is raked back like a rake with a license to seduce. This makeover technique is called "re-lookage" a wonderful example of the Franglais Madame X favors. "I often use Alain Delon as an example of how to dress," she said deadpan, adding that she believes clothes do indeed make the man. "He's a successful role model. You might or might not like him, but he's not your run-of-the-mill actor, and he did it himself, so it means you can transform a man. When you work at it, when you have the will to change yourself, you can."

Dr. Cirillo may have his silhouette, but Madame X has two secret weapons of her own. The first is the small black Belgian sheepdog which snorted and padded around the office as we spoke. Parisians are dog obsessive; Madame X loans her pet to her clients so they can easily pick up dog-owning females anywhere.

The second weapon comes in the form of fieldtrips to one of Dr. Cirillo's stomping grounds – Rome. She met her husband there, an Italian who picked her up in a café. This explains why Madame X is convinced that Cirillo's clients are total basket cases.

"I take a bunch of Parisian men, we fly to Rome, go the center of town, and I and my women helpers are the bait," she explained. "We sit at a café and demonstrate how Roman men pick us up. We get all dolled up, we sit down, with our clients nearby, and then we wait. And I assure you we don't wait long. Go sit at a Paris café and unless you're wearing a miniskirt pulled up to your panties you can wait two hours before a guy will even talk to you."

So, I asked, despite Cirillo's basket cases, the secret of being a great lover is to be Italian? I could just imagine the Bill Gates look-alikes at Madame X's future American campuses exchanging their pen-protectors for Dolce Vita suits, worn boldly to help them shark in on single gals slurping 20-oz lattes at the local Starbucks.

"I'm not going to teach American men to pick women up like Roman men," she protested. "The essential thing is to be likeable instantly in the first seconds when approaching someone."

I soon understood why Madame X was hoping to open a school in America, specifically in California, a Mother Lode of dot-com nerds, luckless Bohemian Bourgeois and geeks surrounded by post-feminist *castratrices* with sharp sheers, fat wallets and dating contracts *(You shall not touch me until I specifically request you to do so…)*. One question remained in my mind, however: was she qualified? Madame X has traveled to, but never lived in America. She speaks fluent though flawed English and demonstrates a deep understanding of American culture. "My impression," she confided, "is Americans don't know how to flirt. There isn't a single American who knows how to flirt, and I mean the mating dance, the seduction dance, they don't know how to do it. They don't have good table manners either. I'm not saying all Americans are like that – some aren't of course but… The guys in Silicon Valley, in front of their computers all day, they barely know how to hold a fork. American guys can be jokesters, bon vivants, and suddenly they reach out and grab your ass and say *I want to fuck you* or whatever. They're capable of behaving like real hicks. Whereas the bourgeois American guy is calmer, more Puritanical."

Once I had left her office I formulated in my mind the "Madame X Method" in three easy steps. One: if you're a man, have Roman gene-implant therapy. Two: if you're a woman, fly to Rome and drink your latte there (despite the fact that no grown Italian drinks latte, which simply means "milk"). Three: if the first two methods don't work, buy a dog. In any case, do not bother coming to Paris in search of romance. Apparently the women nowadays are viragos, the men wimps.

PARIS PHENOMENA

Jardin des Plantes, 1997

In the Spring

"When good Americans die they go to Paris."
Oscar Wilde, *A Woman of No Importance*, 1893

Il fait beau, c'est le printemps, ran the lusciously enunciated, taped dialogue at the Pompidou Center's language laboratory. "The weather is beautiful, spring is here," I repeated, joining my own to a dozen eager voices as snow fell beyond the windows. Wherever I went that first April in Paris – now two decades ago – through sleet, rain, wind and snow, I would cheerfully say my *bonjours* in grade-school French, adding with a wink *c'est le printemps.* As if in answer the cloudy sky would blow for a few minutes into a blue expanse shot through with light, brightening the wet tin-and-tile mansard roofs time and again, like pebbles on a beach.

Cynics will remind you that the tune *April in Paris* got its name because the lyricist needed a two-syllable word for his refrain, and "May" or "June" wouldn't do. So what if the "thrill" of a wintry Paris April rhymes with "chill"? Springtime in Paris is a celebration, a chant, a hope, a modest dream that keeps millions going. Even people who have only visited the city in their imaginings know about it. They have sniffed and tasted a Paris spring in books, movies and paintings, and felt it warming their skin from Moscow to Manhattan. To Romantics and adepts of Shakespeare a Paris spring means sweet lovers loving on the Seine. To foodies it's the arrival of the year's new Michelin *Guide France* to hotels and restaurants. To footloose walk-aholics like my wife Alison and me, spring stands for flower-spangled gardens and sunny hikes. Of course, to those who view life through jade-colored lenses, and see horizontal pollution where cobbles glisten, it means rain, wind and the first crowds of noxious tourists.

I actually like spring rain: when it stops and the puddles grow still, you see two cities at every glance, the one reflected in the puddle often framed serendipitously. I like to think of post-Impressionist painter Gustave Caillebotte's *Rainy Day in Paris,* the umbrellas of the passers-by held high like the masts of ships navigating the gleaming boulevards, with buildings, carriages and people mirrored in them, plus much more of a commentary on bourgeois life than meets the eye at first glance.

W. Somerset Maugham's hero in *On the Razor's Edge* reveled in the "light, transitory pleasure, sensual without grossness" of a Paris spring that filled him with the glow of youth. Émile Zola wrote of "the charm of awakening desire, the thrill of hope and expectation." So just this once, let the pseudo-sophisticates fret about clichés, and try to spoil your enjoyment. The season will always have a special significance to me: every year the magic of those first months I spent in Paris, months full of adventure and promise, returns however fleetingly and flowers like the city's horse-chestnut trees, the quintessential symbol of springtime in Paris.

Though the city is a year-round destination nowadays, the number of visitors still spikes at Easter and mid-summer, the beginning and end of spring. In January, when April, May and June seem a lifetime away, I start receiving postcards and, these days, e-mails, announcing friends' spring itineraries. Will it be cold, they ask? They forget that Paris exists geographically (and not simply in their dreams) and is north of Saint John's, Newfoundland, north of Montreal, Boston, Vienna and Budapest. To be even-handed when I write back I copy out statistics from encyclopedias and guidebooks. "The average temperature in March," I say, "is 50.4 Fahrenheit, April 60.3 and May 61.9, while June hits 74." And I leave it up to them to judge whether that's warm or not. I often wonder whether these friends imagine, from where they write in sunny Rome or Los Angeles, the effect their messages have. In the dead of a leaden Paris winter, the mention of "spring" steels residents against the unremitting gray. In the mind's eye the Champs-Elysées bursts into elapsed-time leaf, rowboats in the Bois de Boulogne nose along lazy lakes, and ten thousand sun umbrellas sprout like kaleidoscopic mushrooms at street-corner cafés.

Anticipation, the weathering of that seemingly interminable Paris fall and winter, is what makes the spring so special here. It's as much a question of your state of mind as of meteorological phenomena. After a few false starts in February and early March, when picnickers are snatched off benches by icy claws, a sudden change occurs. The roast-chestnut sellers stow their steel drums and shopping carts, reappearing with fresh-cut mimosa in hand. Lap dogs appear sans doggie jackets. Tulips and forget-me-nots pop up in the Luxembourg Gardens. Bright little sailboats skim on pools in the Tuileries. The bell-weather youths of the Latin Quarter dress even more cavalierly than usual – a shirt and a loose knit sweater, or a thin blazer with a scarf tossed defiantly around a ruddy neck. No-nonsense northern and eastern Europeans pour out of the tour buses behind Notre-Dame wearing warm, practical clothes, which they quickly shed when they find they are no longer in Helsinki, Warsaw or other places with weather much harsher than Paris'. They rush, camera in hand, from the flying buttresses behind the cathedral to the Seine-side garden to be photographed in front of the cherry blossoms. The Italians, hidden in fur and shearling coats, shiver happily no matter how hot it gets.

On either bank of the Seine, the first things to sprout are not crocuses and daffodils but sidewalk tables and faux cane chairs. Locals eye them cautiously, hesitating because no one recognizably French has yet dared to sit outside. Clever café-keepers – notably on the Île-Saint-Louis, in the Place des Vosges and around Saint-Germain-des-Prés – beat the elements early by investing in Plexiglas windscreens and glowing outdoor gas heaters. These are a surprisingly effective cross between a Second Empire lamppost and a Coleman stove, and they have caught on all over town. No wonder: "The café," states my surprisingly up-to-date, 1912 Ward, Lock & Co. Paris Guide, "is the preeminently French institution.... Verlaine, the great French poet, never wrote a poem anywhere else!"

Indeed, the café still doubles as office and cozy living room in cold months, turning into a lively garden party the rest of the year. No true Parisian will be kept from his great spring communion for long. Once a fearless few have begun to brave the elements by sitting out of doors, the terrasses soon overflow. Waiters in their old-fashioned black-and-white penguin uniforms dash to and fro bearing beer, espressos and steaming hot chocolate.

Another bell-weather of spring is the city's outdoor-markets. If you arrive early enough you'll see the greengrocers arranging their fruit and vegetables into color-coded pyramids, domes or Cartesian rows. Next to the last winter cabbage and mud-spattered cauliflower nestle tiny zucchini swaddled in protective wrappers and crisp sweet peas from the hothouses of Provence. New potatoes with skins as pale as a Parisian's wait to be eaten unpeeled in a single bite. Flanking the mounds of cold apples and still-hard pears are baskets of berries, anemic cherries and the first ruinously expensive melons coaxed from the fields of Cavaillon 500 miles south. So gorgeous is the display that you hesitate before buying, unwilling to deconstruct these succulent still lifes. *Bon melon!* shouts the grocer as you pass by, promising the first taste of honeyed sweetness, nectar and joy. Seduced by his spiel, you buy an unripe melon, fully aware that you'll be disappointed, but happy to be taken in, as you are each year.

Once spring is in the air, the plein air painters appear in numbers: glimpsed through trees about to bud, monuments materialize on their easels. I find it difficult to visit museums or galleries in spring unless the works on show are divorced from nature. Instead I choose a vantage point on the edge of town, or an open spot within it, and settle in to watch the greatest exhibition of all – the spring sky and changing cityscape. There are no waiting lines and the show is free. The Pont Saint-Michel, or the Champs-de-Mars, the overlook at Père-Lachaise cemetery, the panoramic park at Belleville or even meretricious old Montmartre are my favorite spots. The shifting light seems to parade the masterpieces of the Louvre and d'Orsay across the heavens. There are swirling, puffy Tiepolo cloudscapes over the Italianate Institut de France and the lacey Pont des Arts. Billowing Renoirs clothe the ridiculous cupolas of Sacré Coeur. Giddy Pissarros and Signacs float over the Grands Boulevards, Seine and Tuileries. At dusk the mauve Monets and the flaming blues, pinks and reds of Fauvists like Derain clamp down on this old gray city that is itself an artwork in progress.

The Lac Daumesnil in the Bois de Vincennes on the second, third or fourth Sunday in April, depending on the calendar year, offers one of the oddest spring double-headers I know: the traditional Foire du Trône funfair, and the Buddhist New Year's celebrations held next door at a municipal temple. At the funfair, bumper-cars bang and merry-go-rounds spin to the nostalgic wheezing of accordions, with the smell of french fries hanging thick enough to slice. Under the Pointillist clouds of horse-chestnut trees lovebirds peck, kids run wild clutching cotton candy, and anglers fish for muddy *goujon* they will never eat. Here are the celebrated rowboats of Paris, each with a name, and here, too, are the swans and ducks and sculpted flowerbeds splashed with primrose, narcissus and daffodils. A few hundred yards down the lake the gongs and chants of Buddhists fill the air. The atmosphere is scented with spices, frying spring rolls and roasting meats. The peaceful co-existence of these two fundamentally different festivities, the complete absence of fear or anxiety among the picnickers and pedestrians of every imaginable color and age, makes me think of e.e. cummings' celebration of Paris as a spiritual place "continuously expressing the humanness of humanity."

Sure, Paris is no paradise, though you might be excused for thinking so now and again, especially in the spring. The joyous, homespun rites of *le printemps* possess none of the primordial horror of Stravinsky's music, which seems to suit so many modern megalopolises to a tee. Take, for example, the Parisian version of April 1st. Each year I receive an urgent telephone call offering me a lucrative book contract, a free trip to a nudist colony in Malta, or something similar, and I invariably fall for the gag. When I go down into the Marais street where we live, not far from the Lycée Charlemagne, a big high school, I inevitably wind up with a large paper fish plastered to my back, cleverly out of view. *Poisson d'Avril!* shout the mischievous but harmless teenagers. April Fool's Day! Then I realize that the book contract and the titillating trip to Malta are bogus, and I console myself with an April Fool's Day treat. The bakers of Paris vie with each other to make the most mouthwatering pastries, cakes and breads in the shape of fish, and the day becomes yet another excuse to celebrate life and stuff yourself with food. This April Fool's Day I might just spread the word that I'll be running in the Paris Marathon, to work off the cakes, cookies and winter fat, but I somehow don't think anyone will believe me.

Perhaps the best spring fête of all is May Day. The museums and public buildings close in honor of the workingman and woman, and not even the most skillful misanthrope or puritanical workaholic can avoid the day's festivities. *Muguet* hawkers appear on every corner, their ingeniously packaged lilies-of-the-valley arrayed in water-filled phials, moss-stuffed pots or elaborate baskets. Come rain or shine, several hundred thousand merrymakers, most of them leaning to the political left, converge on the Place de la Bastille with their bullhorns, wearing sprigs of lovers' muguet in their lapels. *Il fait beau,* chant the schoolteachers and students, the factory workers, bus drivers, grocers and nostalgic socialists with their banners of fallen idols. *C'est le printemps.*

Train Bleu restaurant, 2005

The Janus City or Why the Year 1900 Lives On

"If you love life you also love the past, because it is the present as it has survived in memory."

Marguerite Yourcenar

"Paris is a museum, and that is a privilege. But if it wants to be loyal to its history, it needs to innovate, to dare – it needs to move into the 21st century."

Betrand Delanoë, Mayor of Paris, 2005

It was a mild morning by Paris standards – five degrees centigrade. The previous night's storm had blown itself out, like the countless Réveillons de Saint Silvestre, those midnight New Year's bashes that on this occasion linked the 31st of December 1899 to the 1st of January 1900.

Had you arisen early, before the capital's bleary revelers, and ridden to the observation deck at the eleven-year-old Eiffel Tower's top, you would have gazed down on a strangely familiar city. Familiar in its layout of cannon-shot boulevards lined by Haussmann-style apartment buildings, its Arc de Triomphe, Garnier Opéra and Bastille Column, its topography of sinuous river and gentle hills topped, at Montmartre, by the great white wedding cake of the new Sacré Coeur basilica.

Familiar, yes, yet wonderfully, disconcertingly different.

Once Parisians had awakened to that first day of the 20th century, hung-over from champagne, absinthe and ether (or exhausted from serving the privileged classes who fêted through the night), the boulevards and Champs-Elysées had begun swarming, as they always did.

They swarmed with a cacophony of carriages – tens of thousands of *fiacres* and *cabriolets* jolting over the wooden or stone cobbles. Steam-powered, electric or horse-drawn streetcars lurched among the waves of hurried workers, of *boulevardier* hucksters and strolling *flâneurs* populating this metropolis of over three million. Nearby on the river, *bateaux-mouches* buzzed like flies (hence the *mouche* in their name), moving from bank to bank, avoiding barges and small freighters, using the Seine as another of the city's thoroughfares.

Had you brought binoculars with you to the tower's top, you might have spotted some society gentlemen removing their redingotes and top hats, preparing to duel on the Île de la Grande Jatte or, perhaps, in one of the newly landscaped *bois* edging Paris – the Bois de Boulogne or Bois de Vincennes. Duels were still de rigeur for the offended gentleman. Even the sensitive, the hypnotically intellectual Marcel Proust fought one.

Looking to the left or right of Sacré Coeur, on rutted lanes like the Allée des Bruyards, you might have caught sight of a yoked water-bearer bent under the weight of buckets, for running water was not yet available to all. Or maybe you'd see a lamplighter turning off a *bec à gaz* in the many neighborhoods not yet served by electricity.

Had you sniffed at the air you would have smelled the plumes of noxious smoke curling from factories scattered across town, in the courtyards of crumbling palaces, everywhere in fact, except perhaps in the fashionable 7th, 8th and 16th arrondissements. There the mansions of the *grandes familles* and the new rich vied to outdo each other in ostentation and ornament.

You would not have had to look far to find the city's sprawling slums. Work was still underway on January 1, 1900 to clear the gypsy encampments and shantytowns from the Champ de Mars at the Eiffel Tower's base. The undesirables simply had to be removed in haste, en masse. The areas in the shadow of Eiffel's re-gilt tower were being landscaped and beautified, part of that greatest of turn-of-the-century Paris events, the Exposition Universelle 1900.

Indeed anyone glancing down from the Eiffel Tower – symbol of that other great world's fair, of 1889 – would probably have concentrated his attention not on the damp, wintry city but on the vast work sites of the Exposition Universelle.

Paris had not wanted to host the exposition until a rival plan was put forth by the Germans. But national pride soon prevailed over common sense. By the mid-1890s Paris was piled end to end with rubble and pocked, over an area two and a half miles wide, with holes.

The holes had been dug to build the foundations of dozens of new buildings, fair pavilions and infrastructure, most of which were soon to disappear, with the notable exceptions of the heavily gilded Pont Alexandre III, and the Grand and Petit Palais, the Exposition's centerpieces.

But the most spectacular holes had been burrowed lengthwise – for the new, electrified *Métropolitain*. The city's first subway line linked

Porte Maillot in the west to the Place de la Bastille on Paris' eastern edge, and was considered one of the marvels of the civilized world. "What an age! What a century! What a triumph of engineering! *Nom de Dieu!*" exclaimed English chronicler John F. MacDonald, tongue firmly in cheek. "What miracle could compare to this one – *le Métropolitain?*"

Electricity was still a novelty in 1900, a metaphor for the positive elements of modernity, and it became the theme of the Exposition, which drew 50.8 million visitors over a period of six months. The fair's lighting and machinery were powered entirely by dynamos housed in the wildly gaudy Palais de l'Electricité. The huge colonnaded building glowed with 5,000 multi-colored Fairy Lights. Its crown was the Fée de l'Electricité (the Spirit of Electricty) riding in a chariot that showered colored sparks and flames. *La Ville Lumière,* the City of Light, was born, both as Paris' nickname, and as a self-conscious word-concept meaning "the spiritual and material beacon to the world."

"The city was at that moment," wrote Nigel Gosling in *Paris 1900-1914 The Miraculous Years,* "the vessel which held the whole of western civilization within its twenty arrondissements."

On this drizzly dawn of the 20th century, Paris did not know it was living in the Belle Époque. That nostalgic name was coined later, once the years of the Third Republic, stretching without a European conflict from the end of the Franco-Prussian War and Commune (1870-71) to the beginning of World War One (1913), were over. It was an "Empire without an Emperor," as the saying then went, for the vast majority a suffocating, hidebound, class-conscious world, but also a world on the brink of profound change.

In the year 1900 no one yet spoke of Art Nouveau, either. Originally the term designated a design boutique, opened in Paris by Englishman Siegfried Bing to sell avant-garde furnishings by William Morris in what people called The Liberty Style.

Even the term *fin-de-siècle* meant just that – "end of the century." Still to be invented – by later generations – were the compound adjective's iffy connotations: delirious decadence, tortuous mores and manners, an attitude and world-view that matched the riotous, creeping tendrils of the period's politics, social strictures, art, architecture and literature.

On that cool January morning of 1900 most Parisians were simply too busy staying alive in their own age to worry about what "fin-de-siècle" might mean. Even the writer whose work now exemplifies the period for us, Proust, was then only nineteen and had not yet written a single line of his sinuous prose.

Then as now, everything and its opposite were possible. Paris at the turn of the last century, as writer Hubert Juin notes in *Le Livre de Paris 1900*, was a "Janus city." Like the twin-headed Roman god of thresholds, of beginnings, it looked backward to the 19th century and forward to something it vaguely and uneasily thought of as *la modernité*.

Today's living memory stretches back to the 1920s, perhaps as far back as World War One, but even a centenarian could not remember for us the mood and events of the year 1900. So while much of the physical city of fin-de-siècle Paris remains, in this 21st century of ours we are cut off from personal recollections. We must rely on documents to usher us into this recent past.

To feel what it was like to wake up on January 1, 1900, and throw open the shutters on this strangely familiar city, I headed to the Bibliothèque Historique de la Ville de Paris, the city's historical library, housed in the 16th-century Hôtel de Lamoignon. After the ritual to-and-fro, I convinced the head librarian there to allow me to peruse several newspapers printed that New Year's day over a century ago. Alas, *Le Temps* had disappeared and *Le Petit Journal* was too fragile to touch. But if I was very careful I could have a look at *Le Figaro*.

The leather spine of the huge volume containing the year's *Figaro* had crumbled. The brittle newsprint had an orange cast and reeked of antique dust. Fittingly, that first day of a workaday century was a Monday. The paper's front page featured six columns. Two on the left were occupied by *Le Soldat-Labourer*, an editorial on France's colonial empire. The empire stretched then from Africa to Asia. The editorialist asked "will we be able to administer our domain so that our growing wealth and power will not, in future, occasion our ruin?"

A small item in the fourth column titled *Hors Paris* gave news of the steamboats sailing from Marseilles to Sudan or Tonkin. *Les Échos* informed Parisians that the high-pressure system would continue, with temperatures in the capital of 5C, 16C in Biarritz and –14C in Moscow. *A Travers Paris* announced the successful crossing of the Sahara by Foureau-Lamy; recounted the Prime Minister's Christmas shopping spree; and listed the heads of Paris' five academies. Finally, the Automobile Club de France, recently formed, made a membership appeal to owners of *voitures sans chevaux* – horseless carriages.

Much of the paper's far right column concerned the latest discoveries at the Institut Pasteur in the field of blood cells, aging and sclerosis.

At last my eye fell upon the half-page, column-five piece titled *L'an*

1 du XXème siècle. The writer's principal concern was to determine whether this was the first year of the 20th or last year of the 19th century. His reasoning was as follows: if you count from the birth of Jesus Christ, the last year of the first century was 100, not 99, so that 101 A.D. (and not 100 A.D.) was the first year of the second century. Therefore 1900 was the last year of the 19th century. "To say the contrary is as absurd as saying the 31st of December is the first day of the next year," he concluded. "If only it were true that 99 was 100, then 2 times 99 = 198 and not 200, and so forth, so that at the end of 1,000 years the world would be 10 years younger!"

Amusingly, in J.F. MacDonald's *Paris of the Parisians* (published in 1900), which I came across later that day, the essay *Nouvelle Affaire!* detailed this same debate raging in Latin Quarter cafés throughout early 1900. Habitués were divided into two hostile camps, "new-century men" versus "old-century men." All discussions began with the challenge "What's your age, sir?" If you stated you were thirty, one group would agree while the others would shout, "Ah no, you're twenty-nine!"

I flipped to the January 2, 1900 issue of *Le Figaro* and discovered a report on a mathematician who, at an unnamed café, calmly demonstrated that the old-century, new-century debate was simply a question of *arithmetic* or *chronology*. The article ended "and the two men came to blows..."

Pure silliness? Probably not. Old-century men were inclined to look back with horror or delight to the Dreyfus Affair; the Panama Canal scandal that ruined countless French shareholders; the loss of Alsace and Lorraine to Prussia; the Commune (17,000 dead in Paris, most of them rebellious poor, in a matter of weeks); the fall of the Divine Right kings and the end of Enlightened Emperors; the rise of organized labor; the composition of salons and café-society rivalries; the death of Delacroix and Victor Hugo.

New-century men spoke of the Exposition, of electricity, of horseless carriages, of the Lumière Brothers' moving pictures, of further colonial domination and economic expansion, of Cézanne, Caillebotte and Jules Verne.

But that is too neat a picture. These were the anything-goes days of *Le parti opportuniste* – a political party whose credo was to leap at every opportunity that arose (only later was the term "opportunist" freighted with negatives). Some monarchists were in fact progressive, and some progressives were anti-Semites and distrusted democracy. Then as now the political left and right blurred.

In the same way that many Parisians of 1900 looked back fondly on the days of the Ancien Régime or the First and Second Empires, conveniently forgetting the misery and bloodshed, today the distorting lens of nostalgia does not encourage us to look clearly at the disconcerting complexity of that 1900, turn-of-the-century, fin-de-siècle Paris.

Belle Époque? Yes, for the happy few, perhaps, most of them men: the world was a man's place. Even rich or noble women could not vote. A single woman lawyer, the first in France, was admitted to the Paris bar in 1900. Working women, men and children alike were lucky if they spent only sixty or seventy hours a week in sweatshops and factories. Newspapers and popular magazines gave advice to the middle classes on how to manage their servants, how to keep them from stealing, moonlighting or indulging in prostitution.

Prostitution was a way of life for servants, dancers, models and seamstresses – the quaint figures of all those Degas' canvases we now love – because their salaries could not feed, house and clothe them. Today most people have forgotten that in 1900 *le mal du siècle* was not some philosophical unease. It referred to syphilis, incurable then, the scourge of everyone from Émile Zola's fictional heroine Nana, to countless real life men and women of all classes, including Gustave Flaubert and Freidrich Nietszche (both died of it). Sexual repression and licentiousness literally went hand-in-glove: some titillating 1900 models for object-women reached above the elbow and had thirty-two buttons on each glove.

It was in the Belle Époque that the upper classes in particular, frustrated by the stifling customs of the Second Empire and Third Republic, began experimenting with their sexuality. Orgies, Sapphism, pederasty and cross-dressing became fashionable not only with the so-called *hors natures* but also among straight women and men. Absinthe, ether and alcohol – as captured by Toulouse Lautrec, Picasso and others – were the drugs of choice both in private and at the city's cafés, bars and music halls.

As regards the quality of life in what we now think of as the quiet, genteel Belle Époque, Hubert Juin provides a fascinating statistic. On a single day in 1900 some 60,000 vehicles, 70,000 horses and 400,000 pedestrians crossed the Place de l'Opéra. In the course of the year, 150 people were killed and 12,000 injured by horses and streetcars in Paris alone. Readers of Proust will recall how in *Swann in Love* the desperate Swann wishes his debauched démi-monde lover Odette de Crécy (mistress of men and women alike) would conveniently die in a traffic accident, so dangerous was it merely to step down from her carriage. Street cobbles were made of wood not for aesthetics or safety but in a mostly unsuccessful attempt to attenuate the nightmarish noise of metal-rimmed carriage wheels.

The Seine? A picturesque river dotted with sailboats, indeed, but also an open sewer: garbage collectors dumped their loads into the river from the Pont des Arts.

It was this mixture of wealth and misery, of forward-looking optimism and retrograde nostalgia that somehow transformed Paris in 1900 into a crucible of creativity and a magnet for the world's greatest talents.

With that thought in mind I resolved to revisit a handful of my favorite 1900 Paris locales. Near a café called Le Paris-Londres, on the Place de la Madeleine, I took the spiraling staircase down to the famous subterranean Art Nouveau *toilettes publiques*, a lavish cavern of carved wood, brass and mirrors, with floral frescos and stained glass windows in each *cabinet*. I awoke the sleeping Madame Pipì, as the French still coyly call bathroom attendants, and once I'd tidied up as a fin-de-siècle gentleman would've, I set off for one of my regular Paris haunts, the Gustave Moreau Museum.

Though built in the mid-1800s, this house-atelier of the mad symbolist painter (much admired by everyone from Klimt to Picasso) has remained largely unaltered since Moreau's death in 1898. Prominently displayed was the jewel-like, gold-embossed rendition of the temptress Salomé – perhaps Moreau's most famous painting, an icon of what fin-de-siècle men thought of dangerous, Siren women.

A half-mile away from the museum, in the Rue du Faubourg Montmartre, I peeked into Chartier, surely one of Paris' most handsome turn-of-the-century restaurants, specifically designed for a working-class clientele. Beneath an immense skylight hang brass chandeliers with white glass globes. There are brass coat racks and carved panels, bentwood chairs, vast mirrors and kitsch paintings. A century after it opened, the same kind of food is still on the handwritten menu, presumably because Parisians still like it.

Another quarter mile east is a second Belle Époque gastronomic institution, Julien, built for the 1889 Exposition Universelle. With its lapis lazuli peacocks, stained-glass skylights and rampant floral-theme plasterwork it's the prototype of the period's architecture. Here, too, the food hasn't changed much and neither has the bustling, smoky atmosphere.

It was too early to have dinner, but a coffee at Angélina, on the Rue de Rivoli, seemed to me like a good idea. Unchanged since 1903 (except for a few Art Déco lamps from the 1930s, and a change in the color of the upholstery), this temple of straight-laced *gourmandise* used to be Coco Chanel and Marcel Proust's hangout, though the plaster-encrusted mirrors now reflect a distinctly New World and Asiatic clientele.

While sipping my coffee I thought about all the places in Paris I could visit if I continued my whirlwind 1900 tour. There was La Pagode, the crazy movie theater made from a Japanese pagoda and opened in 1896, and of course the 1900 Grévin museum with its theater. Forget the waxworks housed there; the Palais des Mirages, a mirrored hall hung with sculpted elephant heads and snakes, with Fée de l'Electricité lighting, was rescued from the 1900 Exposition Universelle and has been displayed here ever since.

What else was there from the year 1900? The daunting list of sights seemed to stretch forever, from the Samaritaine and BHV department stores to thousands of buildings lining the streets. The list was as infinite, in fact, as the city's seemingly endless turn-of-the-century boulevards. Baron Haussmann's creative destruction of Paris may have begun in the Second Empire (1853-1870) under Napoléon III, but it was still underway in 1900. No, there was no easy way to draw a line and say, here the 19th-century ended, and here the 20th began, just as today it's impossible to say oh, how clean a break we've made with December 31, 1999.

Hungry by now, I decided to ride the *métro* again, down to the Gare de Lyon, and dine there at Le Train Bleu. Both the train station and its luxurious upstairs restaurant were built, like the subway, for the 1900 Exposition Universelle. Unlike the subway and station, however, Le Train Bleu, a landmark, really has not changed.

A dizzying pantheon of plasterwork putti, overflowing amphorae, and fruit-and-floral garlands cling to the heavily gilded neo-Rococo ceiling. Brass, cut-crystal and carved wood, framed by painted panels showing destinations served by the trains on the tracks below, round out the décor of the dining room, which is a hundred yards long. I settled into a comfortable booth in what is one of the city's only authentic non-smoking sections with a view (not of toilets) and, after tucking into a Belle Époque dish of *sole meunière* washed down with a bottle of cool Sancerre, everything became clear. Why were Parisians and visitors obsessed with 1900 and the Belle Époque? The answer was easy: because many people are still living in the period.

As we see the portals of the year 2000 receding in our rear-view mirrors, the two-faced god of thresholds seems to be staring fixedly at a bygone Paris, unwilling or unable to shake off the past. Perhaps Janus is merely reminding us that in this old Europe of which Paris is still the cultural capital, to look forward we must first look back.

Reflection of merry-go-round, Tuileries, 1999

La Ville Lumière
Paris, City of Light

"Museum cities are like old cocottes–only fit to be seen in a soft light."
Robert Doisneau, 1989

Webster's defines "cliché" as a "trite expression" and "trite" as "worn out by constant use." Happily, the title *Ville Lumière* or City of Light is neither a cliché nor trite. Though it is constantly used in reference to Paris, it has become a nickname, a sobriquet, an endearment.

For me, the images it evokes are rooted in history yet very much alive.

Say *Ville Lumière* and some will see old-fashioned street lamps spilling pools of light along the Seine where lovers stroll hand in hand. Others will think of the Champs-Elysées and Eiffel Tower ablaze. Still others will envision night-lit monuments perched on hills – the Panthéon, Sacré Coeur, Trocadéro – and a cityscape bathed in an otherworldly glow.

Personally I've often imagined the expression had more to do with the welcoming lights of the city's cafés, its bookshops, museums and universities, where minds meet and tongues wag into the night.

Professors and philosophers like to say that the appellation *Ville Lumière* isn't about physical sources of light at all. Rather it's a metaphor for political, spiritual, cultural and intellectual energy. Louis XIV, an enlightened despot, was known as the Sun King (though he abandoned luminous Paris for swampy Versailles). The 18th-century's Enlightenment found fertile ground here for its philosophical, social and political ideals: empiricism, skepticism, tolerance and social responsibility. Voltaire, Diderot, Jean-Jacques Rousseau and other proponents were called *les lumières*.

In his writings on the French Revolution, historian Jules Michelet (1798-1874) was probably the first to call Paris *la Lumière du Monde* – Light of the World, a beacon for humanity. During Michelet's lifetime, Paris underwent radical change: its population more than doubled. By the second half of the 19th century (starting with the Second Empire in

1852), Paris had indeed become the most stimulating, the most modern and best loved of European cities.

In some ways it was an ideal city, a military man's Utopia conceived by Emperor Napoléon III and engineered by his prefect Baron Haussmann. It was anything but ideal, though, for nostalgics or romantics. In *Les Fleurs du Mal* and other works, Charles Baudelaire scented death and urban anguish in Haussmannization – the radical modernization that resulted in the demolition of the medieval city. "Old Paris is gone," Baudelaire wrote in *The Swan*. "No human heart changes half as fast as a city's face."

Haussmann's was an ideal cosmopolis for those who believed in order, uniformity, and the hygienic properties of open air and sunlight. At Napoléon III's behest, the prefect brought down some 25,000 buildings in fewer than twenty years. Broad cannon-shot boulevards and regular street alignments with uniform facades rose where a tangle of dark alleys had once been.

With few exceptions the Impressionists and early photographers who documented this remade world were fascinated by its novel cityscapes and seemingly endless perspectives. They sought above all to capture the effects of a new kind of light that was at once physical and spiritual. It was the light that sifted through the trees planted on the new boulevards. Or the light cast by the hundreds of *réverbère* gas lamps installed in the 1860s on the sidewalks of those boulevards. Light streamed into the tall french windows of modern buildings. Lights burned round the clock in the new cafés, theaters and train stations that sprang up all over town. By association, *la lumière* was also the enlightened attitude of the inhabitants of this marvelous new world.

The late 19th-century's Universal Expositions, in particular that of 1889, which marked the centennial of the Révolution and the building of the Eiffel Tower, seemed at the time to herald a new age of technological progress and scientific reason in parallel to the artistic flowering of the Belle Époque. We may marvel today at their ingenuousness, but most of the spectators of all classes and walks of life who crowded around to watch the Tour Eiffel's inauguration in 1889 were astonished, transfixed and delighted. The world's tallest structure, it was lit by 10,000 gas lamps. Fireworks and blazing illuminations drew the spectator's eye to various levels. A pair of powerful electric searchlights – among the earliest of their kind – raked the city's monuments from the summit at a height of 984 feet. Some say it was this signal event that engendered the name *Ville Lumière*, but there is no written record to prove it.

Admittedly not everyone was bowled over by the tower, its lighting display or what it stood for. Caricatures and political cartoons of the period show strollers shading their eyes at night, blinded by Paris' newfound modernity. One cartoon's caption noted that from then on, people would need to use seeing-eye dogs to go out for an evening stroll. By the 1890s, most of the city's gas lamps had already been replaced by even brighter electric lighting (though the last gas *réverbère* in central Paris was removed only in 1952, and one still exists, just outside the city limits).

It's no surprise then that at the Belle Epoque's zenith, which coincided with the *Exposition Universelle* of 1900 and its further technical wonders, a novelist named Camille Mauclair wrote a book titled *La Ville Lumière* – City of Light. This is the earliest documented use of the term as applied to Paris. The book was published in 1904 and has been out of print for decades. No one seems to remember precisely what it was about. Georges Frechet, *conservateur* at the Bibliothèque Historique de la Ville de Paris, has suggested that the novel probably drew inspiration for its title and content from both the 1900 Universal Exposition (one of the exhibits, La Fée Electricité, was a celebration of the miracle of electricity) and the intellectual ferment generated by the period's artists, performers and writers, Stéphane Mallarmé foremost among them.

But what of the actual lighting of Paris? Though it has been "modernized" repeatedly, Paris intra-muros – meaning the city within the Boulevard Périphérique beltway – retains many Second Empire features. Other than minor damage in 1870-71 caused by the Franco-Prussian War and Commune struggle, it was never bombed or burned. Real estate speculation has caused the greatest damage.

But this apparent changelessness goes beyond the physical. Jean-Paul Sartre described Baudelaire as a man who "chose to advance backwards with his face turned toward the past." In many ways the same can be said of the city and many of the people who reside in it. With all due respect to the memory of photographer Robert Doisneau, Paris isn't a "museum city" yet – and is far from dead. But the weight of history, institutions and above all culture forces inhabitants to glance back while moving forward.

Sartre's observation seems particularly apt when applied to the nuts-and-bolts of lighting the Ville Lumière, and the philosophy, if one can call it that, underlying the myriad of light-related technical and bureaucratic constraints at work. For a down-to-earth example, consider the many light fixtures on Paris streets that were installed before or during the Second Empire. Haussmann-style lamps are still manufactured today. There are also Art Nouveau fixtures and others added in the 1930s. Are they obsolete? No one would dream of removing them. Why? Atmosphere. The atmosphere Paris' old-fashioned lamps create is warm, welcoming and infused with nostalgia. Nostalgia is both a state of mind and a cultural ID card. No other city goes to such lengths to create a retro "light-identity", an ambience that immediately declares, "You're in Paris, the City of Light." In many places you could be walking alongside Baudelaire or Brassaï or Sartre through a crepuscular time tunnel.

This is something most residents and visitors alike take for granted. But behind the scenes, a score of *éclairagistes* and *concepteurs-lumières* (lighting designers) – plus architects, engineers and some 400 technicians – are hard at work round the clock creating Paris' evening magic.

Raise your eyes from just about anywhere in town and you'll see how lighting designer Pierre Bideau has illuminated the Eiffel Tower with hundreds of small sodium lamps. The tower's golden lacework glows from within, recalling the gas lighting of 1889. Louis Clair has turned the church of Saint-Eustache (at Les Halles) into a magic lantern, with light tracing the flying buttresses and spilling outward through stained glass windows. Clair's delicate lighting of the Rotonde de la Villette underscores the curves and colonnades of architect Claude-Nicolas Ledoux's fanciful 18th-century canal-side customs house.

Roger Narboni and Italo Rota – two other bright stars in the French lighting firmament – have worked together or separately to capture with lights the physical and spiritual essence of Notre-Dame cathedral, the Louvre, a handful of bridges over the Seine, and famous avenues such as the Champs-Elysées. But there are dozens of other equally impressive night-time scenes: the Place Vendôme and its storied facades look to me like a stage set; the fountains of the Place de la Concorde or the Boulevard Richard-Lenoir splash both water and light.

What these projects share, their planners assure, is the goal of bringing forth the history and symbolism of each site. Flamboyant or experimental lighting displays that might seem marvelous in America, for example, simply don't work here on anything more than a temporary basis. True, avant-garde French light-sculptors like Yan Kersalé do create works in Paris for special occasions (July 14th extravaganzas, bicentennials and so forth). And many French lighting designers rightly consider themselves artists or *créateurs*. But for them to succeed here, their talents must be solidly anchored to the city's multi-layered historical reality. To transpose Sartre's celebrated description of Baudelaire – moving forward with his eyes on history – they must light the future by illuminating the past.

"If you don't know exactly where you're going, at least you can look back to the past and form some ideas," said François Jousse, musing about the Parisian worldview in general and how it applies to lighting in particular. Jousse is the chief engineer of Paris' municipal lighting and street maintenance department, a title that describes only a few of his functions. I met him at his office in a nondescript building near Paris' beltway.

Modest yet contagiously jovial, the bushy-bearded Jousse is famous among French lighting professionals for his expertise on everything from the performance of electric bulbs to the philosophy of monument illumination or the history of lighting since Antiquity. Indeed if any one person is responsible for setting the city's nocturnal mood it's Jousse.

Individual monuments, buildings and bridges may take on a beautiful sculptural quality at night, Jousse readily admitted to me, but what most intrigues him is the night-lit city as a physical, spiritual and emotional whole – the grand display case of Paris and its lifestyles. "Drive into town at night from the suburbs and you feel the difference immediately," he told me, his eyes twinkling. "From the linear, traffic-oriented lights leading you through and out of the suburbs you enter the floating blanket of Paris light – a destination, a place, the arrival point." He stroked his beard and leaned back into his unfashionable office chair, readying himself for a stroll through centuries past.

As far back as the Middle Ages, lanterns or candles marked the city limits and the three most strategic points in town, Jousse explained. They were above all symbolic: the Louvre's Royal Palace; the Tour de Nesle (a watchtower that once stood on the Seine); and the cemetery of the Saints Innocents, a favorite meeting place near Les Halles for thugs and lovers. Over the years, oil lamps were added around town. But it was the Sun King who lived up to his title and in 1669 inaugurated the first systematic public lighting scheme (he even had a commemorative lantern medal minted to celebrate it). By the 1780s, a pulley system had been devised to hang new, elegant lamps over the streets. And then came *le déluge* of 1789. "The refrain in the Revolutionaries' song *Ah! ça ira* is all about hoisting aristocrats from the lampposts," Jousse laughed. "And those new pulleys came in very handy."

Paris' nighttime identity as we know it today was largely defined with the advent of modern outdoor lighting in the mid-19th century. Ever since, the city's street lamps have been erected at the same heights: 6, 9 or 12 meters (the Champs-Elysées' new fixtures, designed by Jean-Michel Wilmotte, are exceptions at 11.5 meters). Lampposts are staggered along the sidewalks on both sides of the street to create overlapping, gentle pools of light. The light laps at the buildings and hints at the roofline above the tops of the posts. The overall effect is to give Paris a human dimension, making it an inviting yet safe place to enjoy after the sun goes down.

"It's the little things I like most," said Jousse, echoing the sentiments of many Parisians. "For example, there's a 19th-century wall fountain on the Rue de Turenne not far from the Place des Vosges that no one notices during the day. Even at night, drivers don't see it. But when it's lit with two small spots, it's a wonderful discovery for strollers."

Beyond the poetry and aesthetics, skillful lighting is one way to diminish vandalism in rough neighborhoods. Jousse is proud that since his technicians have illuminated a contemporary sculpture in the 18th arrondissement's notorious Goutte d'Or quarter near Barbès, the locals have adopted it as their own. At the Porte de Clignancourt, under the sinister spaghetti bowl of freeways where the city's main flea market is held, Jousse and his lighting technicians have lit a wall that was erected as a safety measure, to divide a wide sidewalk. Now, instead of being viewed as an ugly obstacle, the wall is a noctambulist's landmark, a kind of luminous welcome mat on the city's edge.

Half a dozen other cities probably have more and brighter lights than Paris. New York is a forest of flaming skyscrapers and throbbing, colored bands. Parts of Tokyo and Berlin look like immense, garish outdoor advertisements, the objective correlatives of our consumerist age. These forward-looking cities also sparkle as among the world's great artistic, intellectual and economic centers. Yet no one would dream of calling any of the three the City of Light, and not only because Paris claimed the title a century ago. There's another, intangible reason.

Something about the city's quality of life, the skeptical outlook of so many residents, and the sparkling yet sardonic essence of Paris, makes the name *Ville Lumière* ring true. So even if it sounds like a cliché to some, others – including me – will go on using it for as long as the city shines.

Statue, Tuileries, 1994

Philosophy au Lait

"Yesterday it was Jurassic Park; tomorrow will it be Homo-Sapiens Park?"
Budding philosopher at the Café des Phares

"I think, therefore I drink," quipped my studious-looking neighbor at the Café des Phares, the so-called Philosophy Café whose terrace spills onto the Place de la Bastille. "One *petit crème* for the *petit* Descartes," chuckled a nearby jokester as the waiter turned to me.

"Monsieur?"

I wrung my memory for a clever *mot* – from Plato perhaps – with which to order my late-Sunday-morning coffee. "An *express* to raise me out of the Cave of Illusions," I said, blushing. The waiter moved off without batting an eye. As always, the café's small round tables were elbow-to-elbow in a blue fog of cigarette smoke. The day's newspapers hung from sticks. Mirrors quivered with humanity. It was the archetypal Paris café scene, of the kind abhored by those who wish the city and its residents would stop living with one foot in a sepia photograph. I glanced outside and couldn't help smiling at the beehive formation of latecomers thronging the sidewalk, trying to get in.

The Café des Phares' name means "lighthouse" and the symbolism of its storming-of-the-Bastille location is lost on few. It is the mothership that spawned dozens of *Philocafés* in Paris, the provinces and abroad (in Europe, Japan and America).

The concept – an open-mike, improvised public debate on philosophical quandaries – was the brainchild of the late Marc Sautet, a would-be professor alienated by the French university system. His goal was to make philosophy accessible to everyone, highlight its cathartic and therapeutic value, and earn a living. Predictably when the permatanned, blue-eyed Philosopher King took the Bastille by storm he was savaged by the press, and by mainstream philosophers ("nonsense propagated by a sophist..."), few of whom could be troubled to participate in his 11am Sunday salons. Undaunted, Sautet published the book *Un café pour Socrate* and, perhaps inspired by Lucy and Snoopy, hung his shingle on a *Cabinet de Philosophie* at a chic Marais address. Soon dozens of philo-moderators, some with impressive academic credentials, were leading enthusiastic if motley groups of apprentice philosophers across the country.

Sautet's apotheosis came when he and best-selling philosophy writers Jean-Luc Marion, André Comte-Sponville and Luc Ferry were guests on culture arbiter Bernard Pivot's then-popular TV show *Bouillon de Culture*. Philosophy is a perennial favorite in France: high school students study it and their Bac graduation exam questions make front-page news. Radical-chic, telegenic Nouveaux Philosophes such as Bernard Hénri-Levy – BHL for short – have even made "philo-films" (BHL's credits include *Le Jour et la Nuit,* widely considered one of cinema history's all-time dogs).

To Academe, though, Philocafés remain suspect, a plebian Collège de France (where distinguished professors lecture, free, to the rapt and reverent, most of them retirees). Instead of welcoming the maverick Sautet and his adepts, France's legions of savants began lacerating themselves over the *succès de scandal* of the *Phénomène Philocafé*. Was it, they asked earnestly, because the Age of Ideology died in 1989 with the fall of the Berlin Wall? Or could it be a manifestation of "collective despair" linked to globalization, waning family values and chronically high unemployment? Perhaps it signaled a fin-de-siècle crisis of the spirit, the conjugation of lost piety and the advent of the Second Millennium, or a revolution against "Anglo-Saxon values" embodied in commercial TV, the movies and the Internet?

Strangely, few French intellectuals asked themselves whether the popularity of philosophy cafés could be put down to the simple fact that they offer good, ribald fun, in keeping with the best Parisian café tradition. That is precisely what you sense on a Sunday morning at the Café des Phares, still the city's liveliest Philocafé after over a decade of tongue wagging. The ritual pecking of cheeks and passing of cigarette packs starts at 10am, when several dozen regulars show up to make sure they'll find a spot inside, near the bar. That's where the action is. A hundred or more casual participants ebb and flow between the bar and the sidewalk terrace, where they hear the debate through loudspeakers. Cellular telephones disappear as budding philosophers brandish their notepads and reference books – everything from Plato's *Republic* to Heidegger's *Sein und Zeit,* Sartre, Foucault, Camus, the Larousse dictionary, even The Bible.

At the appointed hour a philo-moderator rises to his feet, tests the mike and, in consultation with a roundtable of regulars, sets about finding the theme of the day. It's like a college-town literature workshop and a Quaker meeting rolled into one, with a pinch of Karaoke and a splash of pop-psych.

"Yesterday it was Jurassic Park," suggested the first speaker, "tomorrow will it be Homo-Sapiens Park?" The theme was met by baffled groans.

"Nothing is to be hoped for, everything is to be experienced," offered another speaker. More grumbling from the peanut gallery.

"Could it be that unemployment isn't a problem, but rather a solution?" asked a provocative old Hippie. This quandary, too, was discarded. Too political.

Meanwhile coffee and beer were floating by on trays, and a Philocafé regular had begun squeezing between the tables, hawking a stack of *Philos*, a monthly newsletter justly celebrated for its turgid, impenetrable prose. "All roads lead to Rome," warbled the moderator's disembodied voice through the mike. "How about considering the real meaning of this ancient saying?"

The question seemed genial enough so was accepted as the theme of the day.

"Because of the Paris marathon," began an eager woman, "it took me two hours to get here this morning, and I thought to myself, traveling toward an objective is sometimes difficult, so perhaps the hidden meaning in 'all roads lead to Rome' is that if you try hard enough you can reach your goal...."

"Rome meaning the seat of all power?" asked someone.

"The Vatican? The church? A symbol of oppression?" questioned a second.

"The incarnation of totalitarian moralism, the first manifestation of religious globalism..."

"This evokes the schism of the Popes in Avignon, and is anti-papal..."

"Nonsense! The quote is much older, it refers to Imperial Rome!"

Soon the debate was rolling along, the mike passing from hand to hand. A pipe-smoking professor with wrinkled trousers had his say, then a bird-boned sophisticate wearing a Hèrmes scarf. "All roads lead to infinity," quipped a youngster hidden by the cigarette and pipe smoke, "Rome is finite, therefore the saying isn't valid!"

The permutations of this millennial cliché turned out to be manifold. Roads are experience and all experience is valid. Roads are the ways of the Lord, and they're unknowable. Rome is shorthand for beauty, love, art and death, and all roads lead to death, preferably via sex. The road to knowledge passes through sin, Rome is sin, therefore.... A bookish man quoted 16th-century chronicler Montaigne ("By different means we arrive at the same end") while an irreverent wit paraphrased Jorge Luis Borges ("If you put a monkey at a typewriter for eternity sooner or later he'll write Shakespeare's entire oeuvre"). Things were beginning to spin out of control. Someone I couldn't see started a convoluted philosophical argument but lost his train of thought, stuttering and spluttering like a motorcycle out of gas. Amid cruel mocking the mike passed to the next apprentice philosopher.

"All roads lead to sex," said a Rabelaisian man in his thirties, picking up the libidinous sub-text abandoned earlier.

"All roads, or just sex-tions of them?" teased a voice. "Errantry or Eros?"

"In the dark, all women are beautiful!"

"And all men are desirable!"

A handsome young fellow in a tweed jacket made eyes at the soulful-looking young woman across from him. She rewarded him with a coy smile and a riffle of her notepad. Several other potential couples chatted away, oblivious to the debate. Eventually the moderator's voice of reason intervened to put things back on track. My neighbor leaned over and remarked, "Isn't this silly and pretentious?" Before I could answer a gaunt intellectual leaned over me from the other side and sniffed, "It lacks rigor, it isn't philosophy at all." Just then a middle-aged woman with a blonde bouffant pushed by, loaded with groceries from the Boulevard Richard Lenoir outdoor market whose stands I could see across the square. The smell of ripe cheese wafted up as she reached for the mike. "She's been haggling over chickens and eggs," quipped my jocular neighbor, suppressing hilarity. Suddenly a roller-skating teenager slalomed past, crashing into a table before being rescued by her philo-mom.

Finally an authoritative voice with a distinctly Italian accent began thundering through the microphone like an opera singer. "So far the lesson," he sang, "seems to be that any sentence can lead us all anywhere!" A collective guffaw went up, and by the time I managed to flag a waiter, several couples had been formed, strangers had laughed, argued, triumphed and failed together, and lots of drinks had been sold. At their worst Philocafés are innocuous, I decided. Posing, and pretentious philo-babble, never hurt anyone, after all. At their best they can be stimulating and fun. In any case they're money-spinners. *"Ça tourne rond,"* beamed my waiter as I paid for two distinctly upscale espressos. The babble is good for business.

Dog at a bistro table, 2004

The Michelin Man Cometh: The Star System

"The citizen these days worries about only two things, panem et circenses *(food and entertainment)."*

Juvenal, AD 60-130

"Qu'ils mangent de la brioche (Let them eat cake)."

Marie Antoinette, 1755-1793

"Twenty-five," said the baker knocking baguette flour off his apron. "Twenty-five?" queried the pudgy Frenchman in line in front of me.

Across the street at the neighborhood café I usually go to I heard a similar refrain. "Twenty-five?" "Twenty-five!"

As I strolled amid the pyramids of spring onions and hothouse melons at the Boulevard de Ménilmontant open market a butcher reluctantly left his morning copy of *Le Parisien* and cleaved some meat for a moist-eyed man who looked like a walking pork chop. "See, there are twenty-five this year," said the pork chop. "Maybe the ratings aren't fixed after all." The butcher grunted and shook his head: he wasn't convinced.

These Parisian gourmands were not talking about soccer league standings or a rugby score. The magic number they were evoking could be twenty-five one year, twenty-three or twenty-six the next. Their coded language was in fact a telegraphic reference to the total number of restaurants in France with three Michelin stars.

As happens every March, the news was on the radio, on TV, in all the papers and on the collective tongue of the capital: the Michelin red guide to hotels and restaurants in France had arrived. Michelin: the bible of gastronomes, assembled by an unknown number of secretive inspectors who prowl the country in search not only of humbug and bedbugs but also of the Delicious, the Luxurious and the Sublime. After a long and fraught winter, few things re-ignite the fires of French foodies – and even normal citizens – quite like it.

Each March or late February I make my rounds of the same butt-littered cafés, listening for the predictable Gallic reactions to the guide's release. Barmen, chefs, gourmets, bakers, candlestick makers, food purveyors and publishers (in search of lucrative cookbook contracts) wait with salivating trepidation for the news. Though it also lists hotels the real attention-grabbers are the establishments that belong to the so-called Michelin Star System. Officially the guide has this to say about the awarding of stars: three stars mean "exceptional cuisine, worth a special journey"; two stars signify "excellent cooking, worth a detour"; and one star denotes "a very good restaurant in its category... a good place to stop on your journey."

An alternative reading of these categories, in reverse order, might be: one-star restaurants are nifty little luxury places with noticeably good food and coddle-the-client service; two-stars are seriously luxurious with even fancier food, more waiters and maître d's, and often valets or other personnel in silly outfits to greet you in a private parking lot; three-stars are veritable temples of gastronomy with an army of maître d's, waiters, coat clerks, bathroom attendants, brass polishing brigades and so on, places where you must plead and wheedle far in advance to get a table upon which you may sacrifice hundreds of dollars for a dining experience orchestrated by an artist-chef, an experience that will remain with you for eternity.

The Michelin guide was first published in 1900 for an elite of motorists. Stars – actually asterisks – were introduced in 1926 as an easy-to-spot symbol denoting an outstanding restaurant. The first twenty three-stars were named in 1933, among them Paris' wood-paneled Lucas-Carton, which still has three. Michelin didn't award three stars abroad until 1972, so honoring a place called "Villa Lorraine" in Brussels (it served French food).

The star system can make prestige and profits soar or plummet: fifteen to twenty-five percent for the first star, twenty to sixty percent for the second and third stars. Little wonder that hundreds of chefs make a yearly pilgrimage, toque in hand, to Michelin headquarters in Paris to review their dossier, or that the star system continues to be the annual target of critics, restaurateurs, and enthusiastic eaters who, like me, wonder whether Michelin is qualified to be the arbiter of taste in the French restaurant world.

Ironically this king making comes from the Paris branch of a down-to-earth company whose main business is manufacturing car tires. Back in the 1990s I had the privilege of interviewing the red guide's reclusive director, Bernard Naegellen. Waiting for him at Michelin's headquarters in the Avenue de Breteuil in Paris' old-money 7th arrondissement, I couldn't help wondering what the great chefs, in to consult their dossiers, would make of Michelin's own taste in décor. The lobby had worn tile floors and chairs covered in creased green-and-ochre vinyl, a style that carried over into the room in which I met Naegellen (since then he has retired and been replaced by Derek Brown, an Englishman some French restaurant critics seem to feel is taking the guide in the wrong direction).

Historically the number of three-star restaurants has varied only slightly since the rating was introduced. It fluctuates between twenty and twenty-five. Every Michelin-watcher has a theory (many outlandish) about how the number is determined. The most widely accepted conspiracy theory involves the so-called "Michelin Mafia" of selected chefs, foodies and Michelin inspectors, coordinated by the Mysterious Monsieur Michelin (the red guide's director). It is the director who ultimately decides which restaurants will receive or lose a third star, but his judgments are made in concert with a team of inspectors. He can't merely reward friends or punish the recalcitrant. Stars are given and taken away only after many years of study, and they go to the restaurant, not the chef, despite what most people think. Was the service perfect every day and night? Was the food exquisite – by Michelin standards – to the appropriate degree? How about the plumbing – in good condition we presume.

Nonetheless, many otherwise sane French citizens believe that a chef must die or lose a third star before another chef can get one. Beyond the humiliation of being ushered out of the club, the loss of a third star can cost a chef considerable income (ten to twenty-five percent, it is estimated). Inexorably the international consultations begin to dry up, the TV and radio interviewers are no longer banging on the door and the juicy cookbook and chef-accessory spin-off contracts shrivel. This can add up to millions of dollars.

The solemn, stodgy, glacially slow, humorless and cryptic guide prefers neutral symbols and little descriptive text. It is known to be the opposite of the mercurial, wordy *Gault et Millau* – the country's other big guide, which sells 100,000 copies or so a year. But there is no question that Michelin remains the arbiter of *la grande cuisine* served at *les grandes tables* run by *les grands chefs*. It also happens to be reliable, easy to use and clean: the inspectors appear to be incorruptible.

After a century and then some of publishing, and desirous to update its image and keep the dust off its shoulders, recent editions of the guide have included various proofs of vigor. The first and most welcome was the addition in the Paris section of a list of good-value restaurants identified with the "Bib Gourmand" symbol – a smiling Michelin Tire

Man's face. The Tire Man, as everyone knows, is nicknamed Bibendum, hence the contraction "Bib." The word "gourmand" needs no translation, though it is worth pointing out that this term means "food-loving" and "hearty-eating." It was chosen over "gourmet", which, as in English, means someone with refined gastronomical tastes. Presumably gourmets will continue to go to the starred restaurants while big eaters with smaller wallets will seek out the Bib Gourmands.

In Paris, Bib was a refreshing novelty because the prices here are so high that it's difficult indeed to eat well without being fleeced. It's regrettable but not surprising that the several dozen Bib Gourmand restaurants in the capital and its surroundings offer meals in the $50 range per person without wine. That is cheap by the Bib's standards – this is the upscale Michelin guide, after all.

Despite innovations such as one-line descriptions of starred restaurants, the guide remains steadfastly conservative and France-centric, reflecting the nation's conviction that its cuisine and culinary sensibilities are the best in the world. Otherwise how to explain the fact that, in Paris alone, there are on average as many three-star restaurants as in the Low Countries, Spain and Portugal, and Great Britain-and-Ireland combined? Tiny Switzerland usually has two three-stars (in its French-speaking cantons), while Germany often has none. The Low Countries (meaning, primarily, Francophone Belgium) have three or four, while Great Britain-and-Ireland and Italy each have two or three. Independently of where they are sited, nearly all of these three-star establishments serve French or French-style food and all are expensive and luxurious. The Italian three-stars in particular are the antithesis of everything Italian – meaning the straightforward, simple, market-based, regional cooking for which the country is renowned.

On average fifteen three-stars in the whole of continental Europe, plus Great Britain-and-Ireland, compared to twenty-five or so in France?

The truth is, France's cultural identity is still largely tied to its produce and cooking. A Chinese restaurant no matter how good is not going to get stars unless it makes concessions to French tastes and techniques. A three-star authentically Thai or Indonesian restaurant is inconceivable.

The culinary buzzword of recent years in France is *terroir*, which means not only "soil" as the dictionaries will tell you. It is shorthand for Our Rural Roots and all the Good Things that spring from them, including Wine, Food, Traditions, Regional Accents and Battered Citroën Deux Chevaux automobiles from the Good Old Days. There's even a Salon du Terroir food fair nowadays, held in Paris in November.

Closely related concept-terms are *vin de terroir* (authentic, earthy, quaffable wine) and *cuisine de terroir,* which includes all the above abstractions and substantives, plus wine, wild herbs, their pungent scents, various ethereal ephemerals, and the myriad of interpretations of same provided by chefs and foodies. In other words, *terroir* means pretty much what you want it to mean.

It just so happens that usually, as the Michelin red guides hit the stands in March, the Paris agricultural fair is underway at the Porte de Versailles convention center. Recent editions of the fair have centered on *terroir*, range-raised folksy-ness, traditional food, wine and politics. The unsinkable president Jacques Chirac, surrounded by a dozen salt-of-the-earth ministers of all political formations, attends the fair to press the flesh and chat with his constituents.

Could it be a further coincidence that each spring, countless radio, TV and newspaper reports heatedly discuss French farming, food, wine and the eating habits of the nation? A few years ago I spotted a surprising statistic in *Le Monde*: inhabitants of the Limousin, Aquitaine and Midi-Pyrénées regions which together comprise about one quarter of the country, spend the longest at table over dinner. Happily, French adolescents still eat nearly eighty percent of their dinners at home with their parents and haven't yet been transformed into obese fast food junkies (though the incidence is rising fast). Four out of five French citizens still manage to eat lunch at home every day, and the ratio reaches an astounding nine out of ten for dinner.

Herein lies the real French paradox: if nearly all French men, women and children are eating *terroir* delicacies at home, who's buying all those Michelin guides, theoretically conceived and compiled by and for the French? Michelin's statistics show that of the approximately 600,000 copies sold yearly of the *Guide France,* on average two-thirds are bought in France and one third in the rest of the world. Of the 1.2 million red guides printed yearly (including France and other European countries), about 650,000 are sold abroad – well over fifty percent. The numbers don't tell us the nationality of guide buyers. But look around next time you're at a *grande table* operated by a *grand chef* famous for his *grande cuisine*. The clientele of such establishments is often made up fifty to seventy percent of foreigners, and in some three-star restaurants the ratio is even higher. You'll probably recognize a cousin from Peoria, or perhaps Osaka, at the next table, for despite economic doldrums and a post-9/11 drop, Americans and Japanese still top the list of big spenders. If you're lucky you might meet a French citizen at a three-star who's not a Michelin inspector or a journalist on an expense account, but I wouldn't count on it.

Since about the mid-1990s, the nadir of a major economic slump dubbed *la crise*, pundits in Paris have been asking the distressing question, "Is the age of *haute cuisine* and the *grand restaurant* over?" The corollary is "Has the Michelin guide been left behind?"

This soul-searching turned into a frenzy of unnatural self-deprecation and criticism when celebrity chef Pierre Gagnaire went bankrupt in the depressed industrial city of Saint-Etienne – the first three-star failure since the rating's creation. Gagnaire's became a national *cause célèbre*. Saint-Etienne's mayor remarked that his city did not want "a restaurant charging [the equivalent of $300] for a meal when people cannot find [a couple of dollars] for their children's school lunches."

Following Gagnaire's demise, fellow three-stars Bernard Loiseau in Burgundy (now deceased) and Marc Veyrat on Lake Annecy announced they were barely able to meet the $60-70,000 monthly loan repayments on borrowings of about $7 million each. In pursuit of three-star status they had overspent on remodeling: Veyrat's Auberge de l'Éridan sports bathroom fixtures gold-plated by Rolex and a kitchen sink speckled with real gold (Veyrat eventually got his three stars, and was further rewarded when his second restaurant, La Ferme de Mon Père, in Megève, also received three stars; he and Alain Ducasse became the first chefs in history to each preside over two three-star luxury operations). Loiseau committed suicide in spring 2003 and his huge debts and reported obsessive fear of losing his stars were often given as plausible, though unproven, motives for the tragic act.

Further revelations of near bankruptcy among starred restaurateurs spurred the Ministry of Culture to pass a law officially enshrining celebrity chefs as artists, and adding *grands restaurants* to France's national cultural heritage known as *Le Patrimoine*. Included was an approximately $20,000 start-up subsidy for young, up-and-coming chefs. The measure also provided for controversial government bailouts, with guaranteed loans to failing star chefs via the French Finance Institute for Cinema and Cultural Industries (IFCIC). This is the bureaucracy that subsidizes the French movie industry. *Cinéma d'auteur* was thus flanked by *cuisine d'auteur* – or *cuisine d'hauteur*, as some pundits remarked.

The outcry was immediate: commentators noted that the law might have a boomerang effect by encouraging ambitious chefs to spend even more lavishly on gilded toilets in quest of Michelin stars, knowing they would be bailed out (so far this has not happened). Ironically, while Jacques Chirac's center-right government ostensibly struggled to dismantle bureaucracies, his Culture Minister, goaded on by a group of three-star chefs (Pierre Troisgros, Michel Guérard, Alain Senderens, Georges Blanc and Alain Ducasse) and Alexandre Lazareff (General Director of the National Center of Culinary Arts) created a welfare system for establishments typically charging $150-$300 a head for a meal.

"We can accept the existence of an elitist cuisine," growled French gastronomy's *éminence grise*, Claude Lebey. "But at the least it should be profit-making. At this rate we might as well subsidize Hermès." Even Pierre Gagnaire, whose plight inspired the measure, called it a bad law. "French society is stuck because the government is expected to fix everything," he told me. "That's impossible! To each his own responsibility." Without government help Gagnaire opened a chic restaurant in Paris a year or so after going bankrupt and quickly won back his three stars.

But the most revealing comment came from Philippe Couderc of *Le Nouvel Observateur.* He termed the law "scandalous... a step backwards towards the Ancien Régime." This is not, as it seems, a gratuitous remark: the elevation of food to the rank of art began under Louis XIV, a prodigious gourmand. Marie-Antoinette's more naive than cynical quip – that if the peasants had no more bread then "let them eat brioche" or cake, if you prefer – remains deeply significant. The Revolution was as much about hunger as it was high-minded *Liberté, Egalité* and *Fraternité*. The Bastille was stormed because it was thought to hold not only arms and prisoners, but flour.

The phenomenon of the *grand restaurant*, born in Paris, dates to the French Revolution, when the cooks of ousted aristocrats at the court in Versailles suddenly found themselves out of work and set up independently in the capital. They distinguished themselves with flair from the humble *cuisetots* (cooks) whose repertories were limited to regional peasant dishes. *Cuisine d'auteur* was born. Their restaurants were the forebears of today's starred establishments, where masters of the sauté pan create culinary performance art. As Pierre Gagnaire once told me, when it comes to Michelin stars and celebrity what counts is "the quality and uniqueness of the chef." It isn't enough to cook great food: top chefs must also be performers, selling "dreams" (Loiseau) or "emotions" (Gagnaire).

So why, with such a glorious pedigree, and a record number of them, are France's *grands restaurants* still failing? The reasons are economic and societal. France has been painfully reinventing itself for the last decade or more. To start, the economy has followed others in Europe and elsewhere into what is hoped is merely a cyclical decline. But the country is plagued by chronic high unemployment, low growth and widespread pessimism even in good years. Gourmets who would have gladly spent lavishly on Lucullan feasts back in the boom decades of the 1950s to '80s now think twice, from guilt about conspicuous consumption or because they can no longer afford it.

Less obviously, French-style *cuisine d'auteur* might be the victim of its own success. An export industry, it is, as Pierre Gagnaire says, "widely copied and pillaged." By definition it can be (and is) produced by skilled *auteurs* anywhere – in New York, London or Sydney. France no longer has a monopoly, and Paris may no longer be the center of the gourmet universe. Many of its practitioners are falling behind dynamic chefs in what were once considered barbarian strongholds. Decrypted, that means three-star inflation. It is as if the Federal Reserve systematically printed money to cover America's chronic debt. For France, the tactic does not solve the underlying macro-gastronomic problems.

The Michelin guide may even be indirectly responsible to a degree for the country's culinary crisis: star status can stultify chefs whose livelihood depends on maintaining their stars and who live in fear of change. More worrying, a Michelin-inspired sense of terror, expressed to me by many starred chefs I've spoken to over the years, often leeks its chill into the dining room.

Increasingly, the extravagant decor and starched atmosphere of many multiple-starred restaurants seems out of step with the times. While Michelin continues to reiterate that its stars are "for the cooking, not the décor," and vigorously denies rewarding only luxury establishments, the fact is that I still know of not a single un-luxurious or affordable two- or three-star place.

As to what "luxury" means to Michelin, one former inspector confessed to me that he thought most *grands restaurants* in France were "hideous" and added that one in particular brought to mind "a high-class brothel." A famous restaurant critic I know, who is no enemy of the multiple-star brigade, told me she found several to be "temples of bad taste" and "theme parks of gastronomy." The starchiness is systemic.

I will never forget my last meal at Joël Robuchon's three-star restaurant near Trocadéro (when Robuchon retired Alain Ducasse took it over then moved on, and it has since disappeared). A savvy Japanese gourmet seated across from me ordered a succulent whole roasted free-range guinea fowl with foie gras. When the waiter had boned and served it and was preparing to whisk the carcass away, the frustrated diner snatched it off the platter, fell upon the bones and sucked them provocatively. "The carcass is the best part," he exclaimed in perfect French to the silent, glaring room full of bejeweled ladies and stuffed shirts. It made my meal. Robuchon has since come out of retirement and, tellingly, opened a "casual" restaurant featuring an eclectic world menu, with seating on bar stools – the opposite of his 1980s-1990s luxury hostelries, though still expensive and, frankly, exquisitely pretentious.

There is nothing intrinsically wrong with the fact that many grand Michelin-starred restaurants have become the culinary equivalent of the Loire Chateaux, or the French answer to Disneyland Paris. Alternatively, and especially in Paris, these establishments are businessmen's clubs where corporate managers wine and dine each other. Despite the decline in the business lunch, "there are still people who feel it's worth it to eat in a *grand restaurant* everyday," Gagnaire told me. "Worth it in terms of quality, prestige, PR, business. It's an investment, like buying fine clothes.... The middle class cannot afford to go to these restaurants anymore."

Recognizing that the real competition is from more affordable and informal bistros, some starred chefs began serving home-style dishes back in the late-1990s, or created "baby grand" spin-offs with a bistro theme. Paris is now lousy with "baby bistros." I have yet to be converted. There is nothing more deadly than a faux bistro.

So is the age of the grand Michelin-starred restaurant really over, and will the counting of three-star establishments continue to thrill Parisians each spring? Doubtless the Darwinian shakeout will continue, particularly among expensive provincial restaurants, which are the most endangered. But haute cuisine, like the French language, is an expression of French culture, and is widely perceived in France as a bulwark against "culinary barbarianism." That is coded language for "fast food." Therefore haute cuisine will be preserved no matter what the cost, whether it should be or not.

"It is impossible to separate the future of [French] cuisine from that of [French] society as a whole," wrote Jean-Claude Ribaut in *Le Monde* a few years ago. And his point is still valid. "A strong economy means an accomplished culture and a triumphant table. Michelin once again keeps alive with delectation the memory of a golden age." Ribaut might have added, though, that until the French economy in general and its luxury establishments in particular can live without life support, those distasteful dollars and yen will continue doing their part.

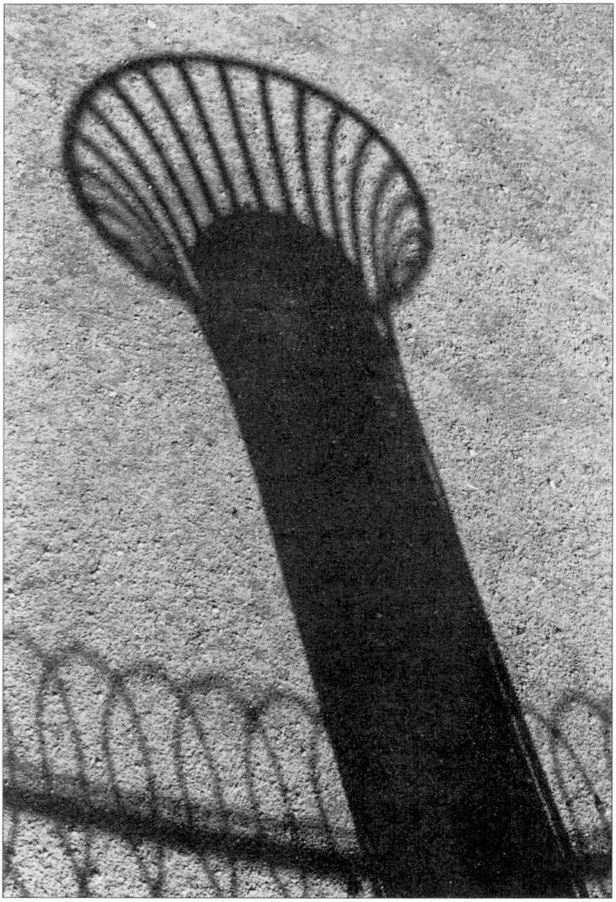

Shadow, Haussmann-era litter basket and wire fence, 1995

Sidewalk Sundae

"Give Parisians water, fresh air and shade!"
Claude Barthelot, Comte de Rambuteau, prefect of Paris, 1830

"[For the 'collective' masses] glossy enamelled shop signs are a wall decoration as good as, if not better than, an oil painting in the drawing room of a bourgeois; walls with their 'Post No Bills' are its writing desk, newspaper stands its libraries, mailboxes its busts, benches its bedroom furniture, and the café terrace is the balcony from which it looks down on its household."
Walter Benjamin, 1934

Say "Paris" and with the predictability of Pavlov's dog millions the world round will bark "Eiffel Tower", "Musée d'Orsay" or "Louvre." For many people, monuments and museums define what the French capital is all about. For me monuments are navigational tools in a cityscape whose character manifests itself in humble, vernacular realities: the alignment of facades, trees and lampposts, and the placement on sidewalks and streets of signs, bus shelters, trash cans, toilets, phone booths, benches and, yes, bollards.

An open-air collection of cultural ID cards, it's the sidewalks of the city and their unsung "furniture" that help make Paris, Paris. Stand on just about any corner in town and you'll know instinctively that you're not in Lyon or Lille, let alone London or Lisbon. Like minor artworks only a curator can love, each piece of Paris' urban décor reflects the spirit and needs of its day, and provides insight into the city's past, present and future.

Take the bollards, for instance, those unsightly lumps of stone or cement that the French lovingly call *bornes*. Unfamiliar to most nations, like the proverbial pearls before swine *bornes* tell more about Parisians and their culture than the contents of most museums. For one thing, *bornes* and their phallic brothers *les bittes*, those serried ranks of spindly brown posts bristling on pavements, are the only effective means of keeping cars from invading the territory of pedestrians. Left to their own devices Parisian drivers would mount *les trottoirs* and park everywhere and anywhere, including on your toes. *Bornes* have been around for centuries: the first Daguerreotype, from 1838, shows rows of them on the Boulevard du Temple near what's now the Place de la République. *Bornes* gave rise to that quintessentially French expression, *dépasser les bornes* – meaning beyond restraint, beyond reason, beyond the control of the bureaucrats whose job it is to enforce *liberté, egalité* and *fraternité*. The argot meaning of *bitte* is obvious enough. Real and metaphorical, blocky *bornes* and penile *bittes* are only one element of a complex system of barriers and signage whose purpose is to restrain, thwart and redirect unruly natives.

In 1910 the poet Guillaume Apollinaire, bemused by the rapidity of technological progress in street lighting, only half jokingly proposed that the City of Light create a museum of lampposts and related equipment. Apollinaire saw perhaps a dozen models of lamp on the city's streets, from ancient oil lanterns mounted on pulleys to pressurized-gas burners on elegant ironwork posts and, of later manufacture, a variety of electric types, including Hector Guimard's praying mantis-like illuminated 1900 Métro entrances. Since Apollinaire's death in 1918 at least another dozen generations of lighting fixtures have been added to the mix. More surprising than this continuing tech evolution, though, is the cultural tendency to adapt the new to the old, to convert a cast-iron gas lamp of the 1850s again and again, for instance, thereby demonstrating an attachment to the past only in part ascribable to economics.

My personal sidewalk epiphany occurred while I was researching the origins of the nickname *Ville Lumière* – City of Light. A bulb flickered on in my brain, highlighting those proverbial pearls scattered before my snout. I began to take notice of Paris' peculiar décor and realized that, just as the City of Light has a luminous identity created by engineers and designers, so too it has dozens of architects, planners and administrators in an array of interlocking departments whose life's work is the creation, placement and upkeep of street furniture that declares "You're in Paris," nowhere else. Now, whenever I step beyond the *bornes* separating my building's courtyard from the public realm, I think about the crucifixion of Saint Andrew as represented in the city's crossbars (they show a capital X on its side and are found at nearly every intersection). I ponder the age-old symbolism of the red (passion, danger), yellow (caution) and green (hope, safety) of stoplights, first used here in 1923. I delight in the double-sided 1850s-style benches draped with young lovers, or garrulous geezers. I weigh the relative merits of granite or asphalt underfoot as I sidestep horizontal pollution, and wonder what Paris was like before it had sidewalks, a comparatively recent invention.

With a curse I blink at the luminous, revolving, flashing outdoor advertising on a thousand panels, poles and columns, and marvel at the hideousness of the so-called *sanisette* pay toilets encased in concrete bunkers.

The ad panels and toilets (plus many other contemporary sidewalk items) were designed for and are operated by JC Decaux, the world's biggest street furniture supplier and Europe's top outdoor advertising agency. In concert with a municipal committee, they hired prize-winning British architect Norman Foster to come up with his glassy bus shelters, international design star Philippe Starck to excogitate faux-Gallic canoe paddles (with potted histories of Paris sites), and Jean-Michel Wilmotte to replace the benches, lighting and signals on the upper end of the Champs-Elysées. Foster bus shelters, intentionally unobtrusive, are now in many cities worldwide. Wilmotte's furniture is nice enough but could be anywhere. And the best that can be said of the Starck paddles is, they supply useful information.

I'm not predisposed to reactionary sentiments. With due respect to current design gurus, generally speaking when it comes to the objects on Paris' sidewalks my feeling is the older they are the better. Whether or not you side with Victor Hugo and despise Baron Georges Eugène Haussmann for the way he destroyed medieval Paris during the Second Empire, sooner or later you'll have to admit that Napoléon III's zealous prefect did an impressive job equipping the city from 1853 to 1870 with site-specific, only-in-Paris fountains, benches, kiosks and newsstands set up under freshly planted trees, on novel sidewalks and in squares or parks, for the delectation of all social classes.

It was Haussmann's head engineer Jean-Charles Alphand and architect Gabriel Jean Antoine Davioud who masterminded the transformation of public areas into "flower-filled salons" where beleaguered Parisians and their horses could quench their thirst, relieve themselves, breathe fresh air, rest in the shade of over 100,000 trees and, if they had time to spare, watch the world go by. Davioud may not be a household name, but city planners everywhere hail him as the unwitting father of "street furniture" (the binomial was coined by Frenchman Jean-Claude Decaux in the 1960s). To his mind, Davioud was merely "decorating" the capital. At a distance of over a century since his death, if Paris can still be said to have its own unmistakable street-level look and feel, that achievement is largely attributable to him.

Despite his lengthy name and Prix de Rome pedigree, Davioud was self-effacing, rarely signing his work. After furnishing Paris' sidewalks, he dashed off blueprints for twenty-four parks and garden squares, detailing everything from the paths, gates and grilles to the tree-corsets, water fountains and amusement stands – an onion dome here, a playful mask there, and plenty of foliage faux and real. Then he turned his hand to the twin theaters at Châtelet, and the fountains of Place Saint Michel, l'Observatoire, and Daumesnil. Dozens of the old green pavilions, rotundas and shelters in Paris are of his conception. So all-encompassing and lasting is Davioud's influence that it's tough to imagine a Paris street before him. But his designs didn't come from nowhere. They were rooted in European history, drawing on the Italian Renaissance and the English reinterpretation of it that followed the 18th-century Grand Tour.

Rewind to the pre-industrial Paris of the Ancien Régime, a city of under half a million, with layout and building styles still marked by the Gallo-Roman Lutetia, with medieval and Renaissance overlays. On the spider's web of alleys spreading outward from Notre-Dame there are few signs and no sidewalks. Gutters in the center of dirt roads run black with sewage. Garbage is piled high against the half-timbered buildings. The air reeks of boiled cabbage and the burning rapeseed oil that fuels the lanterns hung from scabrous facades. In the shadowy rankness, carriages thunder by scattering pedestrians whose only refuges are rows of stone bollards, posts and mounting blocks. There are no benches or trees outside the sealed royal enclave of the Tuileries or the private gardens of the rich. Public fountains are besieged: indoor plumbing hasn't been invented. Most wells are contaminated. Water-bearers serve neighborhoods that have no drinking water. On the edge of this squalor, the sole neighborhood conceived for pedestrians and pleasure-seekers is the Boulevard du Temple, a chaotic esplanade built atop former bastions, where five rows of sycamores from the late 1600s shade theaters and café terraces.

Fast forward from the mid-1700s into the early industrial age, when hundreds of thousands of French provincials driven off the land begin moving to Paris to work in factories. Suddenly, the great unwashed are swarming onto the streets. The number of traffic accidents skyrockets. An anonymous writer in *L'Espion des boulevards* notes that, "The pedestrian lacking agility is a dead man!" Cholera spreads through overcrowded tenements, killing thousands. Old Paris has become a hellhole of disease and famine, wracked by riots culminating in the July Revolution of 1830.

Enter Claude Barthelot, Comte de Rambuteau, prefect of Paris as of

1830. Upon taking office a mere 146 drinking fountains supply a population nearing 1 million. Only three streets have sidewalks. Rambuteau's slogan is "Give Parisians water, fresh air and shade." A chronicler of the day quips that the count "would rather have his own teeth pulled than uproot trees he's planted." It is Rambuteau who begins the process of "sanitizing" medieval Paris: the road that bears his name, driven through Beaubourg in 1838, destroys six streets of the 11th and 12th centuries and scores of buildings. Under Rambuteau, in 1841, the Faubourg Saint Martin becomes the first neighborhood to get a complete set of furniture: sidewalks, lights, benches, trees, drinking fountains and, what is considered a miracle of hygiene, urinals. By the time Napoléon III fires him, Rambuteau can report totals of 1,840 fountains, about 150 miles of sidewalks, hundreds of benches and thousands of trees.

These are the tumultuous years captured on polished metal plates by pioneering photographer Louis Jacques Mandé Daguerre, inventor of the daguerreotype. His studio just happens to be sited high above the Boulevard du Temple. Continuity? In Paris the historic present tense reaches far beyond grammar. If you get out a magnifying glass and study the images Daguerre produced in spring, 1838, you'll see *bornes* edging the road just as they do now in many places, iron corsets supporting saplings, and streetlamps with fishbowl globes held aloft by lyre-headed poles identical to ones in use today.

However hard he tried, Rambuteau's efforts failed to cure Paris' growing pains. The city was rocked by unrest again in 1848. The new government was soon subverted from within, and, in 1852, Charles Louis Napoléon Bonaparte declared himself Emperor. An enlightened despot, Napoléon III was bent on making Paris the world's most modern city. He assigned the task to Baron Haussmann.

The baron's was as much a revolution in social engineering as in urbanism. Since industrial workers' apartments had few conveniences, the Empire supplied basic necessities on the sidewalks. Inclined to build barricades with cobbles piled across narrow crooked alleys, the Empire decided to straighten and widen the streets, get rid of cobbles and knock down residential labyrinths ideal for guerilla warfare. Workers needed a modicum of R&R to keep them from rioting? Give them parks and squares where fountains or artificial waterfalls splashed, while military music, played from bandstands, reminded them who was the boss.

Jokes aside, rioters and road apples were a major preoccupation for

Alphand and Davioud. What these architects didn't have to contend with was the subway, electricity, motor vehicles, telephones and consumerism – five phenomena that brought about a re-jig of the city and radically changed the behavior of its inhabitants, from about 1900 onwards. Gradually virginal Second Empire streets and sidewalks morphed. First came the Métro entrances, grilles, signs and maps. Then, as streets and buildings were electrified, hundreds of circuit boxes appeared. Cars, trucks, motorcycles and buses needed wider lanes, parking spaces, signage, stoplights, gas stations and, later, parking meters. So the sidewalks were narrowed, trees felled and benches removed. Along came the telephone and, overnight, booths sprang up on every corner. More people swelled the capital's population, meaning more street furniture and urinals for busy gents (the total number of *pissoirs* peaked at 1,200 in 1930, when a campaign to eliminate them began). The postwar throwaway consumer culture and its daily tonnage of trash forced city officials to fit garbage cans into an ever-more cluttered puzzle.

By 1975, arguably Paris' modern nadir, the street furniture crisis had become acute. The head of the city's historical library was moved to begin his preface to an exhibition catalogue entitled *Paris, la Rue* with the words, "The traditional Parisian street is dead." He lamented that roads were anonymous people-moving spaces and no longer a lively spectacle unto themselves. Soon after that exhibition I arrived in Paris and stayed in the Rue de l'Odéon. Little did I know that in 1781 the street had been the first ever flanked by sidewalks. I do remember the congestion of most Paris streets and the decaying, battered objects on them so full of character.

Since the mid-1970s the pedestrian's Paris has improved by most measures, despite more cars and motorcycles fouling the air and hogging space. In recent years, sidewalks have been growing wider, with many insulated by bus and bike lanes. The so-called Fontaine Wallace – a graceful cast-iron fountain decorated with dancing caryatids, designed in 1871 – has made a comeback, as have the slightly older (1868) Morris Columns – those comical, onion-domed towers bearing theater posters or, increasingly, JC Decaux advertising. New, free toilets, possibly of a Second Empire style, are slated to replace 1980s bunker models. As part of a campaign to green the city, under the tin-eared name "*vegetalisation*", some 8,000 promised saplings will bring the total of Paris trees back to the 100,000-level of the 1870s. City authorities talk reassuringly about a return to sidewalk "conviviality" with improved hygiene (meaning less dog dirt, and redesigned transparent trashcans to replace the current anti-terrorism, see-through plastic bags). Step by halting step Paris is rejoining the ranks of the world's great cities for walking. Perhaps, who knows, one day a contagious form of civility might even affect French drivers, and allow city planners to uproot those ageless *bornes* protecting people from vehicles.

Luxembourg Gardens, 1997

Vie de Chien: A Dog's Life

"Happy dog-owners please take note: your companion is surely not vicious but since we wish to maintain cordial relations with him and to preclude any unpleasant eventualities we advise you to restrain him during our visits."

Notice to Parisians from the French national electricity and gas utility

Samba! Scirocco! Satan! The trio of Bois de Boulogne dog-walkers called their pets to heel. My wife Alison and I glanced over to see what the commotion was about. The pit-bullish mutt with the spiked collar and shocking name of Satan had tangled pedigreed Samba and Scirocco's precious Hermès leashes. The three animals and their masters struggled briefly and with aplomb to set things right, then disentangled themselves from each other as quickly as they could. The friction was palpable.

When the incident occurred Alison and I were walking along a tree-lined path near a lake on the fancy, Neuilly-sur-Seine side of the park. As Alison pointed out, there was more to this canine leash conundrum than met the eye. In Paris, dog breeds, dog accessories and dog monikers had tales to tell – about their owners' social, educational and marital status, even their political leanings.

"*Satan* is such a suburban name," sniffed Samba's matron as we edged our way by on the lakeside path. Scirocco's glamorous owner agreed, using a gloved finger to indicate the unfashionable outskirts on the far side of the park, where Satan and his tattooed female owner, *la patronne,* as she put it, appeared to be heading. "You never know anymore whom you might meet at the ends of a leash, not even in *le bois,*" Madame Samba acknowledged. The two ageing socialites, who did not seem to know each other previously, now shared conspiratorial confidences as their purebred animals licked and mounted each other.

"Owning a dog," remarked Alison, a Paris native, "is the best way to get to know people here." She was thinking in particular of a pair of American friends of ours whose Paris lives had bloomed once they bought their adorable border collie, Randy. We have often dog-sat Randy, a bouncy black-and-white boy with long hair and a ready smile.

Whenever we do, we seem to meet and exchange civil discourse with perfect strangers – the countless Mesdames and Messieurs of Paris whose last names are in fact those of their dogs. That's why, when we take care of Randy, we become *Monsieur et Madame* Randy – not a bad name to have in a lusty city like Paris.

I'm not necessarily prone to citing statistics, which are massaged by the press, politicians and the vox populi the world round. But when it comes to Parisians and their dogs, numbers talk. According to studies I've read, an estimated 8 to 10 million dogs live in France, a country with about 58 million inhabitants. That means on average there's a dog for every six people. Nearly 500,000 dogs live in the capital (its human population is 2.2 million). That makes Paris not only the City of Light but also the European Capital of Dog Dirt and the world Mecca of the Canine Obsessed. The dog dirt is a major health hazard, number two after car-related accidents, and has been the object of many, so far unsuccessful advertising, poster, radio and television campaigns whose goal is to toilet-train Parisian dog owners.

Randy's owners initially shocked the locals by cleaning up his daily mess. As we've learned, generally speaking, the Parisian love of domestic animals does not extend to humans, so *les crottes* pile up even in fashionable areas, where the city sends out squadrons of motorcycles equipped with dog-dirt vacuum devices, plus extra contingents of street sweepers with their green plastic brooms, to deal with the dirt. I asked several dog-walkers we became friendly with, and even ventured into several pet shops and salons, but no one could tell me how to say "pooper-scooper" in French, or suggest where I might buy one. Perhaps, I reflected, the Academie Française hadn't yet come up with an official French translation yet, and the language police had therefore banned the import or manufacture of such suspect implements. Recently, however, the city of Paris has begun setting up dog toilet areas – essentially, sandboxes and peeing posts – some supplied with plastic bags in suspended dispensers. Theoretically dog owners should pull off a bag, pick up the poop, flip the bag inside out, tie it and drop it in a garbage can – standard practice across the Atlantic.

"There are limits," one dog-owner in our building shivered with disgust at the thought of handling horizontal pollution. Her pocketsize terrier has more than once soiled the cobbles of our courtyard, and I mentioned to her the *crotte* bag concept. "You in the New World sometimes go too far," she scowled.

Maybe. But recently our concierge has put up a sign politely inviting dog owners to remove their pets' *excréments*, and several celebrities and politicos have been photographed by newshounds wielding bags and publicly declaiming the merits of dog-related civility.

As to Parisians' canine obsessions, they are another tale. Dogs are the source of pride, prejudice and big money. Start with the purebred phenomenon. Here as elsewhere in the world, the first letter in the names of purebred Parisian pooches follows calendar years and the alphabet: 2001 was an "S" year, 2002 a "T" year, 2003 a "U" year, 2004 a "V" year, 2005 an "X" year, and so on. That's why there are so many Sambas and Satans around. Those Tommy and Tiger pups you knew yesterday are full grown and replicating today, with Ursula, Unic and and Uranus. Venus, Vulcan and Vegas are already getting to know Xerxes, Xenophon and X-citation. The obligatory letter explains why, as you travel around Paris, you keep hearing the same dog names again and again, or diabolically similar variations on them.

Why so many dog names are formulated in something resembling English is a mystery no one has adequately explained to me. Perhaps it's a subtle way of getting revenge on *les Anglo-Saxons* for a variety of perceived crimes. But I doubt it: Parisians love their dogs more than anything in the world except possibly their cars. *Les Anglo-Saxons* may have invented hero-dogs such as Rin-Tin-Tin and Lassie – real dogs that looked, behaved and probably smelled like animals – but at some point last century the French hijacked dog-worship and raised it to a higher realm, a place in which curls, perfume and manicured paws are the ultimate measure of refinement, civilization, sensuality even. What better toy for an ageing Parisian vamp than a coiffed lapdog – infant and tender lover rolled into a single, loyal, furry package? And for a graying womanizer with hormones on the wane, a lively, bouncing big dog – a golden lab or Rhodesian ridgeback – could be the ticket to some canine-inspired philandering.

For an ethnically mixed American mutt like me, brought up with casually, often monosyllabically, named human friends and mongrel pets rescued from beaches and parking lots, the complexity of Paris' dog world is baffling. I still do a double take when someone here explains earnestly how Parisian dog-owners treat their pets as lovingly as their children – if they have children. The late, great Parisian comedian Colluche once quipped that French families procreate only if they can't afford dogs. An updated corollary might be, if you can't be bothered to invest emotionally in your family, your aging parents for instance, get them a lapdog. Parisian Little Old Ladies and vintage gentlemen, particularly widows and widowers who live to what busy youngsters might consider an overripe age, rely heavily on dogs for company.

Loneliness is a big part of the equation. The other is control. Those many proper little baby-boomer Parisian *filles* and *garçons* with names like Louis-Amadeus, Marie-Astrid, Jean-Luc and Paule-Andrée have grown up, left home, and just might have families of their own one day, families whose tyrannical only-child offspring's references will be not the choir stall or the centuries-old estate in Burgundy, where vacations must be endured. No. Their references will be the cellular telephone, body piercing and tattoos, reality TV, hip-hop, rap, and independent travel to distant places where English is spoken and junk food is considered gourmet fare. If there is a dog in the picture it's probably going to be a pit bull (the favorite breed of rebellious hipsters and suburban delinquents alike). But good old coiffed Samba, Uranus and Venus will never abandon *maman* and won't listen to French techno music, either. After several thousand dollars' worth of obedience schooling, they will wear their ribbons and collars until the day their little paws no longer make that pitter-patter on the parquet.

What most Parisians do with their *chiens*, I've discovered, in part by taking care of lithe-tongued Randy, is precisely what other nations do with children – and husbands, wives or lovers. Want a romantic stroll? Take your partner but don't forget your dog: the Bois de Boulogne is *the* place to show off your Yorkshire, Westie (West Island Terrier) or accordion-muzzled Tibetan Shihtzu in his new hounds-tooth coat. Forget Fifi the passé poodle – the above-mentioned trio of dog breeds is the rage among Parisian pedigree lapdog lovers. Labradors and bulldogs top the purebred big Bowser list for the central-city bourgeois set, with border collies like Randy down the roster but not entirely unfashionable.

Here is a further handful of statistics and prices I've come across and found particularly revealing, given the state of the French economy, with its chronically high unemployment, and the country's increasing variety of complex social ills related to mass immigration, urban alienation, globalization and the ingestion of beef-based fast food in combination with foie gras and goat cheese. France has an estimated 3,200 canine beauty salons, hundreds of them in Paris, and they all seem to be prospering. The fishmonger's or dry goods store, not to mention the authentic local bistro we all once loved, are things of the recent past, but the dog salon trade is booming. Most coif shops are modest neighborhood operations. One of them I heard about, however, is famous for organizing runway fashion shows for hoity-toity hounds. It's called Marie Poirier, after its chic owner, and is located on the Boulevard des

Batignolles in Paris' 17th arrondissement, one of those deeply bourgeois arteries in the vicinity of which well-fed, well-bred dogs abound. At this salon a haircut for Uranus will run you somewhere in the vicinity of $130.00 – or so I was told when I telephoned to enquire. In addition to doggie fashion items like coats and booties costing many hundreds of dollars, you can also purchase swish 4-digit accessories such as gem-studded collars and designer leashes.

Should you need to ride across town with your pet after an intense coif-fashion experience, the cordial woman at the other end of the telephone added, the salon's management will gladly call you a Taxi Canine. I asked her what that was. "Possibly the world's first taxi service specifically conceived to cater to dog owners," said the helpful woman. Apparently people use Taxi Canine because not all standard Paris taxis accept dogs, especially big dogs, and even those cabbies that do like Bowser, sometimes make a fuss about the mess, the smell, the fleas and so forth.

I didn't believe this next item until I started getting to know the local pet world, and had several remarkable encounters of the third kind with canine-o-philes apparently visiting from another planet. To satisfy the country's countless upscale dog-owners there are not only dog kennels and the like. There are also dog-friendly hotels and dog-receptive restaurants, most of them luxury properties. Parisians routinely dine out with their pets, and travel with them, too. Once, at the celebrated, centuries-old Le Doyen restaurant on the Champs-Elysées, the movie star Jean-Paul Belmondo came in carrying two lavishly coiffed lapdogs, one cupped in each bejeweled hand. Alison and I soon tired of watching the aging heartthrob – he was one of my film heroes for his roles in *Breathless* and *That Man From Rio* – but we, the wait staff and most of the other diners at the restaurant remained fascinated throughout our hideously expensive meals by Belmondo's eerily doll-like dogs and the perfect fit they made with the mirrored, gilt décor. It harks back to an earlier age of decadence, the Ancien Régime.

It's a fact that the Michelin red *Guide France* identifies establishments that do *not* welcome *toutous* or *clébards* – French colloquialisms for "doggie." It is assumed, therefore, that all other hotels and restaurants in the land will throw open their doors at a dog's approach, and perhaps even provide a comfortable basket so that old Hector or young Troika can settle in under your starred table, or nestle at the foot of your Queen Marie-Antoinette-size bed. I have never been able to confirm rumors of gastronomes ordering starred meals for their animals and feeding them surreptitiously with the approval of the chef.

Certainly, Parisian butchers stand to attention when they see a dog-owner. As our local meat wizard on the Rue Saint Antoine, Monsieur Lefebvre, puts it, most of his Parisian dog-loving clients nourish their animals as well as, and often better than, their own families. "Scraps?" Lefebvre gasped when I spoke the dreaded word signifying something cost-free, in other words, a product he couldn't sell for a profit. "No, no, they want filets, rib steaks, ground-round..."

Le shopping has become a worldwide leisure activity so it came as no surprise to me to learn that the dog fashion business is big business here. At the top of the gift scale there are real diamond-studded collars or lavish leashes from Chanel, Gucci and Hermès, as you might expect. But what about a dog carry-case from Louis Vuitton starting at about $1,000? When out for a stroll with Randy one day I heard from a fellow dog-sitter about Le Webstore, a website and retail outlet near the Louvre with fabulous dog-couches for a mere $1,500 and up. For considerably less (something on the order of $60) you can pick up a K9 doggie travel kit including a dog Frisbee, a bowl and ball, a doggie wash-cloth and chew toys, all packaged in a nifty nylon pack and sold at the Paris branch of The Conran Shop in toney Rue du Bac, in the 7th arrondissement. I surprised and even shocked myself one day when, instead of looking for a welcome-home gift for Randy's owners – a bottle of champagne or suchlike – Alison and I actually trawled the stores looking for that perfect gift for him, Randy, which we knew would in turn please them. Dog-mania is insidious.

That was when we found out that in Paris you can experience a real doggie department store extravaganza at Le Printemps, that venerable establishment I usually associate with people's grandmothers. Nowadays Le Printemps is dog-lover's paradise, one of the hot spots in town where you can buy Oh My Dog! perfumes and pelt-care products, or Good Doogy good-luck charms, by a company called Dog Generation. While browsing there we found out that, just in case Randy was feeling neurotic or depressed because his owners had left him in our hands, he could see the in-house vet-psychiatrist for a session. I buttonholed a Madame Titus coming out of the canine shrink's office and was assured by her that the therapy session was not mere doggerel. "Titus is much calmer now," she said deadpan, stroking the heavy jowls oozing slime from his massive head. So, apparently, was she.

"You must absolutely be in touch with Le Chien du Monde," insisted a certain Madame Quantum we befriended in the Bois de Vincennes on Paris' eastern edge, and saw many times thereafter one summer. This boutique, apparently, was *the* source for custom bejeweled collars ($250-$1,300) or silk canopy dog beds (about $2,600), and, what was better, said Madame Quantum, all profits went to worthy, animal-welfare causes. The only rub was, you couldn't just pop out to the shop – it wasn't in Paris. "You know, the Riviera is where people live who are really passionate about dogs," assured Madame Quantum. "We keep an apartment in Cannes..." For the dog? "Well, not just…" The boutique in question turned out to be in Nice. "The weather is so much better down there, so much healthier for your *toutou*, isn't that right, Quantum dear?"

As we walked Randy through the bois later that day, Monsieur Odalisque, the affable owner of an ageing German shepherdess we'd gotten to know, told us that the time had come to immortalize his beloved companion. "*Vous savez,*" he sighed, "Odalisque will not live forever…" So he had arranged for a renowned animal portraitist to capture Odalisque while her canines and incisors were still in place.

"Why is that important?" I asked dimly.

"So she can smile," explained Monsieur Odalisque.

The pet painter, it transpired, ran a shop called "Pour Sourire," meaning, literally, "for a smile."

Several months later we bumped into Monsieur Odalisque again near the Lac Daumesnil, a favorite lacustrine rendezvous among Bois de Vincennes dog-walkers. He'd changed his hairstyle and now led on a new red leash a yapping puppy whose name, we learned, was Underdog. "Odalisque is gone," he confided. Apparently the excitement of having her portrait taken had proved too much. Monsieur Odalisque, now Monsieur Underdog, had accordingly telephoned Taxi Canine and requested that they arrange for cremation and transport of Odalisque's ashes in a decorous dog funerary-urn – one of the many services they provide. "They drove us to the pet cemetery in Villepinte," he recalled. This graveyard, it turned out, is the resting place of beloved Parisian blueblood hounds and suburban mutts, the Père-Lachaise of the capital's canine world. "It's a dog's life we live," added Monsieur Underdog, giving the leash a tug. "Now come along boy, enjoy it while you can."

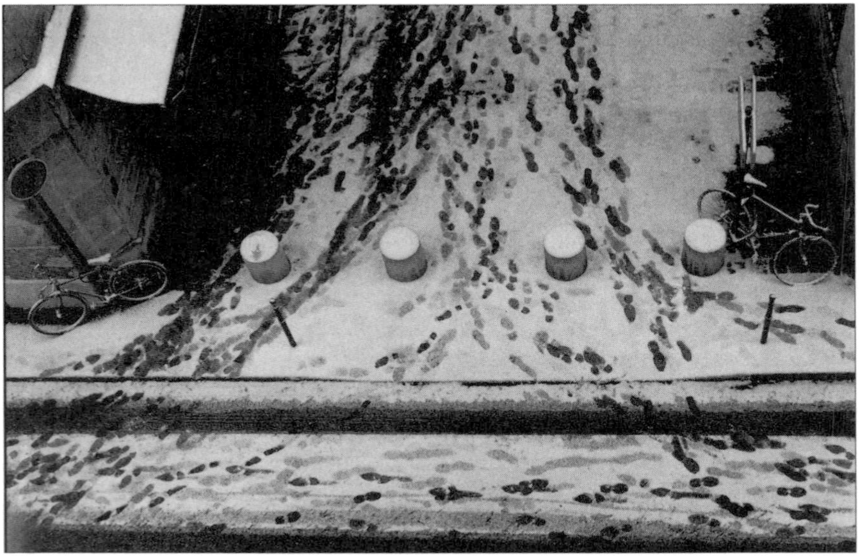

View from Marais window, footprints in the snow, 2005

Why the Marais Changed its Spots

"I wanted to talk about Paris but here I am telling you the story of my life."

Daniel Halévy

Long before moving to it I knew the Marais: as an adolescent I'd read in the crime novels of Georges Simenon about this patchwork of neighborhoods erected on former marshlands between Beaubourg and the Bastille, Temple and the Seine, in the 3rd and 4th arrondissements. Simenon's Marais was a dark, sinister place of dilapidated townhouses, where prostitutes plied their trade while murderers lurked in the shadows.

On my first visit to Paris, in 1976, I walked across the Marais without realizing it. It struck me as a kind of landlocked Marseilles, Genoa or Naples without the wharves and longshoremen of course. The seedy edginess thrilled me – the greasy-spoon restaurants where unshaved louts swilled cheap red and smoked corn-paper Gaulois; the hives of shady traders in courtyards stuffed with cubbyhole stores, factories and crafts shops. It was the *French Connection*, the *Day of the Jackal*, and Simenon's *Ombre Chinoise* in one.

In late 1986 I moved from a maid's room in the maddeningly symmetrical 17th arrondissement, near Place des Ternes, to a two-room apartment above a lampshade factory in a courtyard behind Sainte-Marie, the cupola-topped Reformation Church designed by royal architect Jules Mansard. The Bastille district, with its ramshackle movie theaters and provincial Auvergnat restaurants, was only 200 yards away. From Sainte-Marie I shifted a year or so later into my wife's apartment near Saint Paul, where we live to this day. Headquartered in our building was a packaging materials manufacturer called Relda. The courtyard doubled as a parking lot and loading dock. Trucks came and went from dawn onward in clouds of diesel. Workers wearing blue outfits, the badge of the working class, pushed carts or hand trucks across the scarred, oil-stained cobbles, and seemed to revel in the deafening thunder they made. Our outwardly fierce, full-throated concierge Madame Gambaro kept the peace, directing traffic with mop in hand. Meanwhile the plaster of Paris with which our building is held together turned back into gypsum powder and rained from the cornices framing the courtyard's 17th-century carriage entrance. The timbers holding up our stairwell sagged. Drop by drop our cellar filled with water from leaky pipes, some of them feeding the communal toilets on each landing. The last major documented remodel turned out to have been done in 1784.

Today the cobbles of our courtyard are pristine. The factory and cars are gone. Tour groups file in, admiring the restored cream-colored facades, the trellised honeysuckle, flowering shrubs and leafy paulownia tree with its snap-dragon-like mauve-and-white blossoms. Gone are our old gray shutters, too: the architects in charge of beautifying the Marais claimed there had been no shutters here originally, in 1640, and that ours had been added only in the 1840s. They had to go. The building is eerily quiet by day. By night, however, when the new Marais' cafés and restaurants get into swing on the pedestrian-only square we overlook, it's Bobo-a-go-go – a Bohemian bourgeois playground. The noise makes the old Relda packing factory seem benign.

The story of our building is like that of hundreds of other spots in the Marais. The seedy neighborhood I discovered as a teenager in Simenon, and stumbled across entranced in the 1970s, has undergone a top-to-bottom remake. Museums, libraries and administrative offices occupy restored landmark mansions. Postcard perfect, it is a fictional place lined wall-to-wall with designer boutiques and restaurants devised to please shoppers and tourists. Organ grinders and faux Dixieland bands delight visitors while driving inhabitants mad. So renowned has the neighborhood become that *National Geographic* has reported on this incarnation of "Bohemian Paris."

How and why did the transformation take place? The quick answer is, a combination of real estate speculation and dire need. The area represented hundreds of acres of prime property in central Paris, with many storied sites, most of which were imploding, like our building. The options were either to demolish or restore. In the end the Marais wound up with a dose of each.

Besotted by my adopted neighborhood, for years I pored over every book I could find about it. I interviewed local history experts and longtime residents not simply to write articles but also, and perhaps primarily, in an effort to come to grips with what was happening around me.

The Marais was once a swamp, fed by the seasonal swelling of the Seine. Its past is therefore understandably murky. The area's pre-Roman inhabitants paddled across it in canoes netting fish and swatting mosquitoes (whose descendants entertain us to this day). The Romans engineered a raised roadway through the bogs and some time around 700 AD monks started building the church of Saint Gervais. They also reclaimed abutting land. The city walls of Philippe Auguste and Charles V eventually embraced those lands. To build the *hôtels particuliers* townhouses of the Renaissance and 17th-century "Grand Siècle" for which the Marais is now famous, many medieval constructions had to be razed. The Maison d'Ourscamps (1590) and Hôtel de Beauvais (1655), both in the Rue François Miron near city hall, as well as several other landmarks, rise atop monasteries or medieval residences that probably resembled the turreted, fortified Hôtel de Sens in the Rue de l'Hôtel de Ville (one of Paris' remaining two "medieval" townhouses, completely rebuilt in the mid-1800s by Viollet le Duc). Several of the grandest Marais mansions, including the Carnavalet (the Paris Historical Museum) and Lamoignon (the Paris Historical Library) are from the 1500s. They pre-date the Place Royale, a square known nowadays as the Place des Vosges, King Henri IV's revolutionary urban redevelopment scheme, initiated in 1600 and considered the Marais' centerpiece. The square itself was constructed over the 14th-century Hôtel des Tournelles, abandoned in 1559 after Henri II's accidental death there and demolished soon after.

"If you come back to Paris in two years," wrote a certain Monsieur Malherbe to his friend Peiresc on October 3, 1608, in reference to the Marais' new royal square, "you won't recognize it."

This is one of the lessons the history books teach about the Marais: periodic change is the norm, not the exception.

In essence Henri IV did to the former marsh what Napoléon III's prefect, Baron Haussmann, did to inner Paris some 350 years later: demolished the old city to erect a modern one in its place. Suddenly the new, improved Marais was the rage. The Duc de Sully and Cardinal Richelieu commissioned townhouses near the king's pavilion. Scores of sycophants followed suit. By the time epistolary queen Madame de Sévigné began penning her famous *Lettres* from the Carnavalet, the royal square and its surroundings were synonymous with riotous parties, debauchery and the pursuit of grandeur. The climax came when a spirited sixteen-year-old Louis XIV lost his virginity to Catherine Bellier, wife of the owner of one of the Marais' more sumptuous residences, the aforementioned Hôtel de Beauvais.

Changing fashions, the shift of the court to Versailles and the Revolution of 1789 started the Marais' decline. The industrialization that followed changed the silk and affluence of old to soot and effluent.

Townhouses were divided into tenements and factories. Workers poured in from the provinces. The Marais became a teeming swamp of humanity. By the early 1900s this moldering quagmire of urbanism seemed to be standing in the way of progress. In 1922 Le Corbusier teamed up with a carmaker named Voisin and devised an ingenious plan to raze the Marais (and abutting Beaubourg neighborhood) and replace its buildings with a freeway a hundred yards wide flanked by eighteen high-rise towers. Inertia and World War II saved the area until the 1950s, when zealous postwar developers re-floated the scheme and brought in the bulldozers. Seventy percent of the Marais was officially condemned as unfit for human habitation. Some of the best townhouses would be saved, according to planners, by dismantling and regrouping them near the Seine in a kind of Marais Village theme park. Some homeowners fearing expropriation or anticipating speculation allowed already deteriorated buildings to crumble. A white knight finally arrived in 1962, when the Marais as a whole was classed a historic monument under the so-called Loi Malraux, named for then Minister of Culture André Malraux. "An isolated architectural masterpiece," Malraux proclaimed, "is a dead masterpiece."

Malraux's radical strategy was to free the Marais of "parasite constructions" and "pustules", an ungenerous way of describing the often handsome extensions and glass-and-iron workshops grafted onto historic buildings or dropped into their courtyards. The problem with delousing the neighborhood proved to be that people lived in the parasites and worked in the pustules. Eight thousand apartments and 10,000 jobs hung in the balance. The search began for a negotiated compromise to keep the Marais lively and popular. But the laws of the market prevailed. Between 1962 and 1982 the neighborhood's population declined by 35,000 – nearly fifty percent. Light industry and crafts dwindled. When the City of Paris and the French state began converting restored Marais townhouses into museums or administrative office buildings, the rents and real estate values rose. In the '80s the gay community and Bobo DINKS began arriving. The fashion boutiques, nightspots and touristy restaurants followed in what's now a familiar process worldwide.

The boosters of gentrification have a rejoinder for anyone affected by what they regard as "poisonous nostalgia" for the shabby old Marais. "The neighborhood has come full circle" they say. "It is once more an enclave of the rich just is as it was under Henri IV, Louis XIII and Louis XIV in the Grand Siècle, France's greatest historical moment."

History tells a slightly more nuanced story. I once spent several days under the painted timbers of the Paris Historical Library, tangling with curmudgeonly curators while sifting through dusty documents, many judged too fragile to handle. What I discovered is, Henri IV, in his 1605 letters of patent, ordered that workshops and retail stores should line the arcades of his Place Royale. He wasn't creating an enclave for the rich; he was merely trying to enrich himself further by building rental properties. Another interesting tidbit proves that before the Revolution, most townhouses had a storefront on the ground floor to generate income. Rich nobles' apartments were on the floor above, the so-called *étage noble*, while the bourgeois or less affluent nobles lived above them. Servants or the poor occupied the uppermost stories, which were less desirable in pre-elevator days. Flanking the townhouses were purpose-built craftsmen's lodgings. The result of this organic style of urbanism was that all classes lived and (some) worked side-by-side.

The French have a wonderful expression for window shoppers: *lèche-vitrines*, meaning, literally, window lickers. I went out for a stroll recently and found myself three-deep in shoppers, their tongues out. With them I cruised the narrow Rue du Roi-de-Sicile, Rue des Ecouffes, Rue des Rosiers, Rue Mahler, Rue Pavée and two short blocks of the Rue des Francs Bourgeois – the Marais' drunken parallelogram of a heartland – and therein counted over a hundred fashion boutiques, up several dozen from the last time I'd bothered to count almost ten years ago. Mock 19th-century, pre-aged shop fronts beckon. Erstwhile bakeries smell not of baguettes but of another kind of dough. Kosher delis in the century-old Rue des Rosiers Jewish district (which becomes distinctly less Jewish by the day) have swapped pickles for bangles, as long-time residents sell up, cash in, and move out. With an eviable lack of self-irony, self-styled "pioneer" boutiques from the 1980s such as Lolita Lempicka grumble that their image has suffered from the onslaught of new commercial settlers. Mass-market clothiers, foreign chains and discounters have rushed to plant their tills in the last square yards of the Marais' fertile floor space, and who can blame them?

Paris' gay community began colonizing the vibrant Rue Vieille du Temple and surrounding streets twenty years ago. Now gay bookstores, bars, restaurants, bakeries, hotels, cabarets, cafés and clubs buzz day and night. All told the Marais has nearly 400 gay businesses, many of whose owners and patrons claim they created, and maintain, the neighborhood's perpetual "animation", as if it had been on a respirator before their arrival. Light sleepers and residents who work normal office hours have fled. Sleep deprivation and the laws of the market are hard to fight, especially when the political establishment helps grease the wheels of the real estate agents.

Ironically I washed up here with the first wave of proto-Bobos. When I lived behind Sainte-Marie on the Rue Saint-Antoine, half a dozen greengrocers sold their fruit and vegetables from battered wooden wagons on the sidewalks. They dragged the wagons out before dawn and set up. The last wagon concessionaire, a wizened woman named Madame Jaïs, boasted when she retired that she was a thirty-five-year veteran. Her day started at 3 am and she stayed out, selling cabbages or melons, until 8 pm, six days a week. Who could be surprised to see her go, with no one to follow?

It's hard to lament the passing of such neighborhood icons as Génie Burger, the king of grease (it became a Benetton shop, which soon morphed into a shoe boutique, which morphed into an interior decoration shop). But even for those with a historical perspective and a disinterested view, it's worrisome when the long-established specialty food shop becomes a Chinese takeout joint, the dry goods store is reborn as a chain chocolate boutique, the poultry shop with some of the best chicken in town becomes a second-rate sandwich joint, the florist's withers into yet another Kookaï (which has morphed several times since) and both the local fishmongers metamorphose into cellular telephone stores in a few months. Bat an eye and the flash-in-the-pan boutiques change. The rule seems to be, once the quality shops of yesteryear have sold out, the infinitely replaceable chains and could-be-anywhere businesses continue to roll over. For anyone who witnessed the Mom & Pop disappearing act in America back in the 1960s the scenario is familiar.

One of France's cult crime novel writers moved into our building in the early '80s. Tellingly, a few years back he set a series of best-selling books not in the Marais but in the adjacent 11th arrondissement, specifically the roughshod Oberkampf and Roquette districts, both now being "tarted up," as my English friends put it.

Nostalgia is big business in Paris, but it is also a subtle poison, usually concocted with vague notions and selective memory. Good news – "news you can use as you shop", to quote muckraking reporter Mark Hertsgaard – is what makes the world go round. So I try to view the Marais' current incarnation as a first-time visitor would. It's certainly a cleaner, richer and quieter place than it has been for a long time, at least in daylight. The hard work and imagination of many business owners must be admired. Their shops, restaurants and hotels are brighter and more attractive to passersby than were the utilitarian stores and fleabag holes-in-the-wall of pre-gentrification days. Some of my new Bobo neighbors honestly believe that those blue-uniformed, corn paper-Gaulois-smoking ignoramuses of a few decades ago are happier now out in the suburbs. The Marais was wasted on them.

As to the gritty hangouts seemingly plucked from the docks of Marseille or Naples, most of them have been reborn as mod hotspots excogitated by the likes of Philippe Starck. For my part, I continue to rejoice because the three supermarkets poised between Bastille and Saint-Paul's church have not yet killed off our pair of wonderful cheese shops and trio of independent wine merchants. Whenever I feel a hint of poisonous nostalgia for the place Georges Simenon described as a "backdrop for a Court of Miracles... swarming with a wretched mob," I head to my office in the unwashed, unsung and, frankly, unaesthetic 20th arrondissement, where Algiers meets Bangkok via Zanzibar. Who can tell what the future holds for the Marais? There might be another French Revolution. More likely, the Bobos' bubble will burst. In the meantime perhaps the next local history museum should be dedicated to "recent yore."

Tango by the Seine, 2004

Night Walking

"In the evening, on the way to visit La Marquise, I intended to walk through the Saint-Séverin graveyard; it was closed. I took the little ruelle des Prêtres and I listened at the gate. I heard some sounds. I sat down to wait in the doorway of the presbytery. After an hour the cemetery gate opened and four youths went out, carrying a corpse in its shroud..."

Nicolas-Edme Restif de la Bretonne,
Les Nuits de Paris ou Le Spectateur nocturne, 1788

Night had fallen. Lights began snapping on, illuminating room-by-room the interior of the Île-Saint-Louis mansion. My wife and I stood outside, leaning on the parapet above the Seine, and glanced from the dark river to the mansion's twinkling windows. Tuxedoed men flanked by women wearing evening gowns mingled under a painted ceiling. Family portraits stared down at the merrymakers, at the maid carrying a silver tray, and out to the quayside where we loitered. A *bateau-mouche* cruised downstream, its lights flooding the tableau vivant above us. One by one the tuxedos and tailleurs replaced their emptied champagne coupes on the maid's tray and filed out. Chauffeur-driven limousines whisked them away. The maid peered down, spotted us and pulled the shutters closed.

By silent accord my wife and I moved on, no longer looking at the river but lifting our eyes instead to the mansions on the island, drawn to their lights like proverbial *papillons nocturnes* – a poetic way to say "moths." Around the corner from the townhouse on the tip of the Île-Saint-Louis a lamp winked on in a cozy mezzanine with low ceilings. There were leather-bound books and shaded wall sconces illuminating small oil paintings. We could just make out a liquor cabinet and a stag's head. Someone moved, casting shadows across the walls. We wondered if the owner was smoking a cigar – as if Alfred Hitchcock, his profile silhouetted, had arisen from the grave.

Soon street lamps flickered on around us, pooling yellowish light across the stone sidewalks that ring the Île-Saint-Louis. Further east, facing the Tour d'Argent restaurant, we heard a piano and glanced up to another tiny mezzanine built above a carriage door. A straight-backed piano teacher with her hair in a bun instructed her pupil in what sounded like *Für Elise*. The girl shifted on her stool and played a single bar over and over again before moving on clumsily, battling Beethoven. She wore a hair-band and a long dress with ruffles and seemed in that instant the distilled, awkward essence of French bourgeois girlhood.

As we made our way from one pool of lamp-light to the next, rounding the island counterclockwise as we often do, we imagined a life story for the girl, for her piano teacher, for the cigar-smoking man with the stag's head in his apartment, then for the maid with the silver tray and each of the merrymakers from the mansion on the island's tip.

The *bateau-mouches* babbled by with commentary in four languages, their floodlights splashing images on the facades. They raked light on the requisite lovers hidden along the Seine, and revealed interiors with Pompeii-red wallpaper or gaudy chandeliers, decorated ceiling beams, stucco incrustations and 17th-century chimney pieces. Glitzy and loud, the tour boats and their searchlights nonetheless transformed banal parked cars or sidewalk benches – and strollers like us – into elements of a magic lantern show.

The scene flowered in my mind. I began to realize why, in my years in Paris, I have unconsciously loved night walking.

For one thing, daylight flattens and hardens Paris, emphasizing the smog-blackened gray of its plaster facades, the straightness of its boulevards, the maddening symmetry imposed upon it by Baron Haussmann and Napoléon III during the Second Empire.

Night lighting, instead, brings out the bends and recesses, the jagged edges, the secret interiors, the sinuous quality of the Seine, the flying buttresses and other medieval escapees of modernity.

There are practical reasons, too, why nighttime strolling seems to me the finest way to experience Paris nowadays. The later the hour, the thinner the traffic, the cleaner the air, the more quintessential the scenery and atmosphere, stripped of superfluous color and noise. When the cars and trucks and buses and guided groups fade away – unless they're part of a Paris by Night tour – the city's magic steals back. Even garish Pigalle seems bizarrely wonderful with its sizzling neon signs and florescent teeth flashing meretricious smiles. Seen from afar, the Eiffel Tower becomes an eerie glowing skeleton. The Panthéon's leaden dome hovers weightlessly over a jigsaw puzzle of tin roofs. In winter, when the weather drives Parisians indoors, the nighttime streets and sidewalks are for the taking, and the innocuous voyeurism is unparalleled.

Ever since I had my first twilight epiphany on the Île-Saint-Louis nearly twenty years ago, I've not only begun walking more and later at night: I've also been searching in literature for references to fellow night-walkers. It seems that *noctambulism* has a long and noble history in Paris. A strange sounding word, in English it simply means "sleep-walking." But in French a *noctambule* is a night owl, someone who literally walks about – very much awake – in the darkness, a denizen of the night, a nightwalker, stalker or prowler. To serve such creatures, the RATP transit authority created the *Noctambus* – Paris' late-night bus service whose symbol is an owl.

Everyone knows that Paris is called la *Ville Lumière* or City of Light, but a century or more before it earned that moniker a restless writer named Nicolas-Edme Restif de la Bretonne pioneered the Parisian nighttime prowl. He recorded his adventures from 1786 onwards in *Les Nuits de Paris ou Le Spectateur nocturne,* a rambling account of 1,001 nights spread over a period of many years. I was gratified to learn that Restif de la Bretonne's first and favorite night-walks also began on the Île-Saint-Louis when he lived on the Rue des Deux Iles, the island's waistband. Physically at least, the isle must have been much the same then as it is today: most of the townhouses were already 150 years old (they were built in the mid 1600s), the traffic was sparse, the quays cobbled. In Restif de la Bretonne's day oil lamps with reflectors called *réverbères* hung from the center of the streets casting a feeble glow. As in the rest of central Paris, public lighting on the island today is a mix of handsome 1800s lamps and more recent units. The resultant glow entices not only *papillons nocturnes* but also lovers of the island's Berthillon ice cream.

In my reading and walking I've confirmed that no other city cultivates so zealously its nighttime ambience, a sort of luminous identity card spelling out the words *Ville Lumière.* Ever since the term was coined about 100 years ago (probably inspired by the 1900 Universal Exposition), artifice is what the City of Light has been all about. Several hundred technicians, engineers and lighting designers work fulltime creating Paris's magical nighttime kingdom. They follow a master plan that covers the lighting of everything from pedestrian crossings to facades, monuments and bridges. Lampposts are staggered at studied intervals and heights to produce a luminous blanket. Nothing is left to chance.

Restif de la Bretonne may have invented the genre of nighttime sketches, but to many French people the literary night belongs to Charles Baudelaire. The inveterate noctambulist distilled his shadowy world most notably into *Les Fleurs du Mal* – flowers of evil nourished, with poetic license, not only by the sun but also by the flickering gas lamps of the Second Empire, lamps that lit the wide new sidewalks of Haussmann's boulevards and the cafés and theaters and railroad stations that sprang up on them, where people came and went at all hours of the day and night in what had become the world's first modern metropolis. Coincidentally Baudelaire also lived on the Île-Saint-Louis, at 22 Quai de Béthune (in the Hôtel Lefebvre de la Malmaison), and, later, among the hashish-smokers of the Hôtel de Lauzun (at 17 Quai d'Anjou).

Being able to walk safely at night, under lamps on paved surfaces, was a novelty Baudelaire didn't take for granted: paradoxically for him it meant the death of his beloved, dark old Paris. Today, many of the cannon-shot boulevards that Baudelaire tramped along, ambivalence in his heart, have been around for nearly 150 years and people now think of them as the quaint old quintessential Paris. I don't, and rarely include them (with the exception of the boulevards Saint-Germain, Saint-Michel and Montparnasse) in my nocturnal itineraries. Though some of the grand cafés and theaters of the Second Empire and Belle Époque are still around, the Avenue de l'Opéra, Boulevard Haussmann and dozens of arteries like them strike me as about the worst places in town for an amble. Even skillful illumination fails to give them charm.

Here's something else I've deduced: whether you have prurient inclinations or not, noctambulism inevitably induces voyeurism. Outside, in the dark, you can't help peering up at the apartments, into countless doll's-house tableaux enacted nightly, seemingly for your delectation. Exhibitionism may be part of the equation. Parisians are often unselfconscious and I sometimes wonder if they get a thrill by *not* drawing the curtains.

Beyond the Île-Saint-Louis and its mansions, the most exquisite doll's houses I know for nighttime viewing are found on and near the Place des Vosges, centerpiece of the Right Bank's Marais neighborhood. The square's thirty-six identical pavilions – all of them built in the first decade of the 1600s – offer remarkable architectural detailing, and a chance to indulge your curiosity. There are bull's eye windows in the slanting slate roofs, plus arcades and painted timber ceilings. At times, the magic-lantern effect reveals the fabulous art collections of several famous auctioneers and the rich families who've lived there for decades or centuries.

When the window-shopping culture-vultures who cruise the Marais by day bed down for the night, the area's narrow streets and townhouses provide endless permutations for the intrepid *noctambule*. A head looms in a backlit, arrow-slit window on a tower jutting over the Rue Saint-Paul. Tattered curtains flap in a ghostly old building – recently a squat – in the Rue Pastourelle. Mystery awaits you around every corner.

The Palais Royal is another nocturnal treat, its long, moodily lit arcades little changed since the days of Restif de la Bretonne (though what you now hear echoing are not the clogs of prostitutes or the boots of assassins, but the taps of the well-heeled tripping home from fancy restaurants like three-star Le Grand Véfour).

One of my favorite night circuits wends from the Palais Royal via the colonnaded Bourse (the stock exchange), through ill-lit passageways and alleys to the Rue du Faubourg Montmartre, whose hollow-eyed facades look like craggy cliff dwellings. The road changes names as it mounts in an arc past the church of Notre-Dame-de-Lorette – homely by day, almost pretty by night – and Place Blanche to the famous hill crowned by that marvelously obscene basilica Sacré Coeur.

Over the centuries many French and foreign writers have contributed to the literature of noctambulism. In the 1920s and '30s, Louis-Férdinand Céline *(Voyage au Bout de la Nuit)* trotted obsessively to and fro between Paris and the suburb near Levallois where he lived, ruminating on the horrors of contemporary society. When he wasn't searching for outdoor urinals or gazing at his navel, Henry Miller was taking (or describing) his so-called "obsessional walks" – a kind of revelatory nighttime ramble – around the Place de Clichy and Montmartre, under the night-lit silhouette of Sacré Coeur and its "savage teat" cupolas.

When I walk around Montmartre I can't help thinking of Amedeo Modigliani, nicknamed "Modì", which sounds like *maudit* and means, in French, "cursed" or "luckless." Modì may never have written about the night himself – he used his pencil for other endeavors – but his lustful wanderings are the subject of many a biography. It seems that if the perpetually thirsty and penniless genius couldn't be found painting or sculpting in one of the Montmartre hovels he occupied, he was usually leaping from bed to bed, or mooching a drink in the Place du Tertre.

This square and the streets fronting nearby Sacré Coeur are a zoo from dawn to past midnight, and if you're into high kitsch then be my guest. In the dead of night, though, they emanate a hauntingly beautiful sadness. Nearby roads like the Rue des Saules and Rue Saint-Vincent, instead, wrap around the backside of the hill to a small vineyard. I like to wander there and down the arm span-wide Allée des Brouillards – Fog Alley – which crosses an area once called Le Maquis, a no-man's land filled with ramshackle studios where Modigliani drank and smoked himself toward oblivion. At night you can still spot the occasional artist's atelier in Modì's neighborhood, illuminated from within, or catch keyhole views of the city from streets that tilt and turn, like the Rue Lepic. Recently Paris' lighting engineers have transformed a series of Montmartre outdoor stairways into "light sculptures", a new expression of environmental art that taps into the magic of the night and might even help prevent tired tourists from tripping in the dark.

Cost-free, non-polluting and surprisingly safe, the best thing about noctambulism in Paris, however, is its inexhaustible variety. Another walk that fills me with wonder follows the curving Canal Saint-Martin from the Seine, along the Boulevard Richard Lenoir, all the way to La Villette on the edge of town. On cobbled sidewalks under towering plane trees you pass the Hôtel du Nord *(Atmosphere! Atmosphere!)*, several drawbridges, mossy locks and the circular La Rotonde customs house designed in 1789 by visionary architect Claude-Nicolas Ledoux. Or wander around Belleville, an unsung neighborhood in the 19th and 20th arrondissements, with views from the Parc de Belleville and plenty of un-gentrified urban edge.

When in the mood for tamer surroundings, I walk from the 24-hour cafés of Montparnasse across sleeping Saint-Germain-des-Prés to Notre-Dame on the Île-de-la-Cité and on to the moody Marais. But my favorite night-walk will always remain that slow, meditative trawl around the Île-Saint-Louis, guided by the words of Restif de la Bretonne and Baudelaire, and the lights of the *bateau-mouches*.

Mustard, salt and pepper holders, 2002

Life's a Café

"[T]he sympathy we felt for the young idlers in the Flore was tinged with impatience: the main object of their non-conformism was to justify their inactivity, and they were very, very bored."
Simone de Beauvoir, *La force de l'âge*

At about six o'clock every morning but Sunday, Madame Renée or her husband José would drag the banged up tables and chairs out of their café and set them up on the cobbled *terrasse* under our bedroom window.

At anywhere from 11pm to 2am they would muscle them back in again. Renée did this all her working life and even when still in the womb: her mother ran the café before her. A few years ago Renée and José retired, selling the place to a nearby restaurant. The chair-and-table tradition continues.

My wife Alison and I have lived above the café for eighteen years or approximately 11,007 chair-and-table draggings. We don't feel particularly privileged. There are roughly 10,000 cafés in Paris, which I think should consider renaming itself the City of Caffeine. Up and down the scarred asphalt sidewalks, and across the quaint cobbled squares, café owners do the same dawn and midnight furniture dance for Paris' 2.2 million inhabitants.

That could be enough, you might say, to make us hate Renée, José, their successors and Paris café owners in general? Never. Well, maybe once in a while we'd love to pour boiling oil from our window, and sometimes I do lean out and shout abuse in several languages. But what would Paris be without its cafés? They're the stomach, lungs, liver, bad conscience and, yes, the soul of the city. You buy tobacco in some cafés (*tabacs*), gamble on pari-mutuels or lotteries in others (PMU/Lotto), philosophize, scribble or surf in yet others (*philocafés, cafés littéraires*, web bars), drink and eat in all, sometimes well. Romance buds, hatred flares, revelation dawns, violence erupts, fortune smiles upon lucky winners and smoke gets in everyone's eyes.

If nothing else, cafés animate the city, that's to say they keep it awake with noise and mostly legal stimulants. They've been around for centuries: Paris' first, Le Procope, now a travesty of a café, was founded by the Sicilian Procopio in 1686. Though there are fewer of them today than, say, twenty years ago, cafés are unlikely ever to disappear. Admittedly the coffee in them is often bad, which is one reason why Starbucks, Columbus Café and a myriad of other New World-style competitors are gaining ground.

"For the coffee? Good heavens no, I don't go to a café for that," remarked a friend of mine, a café connoisseur. "Coffee is simply the cheapest thing you can order while occupying a table for an hour or so..."

It was mid-morning. My friend and I were in the Café Jade on the Rue de Buci in the Saint-Germain-des-Prés neighborhood. I always meet my friend in cafés. An English woman who has lived in Paris for the last forty-odd years, she does her entertaining, holds meetings, reviews scripts, edits manuscripts and generally enjoys life in cafés. Now as we chatted about the institution of the café she took a hummingbird sip at the black tar passing for espresso in her cup. It was not her cup of tea, so to speak, but then the tea in Paris is usually even worse than the coffee.

She nodded at the goings-on: waiters whirling among the mushroom-shaped tables, a mixed clientele of ageing regulars from the neighborhood, loners, mavericks, tourists, Sorbonne students, and a businessman seated outside on the shaded *terrasse*, shouting into his cellular telephone. Shops were open around the corner so the street swam with colors and movement. Our table was an eddy in this stream: in safety we snapped up snatches of foreign and French conversation, feasted on the sight of passersby and drank in the kitchen smells of simmering food.

"That's why one comes to a café, isn't it?" asked my friend. "For this – the life, the human contact."

Once the haunt of Paris inevitables like Jean-Paul Sartre, Picasso, Hemingway et al, the Saint-Germain-des-Prés area may have lost most of its *intellos* (intellectuals), artists and retinues of sycophants. But its dozens of cafés live on. Contrary to what most visitors think, the Deux Magots and Café de Flore are the exceptions to this rule. Exquisite tourist traps, they are embalmed, mummified and as such tremendously popular with non-Parisians.

My friend and I hadn't really meant to meet at the Café Jade, a retro hangout. Until a few years ago it had been known as the Café Dauphin. We had forgotten about the changeover. Gone are the Dauphin's booths with their slippery, pumpkin-colored moleskin seats. The Jade has faux-antique wooden tables, instead, and hard-bottomed chairs. A salmon-colored neon tube curls across the ceiling. The awning is a matching salmon pink.

It's ludicrous to lament the passing of the old Café Dauphin and its hideous 1970s decor, uneatable food and black-tar coffee. But as my friend pointed out, the décor, food and coffee are marginal considerations for habitués. It's the feel of the place that counts, the atmosphere, the spidering relationships between waiter and client, waiter and *patron, patron* and client, client and client.

This web is spun over months, years even decades. More than anyone perhaps, photographer Robert Doisneau captured this microcosm of Frenchness in his grainy B&W images. They are images that have become icons and clichés, like berets, baguettes, *pétanque* bowlers and ripe Camembert.

Cheesy cliché or not, today most Paris cafés are still family owned or managed and many are handed down the generations, webs and all. Long taken for granted, these supremely democratic social institutions are a focus of official attention, in part because they are disappearing, in part because a few actually serve decent food and have lured the restaurant critics. Cafés are now reviewed alongside their siblings, the bistros and brasseries. The stumbling café revival also includes festivities. The annual Bistrots-en-Fête, a two-day event held in late September, is a modern Bacchanal featuring dancing, feasting and drinking, often to excess. At the opposite end of the spectrum, the high fashion-lifestyle industry has adopted the revival concept, wedding it to Food-in-Shop, an innovation pioneered in London and New York. Now chic Parisians buy their CDs then linger at the Virgin Mégastore Café; they unburden their pocketbooks at Emporio Armani surrounded by fellow X-rays lapping up foamy lattes; or they toy with the accessories at Lanvin before lunching in the modish Café Bleu. Do-it-yourself types head for the hardware section in the basement of the celebrated BHV department store, now home to Café Bricolò, which is set in a mock-early-1900s *bricolage* (hardware) shop.

Another twist on the caffeine scene got started in the 1990s at the Café des Phares, the first and still most popular "philosophy café" in town. It is perpetually packed by bespectacled *intellos* and studious poseurs carrying tomes by Pascal, Descartes, Camus, Sartre, Deleuze and Foucault, and has spawned dozens of similar hangouts.

Such places are a long way from the Procope of the 1600s or the standard 19th- and 20th-century café type run by what's known as the Auvergnat "mafia." For a hundred years or more most Paris cafés have been in the grip of Auvergnat families. The "mafia" supplies everything from furniture to mortgage loans, lettuce to coffee beans. Here's how the system works: starting in the 1800s the Auvergnat came to the capital from the impoverished Auvergne region centered on the Massif Central. They transformed cafés from their earliest Italianate incarnation into havens of the working class, serving food and drink while carrying on their main business activity of selling coal or wood for heating.

This "mafia" is really a mutual aid society, with nothing to do with organized crime. The rub is that the coffee blends the Auvergnat supply their brethren are generally undrinkable, but everyone has always taken them and those who discontinue do so at risk.

I decided to accompany my English friend to her afternoon café meetings, so followed her into her current favorite among the Odéon-quarter's "literary venues." It's called Les Editeurs, meaning The Publishers, because several venerable publishing houses continue to operate in the vicinity, and donate the books that line the café's shelves. Like the Café Jade, Les Editeurs also received a retrofit, transformed from a kitsch Alsatian eatery. Now it boasts wooden tables and comfortable armchairs, tasteful prints and of course bookcases groaning with donated books. French writers and editors actually do meet here. Les Editeurs has been more successful than most in shedding the moleskin and linoleum and reinventing itself. The upstairs restaurant, in particular, has become popular with scribblers thanks to the tasty club sandwiches and lamb tagine served in what passes in Paris for a nonsmoking section.

As I sipped my mediocre coffee upstairs and listened to the pens scratching away, I reflected on the fact that most of the working writers I know in Paris, whether French, Italian, British or American, are café habitués, with their own personal lists of favorite cafés, but none would be caught dead doing serious work in one. Les Editeurs may be the exception. However I suspect that even here, most of those handsome ink pens and writing pads are used for composing letters back home to Peoria, shopping lists, Sorbonne course outlines and tragically unpublished masterpieces.

I said goodbye to my English friend and rode the 96 bus toward my office, which is in the still-unfashionable 20th arrondissement. My aim was to get some serious work done. En route I attempted to count the cafés we passed. There were about a thousand, I reckoned, between Odéon and Boulevard Beaumarchais, at which point a pierced belly button and an open *Le Monde* closed off my view.

Any student of life will tell you that gluttony takes many forms, including the occasional desire for self-punishment. With that in mind I chose to get off the bus and have yet another coffee, albeit this one a *déca* (decaffeinated). Across the street from the bus stop nearest the Rue d'Oberkampf and Rue Saint Maur is the Café Charbon. To fully appreciate this establishment it's essential to know several Parisian slang words. *Branché* or (*chébran* when spelled backwards) means hip, cool, hot, trendy and so forth, but it is just as often used nowadays as a pejorative, because it suggests a lack of authenticity and an excess of *frime*, as in *frimeur*, the other pertinent term. A *frimeur* is a poseur of a peculiarly pernicious sort, the kind who stars in the very worst of current French cinema, or builds the kind of architectural nightmares favored by state-subsidized Latte Liberals, known here as the Gauche de Caviar.

The Café Charbon has had several incarnations over the last 120 years or so, including a pocket theater and an industrial workshop. But it was never an authentic Auvergnat café selling coal *(charbon)* and wood, as the name suggests. Everything in and about it is strangely marvelous, bona fide 100 percent *frime*. There are War of the Worlds praying mantis-style lamps. The counter is zinc (or, more likely, tin). The floors are covered in broken tiles, just like those of an authentic Avergnat café circa 1950. It is, in short, a retro decorator's dream. The faux element is so well done that most regulars actually think the place was once powdered with coal dust and filled with blue-collar Potato Eaters in funny hats.

Happily the Café Charbon's hardcore *frimeurs* don't show up until after their office jobs, mostly at architectural firms, so a mid-morning or mid-afternoon visit is a treat. I sat in the dark recesses of the place and watched the sneaker-shod, un-uniformed waiters groove with the hipsters perched in booths or poised in front of huge mirrors. Several watched themselves billow smoke from mouth and nostrils, like Stalin-era coal plants. Jazz played on the radio. The waiter did not pester me to consume or move on. I had a table all to myself, with plenty of room. Strangest of all, the coffee was good. Needless to say it was imported Italian coffee, and had no more to do with Auvergnats and their daily grinds than did the décor.

Perhaps I was experiencing the future of French cafés, I told myself. But I hoped not.

Having ingested enough stimulants to keep me awake until the next day's chair-and-table ritual, I was too jittery to get anything done at my office. Besides, by the time I got there it was aperitif hour. Dispensing *l'apéro*, as my French friends call it, is another important function of the café. How could I have overlooked it?

My wife Alison agreed to meet me across town on the glassed-in terrace of Brasserie Balzar, an old Latin Quarter favorite of ours and about a million other locals and visitors. Every table was taken. We couldn't get in for dinner.

"It must be the atmosphere," said Alison, indicating the brasserie's Art Deco interior, the mirrors and cozy tables pushed up to moleskin banquets. "The food certainly has never been great, but who cares?"

We quaffed several ruinous rounds of beer, eaves-dropped on an adulterous couple, and decided it would be all right to continue toward dinner at another favorite of ours, Les Fontaines, near the Panthéon.

Les Fontaines is the antithesis of Balzar and happily has so far been overlooked by most reviewers. It has tacky décor but excellent food. The view of other portly, savvy, ecstatic regular diners obscures the black tuck-'n'-roll vinyl banquettes and jaundice-hued lighting. Les Fontaines is the Paris café to end all cafés, meaning it is comfortable, hideous, noisy, one hundred percent provincial French, and its menu brims over with devastatingly caloric delicacies and wines.

My liver needed a crutch after the chicken heart salad, the pâté, the rabbit kidneys with mustard sauce, the tender sweetbreads and creamy wild mushrooms, the strawberry pie and all that chilled Brouilly. There just wasn't room left for a coffee. So, we decided, what the heck, let's finish the evening at what used to be Madame Renée's, now known as "The café underneath our windows." But by the time we got there it was midnight and the owners were locking up. "Shucks," I exclaimed to one of them, "you won't be waking us up tonight after all." My wife and I yawned, said goodnight, and woke up as always to the table-and-chair dance early the next morning. In Paris, life's a café.